Bret Harte

Prose and Poetry

Bret Harte

Prose and Poetry

ISBN/EAN: 9783742839855

Manufactured in Europe, USA, Canada, Australia, Japa

Cover: Foto ©Andreas Hilbeck / pixelio.de

Manufactured and distributed by brebook publishing software (www.brebook.com)

Bret Harte

Prose and Poetry

EACH VOLUME SOLD SEPARATELY.

COLLECTION
OF
BRITISH AUTHORS

TAUCHNITZ EDITION.

VOL. 1263.

PROSE AND POETRY BY BRET HARTE

IN TWO VOLUMES.

VOL. I.

LEIPZIG: BERNHARD TAUCHNITZ.

PARIS: C. REINWALD & Cie, 15, RUE DES SAINTS PÈRES.

This Collection is published with copyright for Continental circulation, but all purchasers are earnestly requested not to introduce the volumes

COLLECTION
OF
BRITISH AUTHORS

TAUCHNITZ EDITION.

VOL. 1263.

PROSE AND POETRY BY BRET HARTE.

IN TWO VOLUMES.
VOL. I.

PROSE AND POETRY

BY

BRET HARTE.

Authorized Edition.

TWO VOLUMES.

VOL. I.

LEIPZIG
BERNHARD TAUCHNITZ
1872.

AUTHOR'S PREFACE.

THE following pages, compiled by me at the request of Baron Tauchnitz, comprise the only complete and authorized edition of my prose and poetical writings, published on the Continent of Europe.

BRET HARTE.

NEW YORK, Aug. 20th, 1872.

CONTENTS

OF VOLUME I.

TALES OF THE ARGONAUTS.

	Page
The Luck of Roaring Camp	3
The Outcasts of Poker Flat	18
Miggles	33
Tennessee's Partner	49
The Idyl of Red Gulch	62
Brown of Calaveras	76
Mliss	91
Night at Wingdam	127
High-Water Mark	135
The Man of No Account	147
Notes by Flood and Field	153

SPANISH AND AMERICAN LEGENDS.

The Legend of Monte del Diablo	185
The Right Eye of the Commander	203
The Legend of the Devil's Point	214
The Adventure of Padre Vicentio	224
The Devil and the Broker	233
The Ogress of Silver Land	238

CONDENSED NOVELS.

	Page
Handsome is as Handsome does. By Ch——s R——de	249
Lothaw. By Mr. Benjamins	261
Muck-a-Muck. After Cooper	273
Terence Denville. By Ch—l—s L—v—r	282
Selina Sedilia. By Miss M. E. B—dd—n and Mrs. H—n—y W—d	290
The Ninety-nine Guardsmen. By Al—x—d—r D—m—s	301

TALES OF THE ARGONAUTS.

THE LUCK OF ROARING CAMP.

THERE was commotion in Roaring Camp. It could not have been a fight, for in 1850 that was not novel enough to have called together the entire settlement. The ditches and claims were not only deserted, but "Tuttle's grocery" had contributed its gamblers, who, it will be remembered, calmly continued their game the day that French Pete and Kanaka Joe shot each other to death over the bar in the front room. The whole camp was collected before a rude cabin on the outer edge of the clearing. Conversation was carried on in a low tone, but the name of a woman was frequently repeated. It was a name familiar enough in the camp,—"Cherokee Sal."

Perhaps the less said of her the better. She was a coarse, and, it is to be feared, a very sinful woman. But at that time she was the only woman in Roaring Camp, and was just then lying in sore extremity, when she most needed the ministration of her own sex. Dissolute, abandoned, and irreclaimable, she was yet suffering a martyrdom hard enough to bear even when veiled by sympathizing womanhood, but now terrible in her loneliness. The primal curse had come to her in that original isolation which must have made the punishment of the first transgression so dreadful. It was, perhaps, part of the expiation of her sin, that, at a moment when she most lacked her sex's intuitive tenderness and care, she met only the half-contemptuous faces of her masculine associates. Yet a few of the spectators were, I think, touched by her sufferings. Sandy Tipton thought it was "rough on Sal," and, in the contemplation of her condition, for a moment rose superior to the fact that he had an ace and two bowers in his sleeve.

It will be seen, also, that the situation was novel. Deaths were by no means uncommon in Roaring Camp, but a birth was a new thing. People had been dismissed the camp effectively, finally, and with no possibility of return; but this was the first time that anybody had been introduced *ab initio*. Hence the excitement.

"You go in there, Stumpy," said a prominent citizen known as "Kentuck," addressing one of the loungers. "Go in there, and see what you kin do. You've had experience in them things."

Perhaps there was a fitness in the selection. Stumpy, in other climes, had been the putative head of two families; in fact, it was owing to some legal informality in these proceedings that Roaring Camp—a city of refuge—was indebted to his company. The crowd approved the choice, and Stumpy was wise enough to bow to the majority. The door closed on the extempore surgeon and midwife, and Roaring Camp sat down outside, smoked its pipe, and awaited the issue.

The assemblage numbered about a hundred men. One or two of these were actual fugitives from justice, some were criminal, and all were reckless. Physically, they exhibited no indication of their past lives and character. The greatest scamp had a Raphael face, with a profusion of blond hair; Oakhurst, a gambler, had the melancholy air and intellectual abstraction of a Hamlet; the coolest and most courageous man was scarcely over five feet in height, with a soft voice and an embarrassed, timid manner. The term "roughs" applied to them was a distinction rather than a definition. Perhaps in the minor details of fingers, toes, ears, etc., the camp may have been deficient, but these slight omissions did not detract from their aggregate force. The strongest man had but three fingers on his right hand; the best shot had but one eye.

Such was the physical aspect of the men that were dispersed around the cabin. The camp lay in a triangular valley, between two hills and a river. The only outlet was a steep trail over the summit of a hill that faced the cabin, now illuminated by the rising moon. The suffering woman might have seen it from the rude bunk whereon she lay,—seen it winding like a silver thread until it was lost in the stars above.

A fire of withered pine-boughs added sociability to the gathering. By degrees the natural levity of Roaring Camp returned. Bets were freely offered and taken regarding the result. Three to five that "Sal would get through with it"; even, that the child would survive; side bets as to the sex and complexion of the coming stranger. In the midst of an excited discussion an exclamation came from those nearest the door, and the camp stopped to listen. Above the swaying and moaning of the pines, the swift rush of the river, and the crackling of the fire, rose a sharp, querulous cry,—a cry unlike anything heard before in the camp. The pines stopped moaning, the river ceased to rush, and the fire to crackle. It seemed as if Nature had stopped to listen too.

The camp rose to its feet as one man! It was proposed to explode a barrel of gunpowder, but, in consideration of the situation of the mother, better counsels prevailed, and only a few revolvers were discharged; for, whether owing to the rude surgery of the camp, or some other reason, Cherokee Sal was sinking fast. Within an hour she had climbed, as it were, that rugged road that led to the stars, and so passed out of Roaring Camp, its sin and shame forever. I do not think that the announcement disturbed them much, except in speculation as to the fate of the child. "Can he live now?" was asked of Stumpy. The answer was doubtful. The only other being of Cherokee Sal's sex and maternal condition in the settlement was an ass. There was some conjecture as to fitness, but the experiment was tried. It was less problematical than the ancient treatment of Romulus and Remus, and apparently as successful.

When these details were completed, which exhausted another hour, the door was opened, and the anxious crowd of men who had already formed themselves into a queue, entered in single file. Beside the low bunk or shelf, on which the figure of the mother was starkly outlined below the blankets stood a pine table. On this a candle-box was placed, and within it, swathed in staring red flannel, lay the last arrival at Roaring Camp. Beside the candle-box was placed a hat. Its use was soon indicated. "Gentlemen," said Stumpy, with a singular mixture of authority and *ex officio* complacency,—"Gentlemen will please pass in at the front door, round the table, and out at the back door. Them as wishes to contribute anything toward the orphan will find a hat handy." The first man entered with his hat on; he uncovered, however, as he looked about him, and so, unconsciously, set an example to the next. In such communities good and bad actions are catching. As the procession filed in, comments were audible,—criticisms addressed, perhaps, rather to Stumpy, in the character of showman, —"Is that him?" "mighty small specimen"; "hasn't mor'n got the color"; "ain't bigger nor a derringer." The contributions were as characteristic: A silver tobacco-box; a doubloon; a navy revolver, silver mounted; a gold specimen; a very beautifully embroidered lady's handkerchief (from Oakhurst the gambler); a diamond breastpin; a diamond ring (suggested by the pin, with the remark from the giver that he "saw that pin and went two diamonds better"); a slung shot; a Bible (contributor not detected); a golden spur; a silver teaspoon (the initials, I regret to say, were not the giver's); a pair of surgeon's shears; a lancet; a Bank of England note for £5; and about $200 in loose gold and silver coin. During these proceedings Stumpy maintained a silence as impassive as the dead on his left, a gravity as inscrutable as that of the newly born on his right. Only one incident occurred to break the monotony of the curious procession. As Kentuck bent over the candle-box half curiously, the child turned, and, in a spasm of pain, caught at his groping finger, and held it fast for a moment. Kentuck looked foolish and embarrassed. Something like a blush tried to assert itself in his weather-beaten cheek. "The d—d little cuss!" he said, as he extricated his finger, with, perhaps, more tenderness and care than he might have been deemed capable of showing. He held that finger a little apart from its fellows as he went out, and examined it curiously. The examination provoked the same original remark in regard to the child. In fact, he seemed to enjoy repeating it. "He rastled with my finger," he remarked to Tipton, holding up the member, "the d—d little cuss!"

It was four o'clock before the camp sought repose. A light burnt in the cabin where the watchers sat, for Stumpy did not go to bed that night. Nor did Kentuck. He drank quite freely, and related with great gusto his experience, invariably ending with his characteristic condemnation of the new-comer. It seemed to relieve him of any unjust implication of sentiment, and Kentuck had the weaknesses of the nobler sex. When everybody else had gone to bed, he walked down to the river, and whistled reflectingly. Then he walked up the gulch, past the cabin, still whistling with demonstrative unconcern. At a large red-wood tree he paused and retraced his steps, and again passed the cabin. Half-way down to the river's bank he again paused, and then returned and knocked at the door. It was opened by Stumpy. "How goes it?" said Kentuck, looking past Stumpy toward the candle-box. "All serene," replied Stumpy. "Anything up?" "Nothing." There was a pause—an embarrassing one —Stumpy still holding the door. Then Kentuck had recourse to his finger, which he held up to Stumpy. "Rastled with it,—the d—d little cuss," he said, and retired.

The next day Cherokee Sal had such rude sepulture as Roaring Camp afforded. After her body had been committed to the hillside, there was a formal meeting of the camp to discuss what should be done with her infant. A resolution to adopt it was unanimous and enthusiastic. But an animated discussion in regard to the manner and feasibility of providing for its wants at once sprung up. It was remarkable that the argument partook of none of those fierce personalities with which discussions were usually conducted at Roaring Camp. Tipton proposed that they should send the child to Red Dog,—a distance of forty miles,—where female attention could be procured. But the unlucky suggestion met with fierce and unanimous opposition. It was evident that no plan which entailed parting from their new acquisition would for a moment be entertained. "Besides," said Tom Ryder, "them fellows at Red Dog would swap it, and ring in somebody else on us." A disbelief in the honesty of other camps prevailed at Roaring Camp as in other places.

The introduction of a female nurse in the camp also met with objection. It was argued that no decent woman could be prevailed to accept Roaring Camp as her home, and the speaker urged that "they didn't want any more of the other kind." This unkind allusion to the defunct mother, harsh as it may seem, was the first spasm of propriety,—the first symptom of the camp's regeneration. Stumpy advanced nothing. Perhaps he felt a certain delicacy in interfering with the selection of a possible successor in office. But when questioned, he averred stoutly that he and "Jinny"— the mammal before alluded to—could manage to rear the child. There was something original, independent, and heroic about the plan that pleased the camp. Stumpy was retained. Certain articles were sent for to

Sacramento. "Mind," said the treasurer, as he pressed a bag of gold-dust into the expressman's hand, "the best that can be got,—lace, you know, and filigree-work and frills,—d—m the cost!"

Strange to say, the child thrived. Perhaps the invigorating climate of the mountain camp was compensation for material deficiencies. Nature took the foundling to her broader breast. In that rare atmosphere of the Sierra foot-hills,—that air pungent with balsamic odor, that ethereal cordial at once bracing and exhilarating,—he may have found food and nourishment, or a subtle chemistry that transmuted asses' milk to lime and phosphorus. Stumpy inclined to the belief that it was the latter and good nursing. "Me and that ass," he would say, "has been father and mother to him! Don't you," he would add, apostrophizing the helpless bundle before him, "never go back on us."

By the time he was a month old, the necessity of giving him a name became apparent. He had generally been known as "the Kid," "Stumpy's boy," "the Cayote" (an allusion to his vocal powers), and even by Kentuck's endearing diminutive of "the d—d little cuss." But these were felt to be vague and unsatisfactory, and were at last dismissed under another influence. Gamblers and adventurers are generally superstitious, and Oakhurst one day declared that the baby had brought "the luck" to Roaring Camp. It was certain that of late they had been successful. "Luck" was the name agreed upon, with the prefix of Tommy for greater convenience. No allusion was made to the mother, and the father was unknown. "It's better," said the philosophical Oakhurst, "to take a fresh deal all round. Call him Luck, and start him fair." A day was accordingly set apart for the christening. What was meant by this ceremony the reader may imagine, who has already gathered some idea of the reckless irreverence of Roaring Camp. The master of ceremonies was one "Boston," a noted wag, and the occasion seemed to promise the greatest facetiousness. This ingenious satirist had spent two days in preparing a burlesque of the church service, with pointed local allusions. The choir was properly trained, and Sandy Tipton was to stand godfather. But after the procession had marched to the grove with music and banners, and the child had been deposited before a mock altar, Stumpy stepped before the expectant crowd. "It ain't my style to spoil fun, boys," said the little man, stoutly, eying the faces around him, "but it strikes me that this thing ain't exactly on the squar. It's playing it pretty low down on this yer baby to ring in fun on him that he ain't going to understand. And ef there's going to be any godfathers round, I'd like to see who's got any better rights than me." A silence followed Stumpy's speech. To the credit of all humorists be it said, that the first man to acknowledge its justice was the satirist, thus stopped of his fun. "But," said Stumpy, quickly, following up his advantage, "we're here for a christening, and we'll have it. I proclaim you Thomas Luck, according to the laws of the United States and the State of California, so help me God." It was the first time that the name of the Deity had been uttered otherwise than profanely in the camp. The form of christening was perhaps even more ludicrous than the satirist had conceived; but, strangely enough, nobody saw it and nobody laughed. "Tommy" was christened as seriously as he would have been under a Christian roof, and cried and was comforted in as orthodox fashion.

And so the work of regeneration began in Roaring Camp. Almost imperceptibly a change came over the settlement. The cabin assigned to "Tommy Luck"—or "The Luck," as he was more frequently called—first showed signs of improvement. It was kept scrupulously clean and white-washed. Then it was boarded, clothed, and papered. The rosewood cradle—packed eighty miles by mule—had, in Stumpy's way of putting it, "sorter killed the rest of the furniture." So the rehabilitation of the cabin became a necessity. The men who were in the habit of lounging in at Stumpy's to see "how The Luck got on" seemed to appreciate the change, and, in self-defence, the rival establishment of "Tuttle's grocery" bestirred itself, and imported a carpet and mirrors. The reflections of the latter on the appearance of Roaring Camp tended to produce stricter habits of personal cleanliness. Again, Stumpy imposed a kind of quarantine upon those who aspired to the honor and privilege of holding "The Luck." It was a cruel mortification to Kentuck—who, in the carelessness of a large nature and the habits of frontier life, had begun to regard all garments as a second cuticle, which, like a snake's, only sloughed off through decay—to be debarred this privilege from certain prudential reasons. Yet such was the subtle influence of innovation that he thereafter appeared regularly every afternoon in a clean shirt, and face still shining from his ablutions. Nor were moral and social sanitary laws neglected. "Tommy," who was supposed to spend his whole existence in a persistent attempt to repose, must not be disturbed by noise. The shouting and yelling which had gained the camp its infelicitous title were not permitted within hearing distance of Stumpy's. The men conversed in whispers, or smoked with Indian gravity. Profanity was tacitly given up in these sacred precincts, and throughout the camp a popular form of expletive, known as "D—n the luck!" and "Curse the luck!" was abandoned, as having a new personal bearing. Vocal music was not interdicted, being supposed to have a soothing, tranquillizing quality, and one song, sung by "Man-o'-War Jack," an English sailor, from her Majesty's Australian colonies, was quite popular as a lullaby. It was a lugubrious recital of the exploits of "the Arethusa, Seventy-four," in a muffled minor, ending with a prolonged dying fall at the burden of each verse, "On b-o-o-o-ard of the Arethusa." It was a fine sight to see Jack holding The Luck, rocking from side to side as if with the motion of a ship, and crooning forth this naval ditty. Either through the peculiar rocking of Jack or the length of his song,—it contained ninety stanzas, and was continued with conscientious deliberation to the bitter end,—the lullaby generally had the desired effect. At such times the men would lie at full length under the trees, in the soft summer twilight, smoking their pipes and drinking in the melodious utterances. An indistinct idea that this was pastoral happiness pervaded the camp. "This 'ere kind o' think," said the Cockney Simmons, meditatively reclining on his elbow, "is 'evingly." It reminded him of Greenwich.

On the long summer days The Luck was usually carried to the gulch, from whence the golden store of

Roaring Camp was taken. There, on a blanket spread over pine-boughs, he would lie while the men were working in the ditches below. Latterly, there was a rude attempt to decorate this bower with flowers and sweet-smelling shrubs, and generally some one would bring him a cluster of wild honeysuckles, azaleas, or the painted blossoms of Las Mariposas. The men had suddenly awakened to the fact that there were beauty and significance in these trifles, which they had so long trodden carelessly beneath their feet. A flake of glittering mica, a fragment of variegated quartz, a bright pebble from the bed of the creek, became beautiful to eyes thus cleared and strengthened, and were invariably put aside for "The Luck." It was wonderful how many treasures the woods and hillsides yielded that "would do for Tommy." Surrounded by playthings such as never child out of fairy-land had before, it is to be hoped that Tommy was content. He appeared to be securely happy, albeit there was an infantine gravity about him, a contemplative light in his round gray eyes, that sometimes worried Stumpy. He was always tractable and quiet, and it is recorded that once, having crept beyond his "corral,"— a hedge of tesselated pine-boughs, which surrounded his bed, — he dropped over the bank on his head in the soft earth, and remained with his mottled legs in the air in that position for at least five minutes with unflinching gravity. He was extricated without a murmur. I hesitate to record the many other instances of his sagacity, which rest, unfortunately, upon the statements of prejudiced friends. Some of them were not without a tinge of superstition. "I crep' up the bank just now," said Kentuck one day, in a breathless state of excitement, "and dern my skin if he wasn't a talking to a jay-bird as was a sittin' on his lap. There they was, just as free and sociable as anything you please, a jawin' at each other just like two cherry-bums." Howbeit, whether creeping over the pine-boughs or lying lazily on his back blinking at the leaves above him, to him the birds sang, the squirrels chattered, and the flowers bloomed. Nature was his nurse and playfellow. For him she would let slip between the leaves golden shafts of sunlight that fell just within his grasp; she would send wandering breezes to visit him with the balm of bay and resinous gums; to him the tall red-woods nodded familiarly and sleepily, the bumble-bees buzzed, and the rooks cawed a slumbrous accompaniment.

Such was the golden summer of Roaring Camp. They were "flush times,"—and the Luck was with them. The claims had yielded enormously. The camp was jealous of its privileges and looked suspiciously on strangers. No encouragement was given to immigration, and, to make their seclusion more perfect, the land on either side of the mountain wall that surrounded the camp they duly preempted. This, and a reputation for singular proficiency with the revolver, kept the reserve of Roaring Camp inviolate. The expressman —their only connecting link with the surrounding world —sometimes told wonderful stories of the camp. He would say, "They've a street up there in 'Roaring,' that would lay over any street in Red Dog. They've got vines and flowers round their houses, and they wash themselves twice a day. But they're mighty rough on strangers, and they worship an Ingin baby."

With the prosperity of the camp came a desire for

further improvement. It was proposed to build a hotel in the following spring, and to invite one or two decent families to reside there for the sake of "The Luck,"—who might perhaps profit by female companionship. The sacrifice that this concession to the sex cost these men, who were fiercely sceptical in regard to its general virtue and usefulness, can only be accounted for by their affection for Tommy. A few still held out. But the resolve could not be carried into effect for three months, and the minority meekly yielded in the hope that something might turn up to prevent it. And it did.

The winter of 1851 will long be remembered in the foot-hills. The snow lay deep on the Sierras, and every mountain creek became a river, and every river a lake. Each gorge and gulch was transformed into a tumultuous watercourse that descended the hillsides, tearing down giant trees and scattering its drift and débris along the plain. Red Dog had been twice under water, and Roaring Camp had been forewarned. "Water put the gold into them gulches," said Stumpy. "It's been here once and will be here again!" And that night the North Fork suddenly leaped over its banks, and swept up the triangular valley of Roaring Camp.

In the confusion of rushing water, crushing trees, and crackling timber, and the darkness which seemed to flow with the water and blot out the fair valley, but little could be done to collect the scattered camp. When the morning broke, the cabin of Stumpy nearest the river-bank was gone. Higher up the gulch they found the body of its unlucky owner; but the pride, the hope, the joy, the Luck, of Roaring Camp had disappeared. They were returning with sad hearts, when a shout from the bank recalled them.

It was a relief-boat from down the river. They had picked up, they said, a man and an infant, nearly exhausted, about two miles below. Did anybody know them, and did they belong here?

It needed but a glance to show them Kentuck lying there, cruelly crushed and bruised, but still holding the Luck of Roaring Camp in his arms. As they bent over the strangely assorted pair, they saw that the child was cold and pulseless. "He is dead," said one. Kentuck opened his eyes. "Dead?" he repeated feebly. "Yes, my man, and you are dying too." A smile lit the eyes of the expiring Kentuck. "Dying," he repeated, "he's a taking me with him,—tell the boys I've got the Luck with me now"; and the strong man, clinging to the frail babe as a drowning man is said to cling to a straw, drifted away into the shadowy river that flows forever to the unknown sea.

THE OUTCASTS OF POKER FLAT.

As Mr. John Oakhurst, gambler, stepped into the main street of Poker Flat on the morning of the twenty-third of November, 1850, he was conscious of a change in its moral atmosphere since the preceding night. Two or three men, conversing earnestly together, ceased as he approached, and exchanged significant glances. There was a Sabbath lull in the air, which, in a settlement unused to Sabbath influences, looked ominous.

Mr. Oakhurst's calm, handsome face betrayed small concern in these indications. Whether he was conscious of any predisposing cause, was another question. "I reckon they're after somebody," he reflected; "likely it's me." He returned to his pocket the handkerchief with which he had been whipping away the red dust of Poker Flat from his neat boots, and quietly discharged his mind of any further conjecture.

In point of fact, Poker Flat was "after somebody." It had lately suffered the loss of several thousand dollars, two valuable horses, and a prominent citizen. It was experiencing a spasm of virtuous reaction, quite as lawless and ungovernable as any of the acts that had provoked it. A secret committee had determined to rid the town of all improper persons. This was done permanently in regard of two men who were then hanging from the boughs of a sycamore in the gulch, and temporarily in the banishment of certain other objectionable characters. I regret to say that some of these were ladies. It is but due to the sex, however, to state that their impropriety was professional, and it was only in such easily established standards of evil that Poker Flat ventured to sit in judgment.

Mr. Oakhurst was right in supposing that he was included in this category. A few of the committee had urged hanging him as a possible example, and a sure method of reimbursing themselves from his pockets of the sums he had won from them. "It's agin justice," said Jim Wheeler, "to let this yer young man from Roaring Camp—an entire stranger—carry away our money." But a crude sentiment of equity residing in the breasts of those who had been fortunate enough to win from Mr. Oakhurst overruled this narrower local prejudice.

Mr. Oakhurst received his sentence with philosophic calmness, none the less coolly that he was aware of the hesitation of his judges. He was too much of a gambler not to accept Fate. With him life was at best an uncertain game, and he recognized the usual percentage in favor of the dealer.

A body of armed men accompanied the deported wickedness of Poker Flat to the outskirts of the settlement. Besides Mr. Oakhurst, who was known to be a coolly desperate man, and for whose intimidation the armed escort was intended, the expatriated party consisted of a young woman familiarly known as "The Duchess"; another, who had won the title of "Mother Shipton"; and "Uncle Billy," a suspected sluice-robber and confirmed drunkard. The cavalcade provoked no comments from the spectators, nor was any word uttered by the escort. Only, when the gulch which marked the uttermost limit of Poker Flat was reached, the leader spoke briefly and to the point. The exiles were forbidden to return at the peril of their lives.

As the escort disappeared, their pent-up feelings found vent in a few hysterical tears from the Duchess, some bad language from Mother Shipton, and a Parthian volley of expletives from Uncle Billy. The philosophic Oakhurst alone remained silent. He listened calmly to Mother Shipton's desire to cut somebody's heart out, to the repeated statements of the Duchess that she would die in the road, and to the alarming oaths that seemed to be bumped out of Uncle Billy as he rode forward. With the easy good-humor characteristic of his class, he insisted upon exchanging his own riding-horse, "Five Spot," for the sorry mule which the Duchess rode. But even this act did not draw the party into any closer sympathy. The young woman readjusted her somewhat draggled plumes with a feeble, faded coquetry; Mother Shipton eyed the possessor of "Five Spot" with malevolence, and Uncle Billy included the whole party in one sweeping anathema.

The road to Sandy Bar—a camp that, not having as yet experienced the regenerating influences of Poker Flat, consequently seemed to offer some invitation to the emigrants—lay over a steep mountain range. It was distant a day's severe travel. In that advanced season, the party soon passed out of the moist, temperate regions of the foot-hills into the dry, cold, bracing air of the Sierras. The trail was narrow and difficult. At noon the Duchess, rolling out of her saddle upon the ground, declared her intention of going no farther, and the party halted.

The spot was singularly wild and impressive. A wooded amphitheatre, surrounded on three sides by precipitous cliffs of naked granite, sloped gently toward the crest of another precipice that overlooked the valley. It was, undoubtedly, the most suitable spot for a camp, had camping been advisable. But Mr. Oakhurst knew that scarcely half the journey to Sandy Bar was accomplished, and the party were not equipped or provisioned for delay. This fact he pointed out to his companions curtly, with a philosophic commentary on the folly of "throwing up their hand before the game was played out." But they were furnished with liquor, which in this emergency stood them in place of food, fuel, rest, and prescience. In spite of his remonstrances, it was not long before they were more or less under its influence. Uncle Billy passed rapidly from a bellicose state into one of stupor, the Duchess became maudlin, and Mother Shipton snored. Mr. Oakhurst alone remained erect, leaning against a rock, calmly surveying them.

Mr. Oakhurst did not drink. It interfered with a profession which required coolness, impassiveness, and presence of mind, and, in his own language, he "couldn't afford it." As he gazed at his recumbent fellow-exiles, the loneliness begotten of his pariah-trade, his habits of life, his very vices, for the first time seriously oppressed him. He bestirred himself in dusting his black clothes, washing his hands and face, and other acts characteristic of his studiously neat habits, and for a moment forgot his annoyance. The thought of deserting his weaker and more pitiable companions never perhaps occurred to him. Yet he could not help feeling the want of that excitement which, singularly enough, was most conducive to that calm equanimity for which he was notorious. He looked at the gloomy walls that rose a thousand feet sheer above the circling pines around him; at the sky, ominously clouded; at the valley below, already deepening into shadow. And, doing so, suddenly he heard his own name called.

A horseman slowly ascended the trail. In the fresh, open face of the new-comer Mr. Oakhurst recognized Tom Simson, otherwise known as "The Innocent" of Sandy Bar. He had met him some months before over a "little game," and had, with perfect equanimity, won the entire fortune—amounting to some forty dollars—of that guileless youth. After the game was finished, Mr. Oakhurst drew the youthful speculator behind the door and thus addressed him: "Tommy, you're a good little man, but you can't gamble worth a cent. Don't try it over again." He then handed him his money back, pushed him gently from the room, and so made a devoted slave of Tom Simson.

There was a remembrance of this in his boyish and enthusiastic greeting of Mr. Oakhurst. He had started, he said, to go to Poker Flat to seek his fortune. "Alone?" No, not exactly alone; in fact (a giggle), he had run away with Piney Woods. Didn't Mr. Oakhurst remember Piney? She that used to wait on the table at the Temperance House? They had been engaged a long time, but old Jake Woods had objected, and so they had run away, and were going to Poker Flat to be married, and here they were. And they were tired out, and how lucky it was they had found a place to camp and company. All this the Innocent delivered rapidly, while Piney, a stout, comely damsel of fifteen, emerged from behind the pine-tree, where she had been blushing unseen, and rode to the side of her lover.

Mr. Oakhurst seldom troubled himself with sentiment, still less with propriety; but he had a vague idea that the situation was not fortunate. He retained, however, his presence of mind sufficiently to kick Uncle Billy, who was about to say something, and Uncle Billy was sober enough to recognize in Mr. Oakhurst's kick a superior power that would not bear trifling. He then endeavored to dissuade Tom Simson from delaying further, but in vain. He even pointed out the fact that there was no provision, nor means of making a camp. But, unluckily, the Innocent met this objection by assuring the party that he was provided with an extra mule loaded with provisions, and by the discovery of a rude attempt at a log-house near the trail. "Piney can stay with Mrs. Oakhurst," said the Innocent, pointing to the Duchess, "and I can shift for myself."

Nothing but Mr. Oakhurst's admonishing foot saved Uncle Billy from bursting into a roar of laughter. As it was, he felt compelled to retire up the cañon until he could recover his gravity. There he confided the joke to the tall pine-trees, with many slaps of his leg, contortions of his face, and the usual profanity. But when he returned to the party, he found them seated by a fire—for the air had grown strangely chill and the sky overcast—in apparently amicable conversation. Piney was actually talking in an impulsive, girlish fashion to the Duchess, who was listening with an interest and animation she had not shown for many days. The Innocent was holding forth, apparently with equal effect, to Mr. Oakhurst and Mother Shipton, who was actually relaxing into amiability. "Is this yer a d—d picnic?" said Uncle Billy, with inward scorn, as he surveyed the sylvan group, the glancing firelight, and the tethered animals in the foreground. Suddenly an idea mingled with the alcoholic fumes that disturbed his brain. It was apparently of a jocular nature, for he felt impelled to slap his leg again and cram his fist into his mouth.

As the shadows crept slowly up the mountain, a slight breeze rocked the tops of the pine-trees, and moaned through their long and gloomy aisles. The ruined cabin, patched and covered with pine-boughs, was set apart for the ladies. As the lovers parted, they unaffectedly exchanged a kiss, so honest and sincere that it might have been heard above the swaying pines. The frail Duchess and the malevolent Mother Shipton were probably too stunned to remark upon this last evidence of simplicity, and so turned without a word to the hut. The fire was replenished, the men lay down before the door, and in a few minutes were asleep.

Mr. Oakhurst was a light sleeper. Toward morning he awoke benumbed and cold. As he stirred the dying fire, the wind, which was now blowing strongly, brought to his cheek that which caused the blood to leave it,—snow!

He started to his feet with the intention of awakening the sleepers, for there was no time to lose. But turning to where Uncle Billy had been lying, he found him gone. A suspicion leaped to his brain and a curse to his lips. He ran to the spot where the mules had been tethered; they were no longer there. The tracks were already rapidly disappearing in the snow.

The momentary excitement brought Mr. Oakhurst back to the fire with his usual calm. He did not waken the sleepers. The Innocent slumbered peacefully, with a smile on his good-humored, freckled face; the virgin Piney slept beside her frailer sisters as sweetly as though attended by celestial guardians, and Mr. Oakhurst, drawing his blanket over his shoulders, stroked his mustaches and waited for the dawn. It came slowly in a whirling mist of snow-flakes, that dazzled and confused the eye. What could be seen of the landscape appeared magically changed. He looked over the valley, and summed up the present and future in two words,—"snowed in!"

A careful inventory of the provisions, which, fortunately for the party, had been stored within the hut, and so escaped the felonious fingers of Uncle Billy, disclosed the fact that with care and prudence they might last ten days longer. "That is," said Mr. Oakhurst, *sotto voce* to the Innocent, "if you're willing to board us. If you ain't—and perhaps you'd better not —you can wait till Uncle Billy gets back with provisions." For some occult reason, Mr. Oakhurst could not bring himself to disclose Uncle Billy's rascality, and so offered the hypothesis that he had wandered from the camp and had accidentally stampeded the animals. He dropped a warning to the Duchess and Mother Shipton, who of course knew the facts of their associate's defection. "They'll find out the truth about us *all* when they find out anything," he added, significantly, "and there's no good frightening them now."

Tom Simson not only put all his worldly store at the disposal of Mr. Oakhurst, but seemed to enjoy the prospect of their enforced seclusion. "We'll have a good camp for a week, and then the snow'll melt, and we'll all go back together." The cheerful gayety of the young man, and Mr. Oakhurst's calm infected the others. The Innocent, with the aid of pine-boughs, extemporized a thatch for the roofless cabin, and the Duchess directed Piney in the rearrangement of the interior with a taste and tact that opened the blue eyes of that provincial maiden to their fullest extent. "I reckon now you're used to fine things at Poker Flat," said Piney. The Duchess turned away sharply to conceal something that reddened her cheeks through its professional tint, and Mother Shipton requested Piney not to "chatter." But when Mr. Oakhurst returned from a weary search for the trail, he heard the sound of happy laughter echoed from the rocks. He stopped in some alarm, and his thoughts first naturally reverted to the whiskey, which he had prudently *cachéd*. "And yet it don't somehow sound like whiskey," said the gambler. It was not until he caught sight of the blazing fire through the still-blinding storm and the group around it that he settled to the conviction that it was "square fun."

Whether Mr. Oakhurst had *cachéd* his cards with the whiskey as something debarred the free access of the community, I cannot say. It was certain that, in Mother Shipton's words, he "didn't say cards once" during that evening. Haply the time was beguiled by an accordion, produced somewhat ostentatiously by Tom Simson from his pack. Notwithstanding some difficulties attending the manipulation of this instrument, Piney Woods managed to pluck several reluctant melodies from its keys, to an accompaniment by the

Innocent on a pair of bone castinets. But the crowning festivity of the evening was reached in a rude camp-meeting hymn, which the lovers, joining hands, sang with great earnestness and vociferation. I fear that a certain defiant tone and Covenanter's swing to its chorus, rather than any devotional quality, caused it speedily to infect the others, who at last joined in the refrain:—

> "I'm proud to live in the service of the Lord,
> And I'm bound to die in His army."

The pines rocked, the storm eddied and whirled above the miserable group, and the flames of their altar leaped heavenward, as if in token of the vow.

At midnight the storm abated, the rolling clouds parted, and the stars glittered keenly above the sleeping camp. Mr. Oakhurst, whose professional habits had enabled him to live on the smallest possible amount of sleep, in dividing the watch with Tom Simson, somehow managed to take upon himself the greater part of that duty. He excused himself to the Innocent, by saying that he had "often been a week without sleep." "Doing what?" asked Tom. "Poker!" replied Oakhurst, sententiously; "when a man gets a streak of luck,—nigger-luck,—he don't get tired. The luck gives in first. Luck," continued the gambler, reflectively, "is a mighty queer thing. All you know about it for certain is that it's bound to change. And it's finding out when it's going to change that makes you. We've had a streak of bad luck since we left Poker Flat,—you come along, and slap you get into it, too. If you can hold your cards right along you're all right. For," added the gambler, with cheerful irrelevance,—

"'I'm proud to live in the service of the Lord,
And I'm bound to die in His army.'"

The third day came, and the sun, looking through the white-curtained valley, saw the outcasts divide their slowly decreasing store of provisions for the morning meal. It was one of the peculiarities of that mountain climate that its rays diffused a kindly warmth over the wintry landscape, as if in regretful commiseration of the past. But it revealed drift on drift of snow piled high around the hut,—a hopeless, uncharted, trackless sea of white lying below the rocky shores to which the castaways still clung. Through the marvellously clear air the smoke of the pastoral village of Poker Flat rose miles away. Mother Shipton saw it, and from a remote pinnacle of her rocky fastness, hurled in that direction a final malediction. It was her last vituperative attempt, and perhaps for that reason was invested with a certain degree of sublimity. It did her good, she privately informed the Duchess. "Just you go out there and cuss, and see." She then set herself to the task of amusing "the child," as she and the Duchess were pleased to call Piney. Piney was no chicken, but it was a soothing and original theory of the pair thus to account for the fact that she didn't swear and wasn't improper.

When night crept up again through the gorges, the reedy notes of the accordion rose and fell in fitful spasms and long-drawn gasps by the flickering camp-fire. But music failed to fill entirely the aching void left by insufficient food, and a new diversion was proposed by Piney,—story-telling. Neither Mr. Oakhurst nor his female companions caring to relate their personal experiences, this plan would have failed, too, but for the Innocent. Some months before he had chanced upon a stray copy of Mr. Pope's ingenious translation of the Iliad. He now proposed to narrate the principal incidents of that poem—having thoroughly mastered the argument and fairly forgotten the words —in the current vernacular of Sandy Bar. And so for the rest of that night the Homeric demigods again walked the earth. Trojan bully and wily Greek wrestled in the winds, and the great pines in the cañon seemed to bow to the wrath of the son of Peleus. Mr. Oakhurst listened with quiet satisfaction. Most especially was he interested in the fate of "Ash-heels," as the Innocent persisted in denominating the "swift-footed Achilles."

So with small food and much of Homer and the accordion, a week passed over the heads of the outcasts. The sun again forsook them, and again from leaden skies the snow-flakes were sifted over the land. Day by day closer around them drew the snowy circle, until at last they looked from their prison over drifted walls of dazzling white, that towered twenty feet above their heads. It became more and more difficult to replenish their fires, even from the fallen trees beside them, now half hidden in the drifts. And yet no one complained. The lovers turned from the dreary prospect and looked into each other's eyes, and were happy. Mr. Oakhurst settled himself coolly to the losing game before him. The Duchess, more cheerful than she had been, assumed the care of Piney. Only Mother Shipton—once the strongest of the party—seemed to sicken and fade. At midnight on the tenth day she called Oakhurst to her side. "I'm going," she said, in a voice of querulous weakness, "but don't say anything about it. Don't waken the kids. Take the bundle from under my head and open it." Mr. Oakhurst did so. It contained Mother Shipton's rations for the last week, untouched. "Give 'em to the child," she said, pointing to the sleeping Piney. "You've starved yourself," said the gambler. "That's what they call it," said the woman, querulously, as she lay down again, and, turning her face to the wall, passed quietly away.

The accordion and the bones were put aside that day, and Homer was forgotten. When the body of Mother Shipton had been committed to the snow, Mr. Oakhurst took the Innocent aside, and showed him a pair of snow-shoes, which he had fashioned from the old pack-saddle. "There's one chance in a hundred to save her yet," he said, pointing to Piney; "but it's there," he added, pointing toward Poker Flat. "If you can reach there in two days she's safe." "And you?" asked Tom Simson. "I'll stay here," was the curt reply.

The lovers parted with a long embrace. "You are not going, too?" said the Duchess, as she saw Mr. Oakhurst apparently waiting to accompany him. "As far as the cañon," he replied. He turned suddenly, and kissed the Duchess, leaving her pallid face aflame, and her trembling limbs rigid with amazement.

Night came, but not Mr. Oakhurst. It brought the storm again and the whirling snow. Then the Duchess, feeding the fire, found that some one had quietly piled beside the hut enough fuel to last a few days longer. The tears rose to her eyes, but she hid them from Piney.

The women slept but little. In the morning, looking into each other's faces, they read their fate. Neither spoke; but Piney, accepting the position of the stronger, drew near and placed her arm around the Duchess's waist. They kept this attitude for the rest of the day. That night the storm reached its greatest fury, and, rending asunder the protecting pines, invaded the very hut.

Toward morning they found themselves unable to feed the fire, which gradually died away. As the embers slowly blackened, the Duchess crept closer to Piney, and broke the silence of many hours: "Piney, can you pray?" "No, dear," said Piney, simply. The Duchess, without knowing exactly why, felt relieved, and, putting her head upon Piney's shoulder, spoke no more. And so reclining, the younger and purer pillowing the head of her soiled sister upon her virgin breast, they fell asleep.

The wind lulled as if it feared to waken them. Feathery drifts of snow, shaken from the long pine-boughs, flew like white-winged birds, and settled about them as they slept. The moon through the rifted clouds looked down upon what had been the camp. But all human stain, all trace of earthly travail, was hidden beneath the spotless mantle mercifully flung from above.

They slept all that day and the next, nor did they waken when voices and footsteps broke the silence of the camp. And when pitying fingers brushed the snow from their wan faces, you could scarcely have told from the equal peace that dwelt upon them, which was she that had sinned. Even the law of Poker Flat recognized this, and turned away, leaving them still locked in each other's arms.

But at the head of the gulch, on one of the largest pine-trees, they found the deuce of clubs pinned to the bark with a bowie-knife. It bore the following, written in pencil, in a firm hand:—

✝

BENEATH THIS TREE
LIES THE BODY
OF
JOHN OAKHURST,
WHO STRUCK A STREAK OF BAD LUCK
ON THE 23D OF NOVEMBER, 1850,
AND
HANDED IN HIS CHECKS
ON THE 7TH DECEMBER, 1850.

✝

And pulseless and cold, with a Derringer by his side and a bullet in his heart, though still calm as in life, beneath the snow lay he who was at once the strongest and yet the weakest of the outcasts of Poker Flat.

MIGGLES.

We were eight, including the driver. We had not spoken during the passage of the last six miles, since the jolting of the heavy vehicle over the roughening road had spoiled the Judge's last poetical quotation. The tall man beside the Judge was asleep, his arm passed through the swaying strap and his head resting upon it,—altogether a limp, helpless-looking object, as if he had hanged himself and been cut down too late. The French lady on the back seat was asleep, too, yet in a half-conscious propriety of attitude, shown even in the disposition of the handkerchief which she held to her forehead and which partially veiled her face. The lady from Virginia City, travelling with her husband, had long since lost all individuality in a wild confusion of ribbons, veils, furs, and shawls. There was no sound but the rattling of wheels and the dash of rain upon the roof. Suddenly the stage stopped and we became dimly aware of voices. The driver was evidently in the midst of an exciting colloquy with some one in the road,—a colloquy of which such fragments as "bridge gone," "twenty feet of water," "can't pass," were occasionally distinguishable above the storm. Then came a lull, and a mysterious voice from the road shouted the parting adjuration,—

"Try Miggles's."

We caught a glimpse of our leaders as the vehicle

slowly turned, of a horseman vanishing through the rain, and we were evidently on our way to Miggles's.

Who and where was Miggles? The Judge, our authority, did not remember the name, and he knew the country thoroughly. The Washoe traveller thought Miggles must keep a hotel. We only knew that we were stopped by high water in front and rear, and that Miggles was our rock of refuge. A ten minutes' splashing through a tangled by-road, scarcely wide enough for the stage, and we drew up before a barred and boarded gate in a wide stone wall or fence about eight feet high. Evidently Miggles's, and evidently Miggles did not keep a hotel.

The driver got down and tried the gate. It was securely locked.

"Miggles! O Miggles!"

No answer.

"Migg-ells! You Miggles!" continued the driver, with rising wrath.

"Migglesy!" joined in the expressman, persuasively. "O Miggy! Mig!"

But no reply came from the apparently insensate Miggles. The Judge, who had finally got the window down, put his head out and propounded a series of questions, which if answered categorically would have undoubtedly elucidated the whole mystery, but which the driver evaded by replying that "if we didn't want to sit in the coach all night, we had better rise up and sing out for Miggles."

So we rose up and called on Miggles in chorus; then separately. And when we had finished, a Hibernian fellow-passenger from the roof called for "Maygells!" whereat we all laughed. While we were laughing, the driver cried "Shoo!"

We listened. To our infinite amazement the chorus of "Miggles" was repeated from the other side of the wall, even to the final and supplemental "Maygells."

"Extraordinary echo," said the Judge.

"Extraordinary d—d skunk!" roared the driver, contemptuously. "Come out of that, Miggles, and show yourself! Be a man, Miggles! Don't hide in the dark; I wouldn't if I were you, Miggles," continued Yuba Bill, now dancing about in an excess of fury.

"Miggles!" continued the voice, "O Miggles!"

"My good man! Mr. Myghail!" said the Judge, softening the asperities of the name as much as possible. "Consider the inhospitality of refusing shelter from the inclemency of the weather to helpless females. Really, my dear sir—" But a succession of "Miggles," ending in a burst of laughter, drowned his voice.

Yuba Bill hesitated no longer. Taking a heavy stone from the road, he battered down the gate, and with the expressman entered the enclosure. We followed. Nobody was to be seen. In the gathering darkness all that we could distinguish was that we were in a garden—from the rose-bushes that scattered over us a minute spray from their dripping leaves—and before a long, rambling wooden building.

"Do you know this Miggles?" asked the Judge of Yuba Bill.

"No, nor don't want to," said Bill, shortly, who felt the Pioneer Stage Company insulted in his person by the contumacious Miggles.

"But, my dear sir," expostulated the Judge, as he thought of the barred gate.

"Lookee here," said Yuba Bill, with fine irony, "hadn't you better go back and sit in the coach till yer introduced? I'm going in," and he pushed open the door of the building.

A long room lighted only by the embers of a fire that was dying on the large hearth at its further extremity; the walls curiously papered, and the flickering firelight bringing out its grotesque pattern; somebody sitting in a large arm-chair by the fireplace. All this we saw as we crowded together into the room, after the driver and expressman.

"Hello, be you Miggles?" said Yuba Bill to the solitary occupant.

The figure neither spoke nor stirred. Yuba Bill walked wrathfully toward it, and turned the eye of his coach-lantern upon its face. It was a man's face, prematurely old and wrinkled, with very large eyes, in which there was that expression of perfectly gratuitous solemnity which I had sometimes seen in an owl's. The large eyes wandered from Bill's face to the lantern, and finally fixed their gaze on that luminous object, without further recognition.

Bill restrained himself with an effort.

"Miggles! Be you deaf? You ain't dumb anyhow, you know;" and Yuba Bill shook the insensate figure by the shoulder.

To our great dismay, as Bill removed his hand, the venerable stranger apparently collapsed,—sinking into half his size and an undistinguishable heap of clothing.

"Well, dern my skin," said Bill, looking appealingly at us, and hopelessly retiring from the contest.

The Judge now stepped forward, and we lifted the mysterious invertebrate back into his original position. Bill was dismissed with the lantern to reconnoitre outside, for it was evident that from the helplessness of this solitary man there must be attendants near at hand, and we all drew around the fire. The Judge, who had regained his authority, and had never lost his conversational amiability,—standing before us with his back to the hearth,—charged us, as an imaginary jury, as follows:—

"It is evident that either our distinguished friend here has reached that condition described by Shakespeare as 'the sere and yellow leaf,' or has suffered some premature abatement of his mental and physical faculties. Whether he is really the Miggles—"

Here he was interrupted by "Miggles! O Miggles! Migglesy! Mig!" and, in fact, the whole chorus of Miggles in very much the same key as it had once before been delivered unto us.

We gazed at each other for a moment in some alarm. The Judge, in particular, vacated his position quickly, as the voice seemed to come directly over his shoulder. The cause, however, was soon discovered in a large magpie who was perched upon a shelf over the fireplace, and who immediately relapsed into a sepulchral silence, which contrasted singularly with his previous volubility. It was, undoubtedly, his voice which we had heard in the road, and our friend in the chair was not responsible for the discourtesy. Yuba Bill, who re-entered the room after an unsuccessful search, was loath to accept the explanation, and still eyed the helpless sitter with suspicion. He had found a shed in which he had put up his horses, but he came back dripping and sceptical. "Thar ain't nobody but him within ten mile of the shanty, and that 'ar d—d old skeesicks knows it."

But the faith of the majority proved to be securely based. Bill had scarcely ceased growling before we heard a quick step upon the porch, the trailing of a wet skirt, the door was flung open, and with a flash of white teeth, a sparkle of dark eyes, and an utter absence of ceremony or diffidence, a young woman entered, shut the door, and, panting, leaned back against it.

"O, if you please, I'm Miggles!"

And this was Miggles! this bright-eyed, full-throated young woman, whose wet gown of coarse blue stuff could not hide the beauty of the feminine curves to which it clung; from the chestnut crown of whose head, topped by a man's oil-skin sou'wester, to the little feet and ankles, hidden somewhere in the recesses of her boy's brogans, all was grace;—this was Miggles, laughing at us, too, in the most airy, frank, off-hand manner imaginable.

"You see, boys," said she, quite out of breath, and holding one little hand against her side, quite unheeding the speechless discomfiture of our party, or the complete demoralization of Yuba Bill, whose features had relaxed into an expression of gratuitous and imbecile cheerfulness,—"you see, boys, I was mor'n two miles away when you passed down the road. I thought you might pull up here, and so I ran the whole way, knowing nobody was home but Jim,—and—and—I'm out of breath—and—that lets me out."

And here Miggles caught her dripping oil-skin hat from her head, with a mischievous swirl that scattered a shower of rain-drops over us; attempted to put back her hair; dropped two hair-pins in the attempt; laughed and sat down beside Yuba Bill, with her hands crossed lightly on her lap.

The Judge recovered himself first, and essayed an extravagant compliment.

"I'll trouble you for that thar har-pin," said Miggles, gravely. Half a dozen hands were eagerly stretched forward; the missing hair-pin was restored to its fair owner; and Miggles, crossing the room, looked keenly in the face of the invalid. The solemn eyes looked back at hers with an expression we had never seen before. Life and intelligence seemed to struggle back into the rugged face. Miggles laughed again,—it was a singularly eloquent laugh,—and turned her black eyes and white teeth once more towards us.

"This afflicted person is—" hesitated the Judge.

"Jim," said Miggles.

"Your father?"

"No."

"Brother?"

"No."

"Husband?"

Miggles darted a quick, half-defiant glance at the two lady passengers who I had noticed did not participate in the general masculine admiration of Miggles, and said, gravely, "No; it's Jim."

There was an awkward pause. The lady passengers moved closer to each other; the Washoe husband looked abstractedly at the fire; and the tall man apparently turned his eyes inward for self-support at this emergency. But Miggles's laugh, which was very infectious, broke the silence. "Come," she said briskly, "you must be hungry. Who'll bear a hand to help me get tea?"

She had no lack of volunteers. In a few moments Yuba Bill was engaged like Caliban in bearing logs for this Miranda; the expressman was grinding coffee on the veranda; to myself the arduous duty of slicing bacon was assigned; and the Judge lent each man his good-humored and voluble counsel. And when Miggles, assisted by the Judge and our Hibernian "deck passenger," set the table with all the available crockery, we had become quite joyous, in spite of the rain that beat against windows, the wind that whirled down the chimney, the two ladies who whispered together in the corner, or the magpie who uttered a satirical and croaking commentary on their conversation from his perch above. In the now bright, blazing fire we could see that the walls were papered with illustrated journals, arranged with feminine taste and discrimination. The furniture was extemporized and adapted from candle-boxes and packing-cases, and covered with gay calico, or the skin of some animal. The arm-chair of the helpless Jim was an ingenious variation of a flour-barrel. There was neatness, and even a taste for the picturesque, to be seen in the few details of the long low room.

The meal was a culinary success. But more, it was a social triumph,—chiefly, I think, owing to the rare tact of Miggles in guiding the conversation, asking all the questions herself, yet bearing throughout a frankness that rejected the idea of any concealment on her own part, so that we talked of ourselves, of our prospects, of the journey, of the weather, of each other, —of everything but our host and hostess. It must be confessed that Miggles's conversation was never elegant, rarely grammatical, and that at times she employed expletives, the use of which had generally been yielded to our sex. But they were delivered with such a lighting up of teeth and eyes, and were usually followed by a laugh — a laugh peculiar to Miggles — so frank and honest that it seemed to clear the moral atmosphere.

Once, during the meal, we heard a noise like the rubbing of a heavy body against the outer walls of the house. This was shortly followed by a scratching and sniffling at the door. "That's Joaquin," said Miggles, in reply to our questioning glances; "would you like to see him?" Before we could answer she had opened the door, and disclosed a half-grown grizzly, who instantly raised himself on his haunches, with his forepaws hanging down in the popular attitude of mendicancy, and looked admiringly at Miggles, with a very singular resemblance in his manner to Yuba Bill. "That's my watch-dog," said Miggles, in explanation. "O, he don't bite," she added, as the two lady passengers fluttered into a corner. "Does he, old Toppy?" (the latter remark being addressed directly to the sagacious Joaquin.) "I tell you what, boys," continued Miggles, after she had fed and closed the door on *Ursa Minor*, "you were in big luck that Joaquin wasn't hanging round when you dropped in to-night." "Where was he?" asked the Judge. "With me," said Miggles. "Lord love you; he trots round with me nights like as if he was a man."

We were silent for a few moments, and listened to the wind. Perhaps we all had the same picture before us, — of Miggles walking through the rainy woods, with her savage guardian at her side. The Judge, I remember, said something about Una and her lion; but Miggles received it as she did other compliments, with quiet gravity. Whether she was altogether unconscious of the admiration she excited,—she could hardly have been oblivious of Yuba Bill's adoration,—I know not; but her very frankness suggested a perfect sexual equality that was cruelly humiliating to the younger members of our party.

The incident of the bear did not add anything in Miggles's favor to the opinions of those of her own sex who were present. In fact, the repast over, a chillness radiated from the two lady passengers that no pine-boughs brought in by Yuba Bill and cast as a sacrifice upon the hearth could wholly overcome. Miggles felt it; and, suddenly declaring that it was time to "turn in," offered to show the ladies to their bed in an adjoining room. "You, boys, will have to camp out here by the fire as well as you can," she added, "for thar ain't but the one room."

Our sex—by which, my dear sir, I allude of course to the stronger portion of humanity—has been generally relieved from the imputation of curiosity, or a fondness for gossip. Yet I am constrained to say, that hardly had the door closed on Miggles than we crowded together, whispering, snickering, smiling, and exchanging suspicions, surmises, and a thousand speculations in regard to our pretty hostess and her singular companion. I fear that we even hustled that imbecile paralytic, who sat like a voiceless Memnon in our midst, gazing with the serene indifference of the Past in his passionless eyes upon our wordy counsels. In the midst of an exciting discussion the door opened again, and Miggles re-entered.

But not, apparently, the same Miggles who a few hours before had flashed upon us. Her eyes were downcast, and as she hesitated for a moment on the threshold, with a blanket on her arm, she seemed to have left behind her the frank fearlessness which had charmed us a moment before. Coming into the room, she drew a low stool beside the paralytic's chair, sat down, drew the blanket over her shoulders, and saying, "If it's all the same to you, boys, as we're rather crowded, I'll stop here to-night," took the invalid's withered hand in her own, and turned her eyes upon the dying fire. An instinctive feeling that this was only premonitory to more confidential relations, and perhaps some shame at our previous curiosity, kept us silent. The rain still beat upon the roof, wandering gusts of wind stirred the embers into momentary brightness, until, in a lull of the elements, Miggles suddenly lifted up her head, and, throwing her hair over her shoulder, turned her face upon the group and asked,—

"Is there any of you that knows me?"

There was no reply.

"Think again! I lived at Marysville in '53. Everybody knew me there, and everybody had the right to know me. I kept the Polka Saloon until I came to live with Jim. That's six years ago. Perhaps I've changed some."

The absence of recognition may have disconcerted her. She turned her head to the fire again, and it was some seconds before she again spoke, and then more rapidly:—

"Well, you see I thought some of you must have known me. There's no great harm done, anyway. What I was going to say was this: Jim here"—she took his hand in both of hers as she spoke—"used to know me, if you didn't, and spent a heap of money upon me. I reckon he spent all he had. And one day—it's six years ago this winter—Jim came into my back room, sat down on my sofy, like as you see him in that chair, and never moved again without help. He was struck all of a heap, and never seemed to know what ailed him. The doctors came and said as how it was caused all along of his way of life,—for Jim was mighty free and wild like,—and that he would never get better, and couldn't last long anyway. They advised me to send him to Frisco to the hospital, for he was no good to any one and would be a baby all his life. Perhaps it was something in Jim's eye, perhaps it was that I never had a baby, but I said 'No.' I was rich then, for I was popular with everybody,—gentlemen like yourself, sir, came to see me,—and I sold out my business and bought this yer place, because it was sort of out of the way of travel, you see, and I brought my baby here."

With a woman's intuitive tact and poetry, she had, as she spoke, slowly shifted her position so as to bring the mute figure of the ruined man between her and her audience, hiding in the shadow behind it, as if she offered it as a tacit apology for her actions. Silent and expressionless, it yet spoke for her; helpless, crushed, and smitten with the Divine thunderbolt, it still stretched an invisible arm around her.

Hidden in the darkness, but still holding his hand, she went on:—

"It was a long time before I could get the hang of things about yer, for I was used to company and excitement. I couldn't get any woman to help me, and a man I dursent trust; but what with the Indians hereabout, who'd do odd jobs for me, and having everything sent from the North Fork, Jim and I managed to worry through. The Doctor would run up from Sacramento once in a while. He'd ask to see 'Miggles's baby,' as he called Jim, and when he'd go away, he'd say, 'Miggles; you're a trump,—God bless you;' and it didn't seem so lonely after that. But the last time he was here he said, as he opened the door to go, 'Do you know, Miggles, your baby will grow up to be a man yet and an honor to his mother; but not here, Miggles, not here!' And I thought he went away sad,—and—and—" and here Miggles's voice and head were somehow both lost completely in the shadow.

"The folks about here are very kind," said Miggles, after a pause, coming a little into the light again. "The men from the fork used to hang around here, until they found they wasn't wanted, and the women are kind,—and don't call. I was pretty lonely until I picked up Joaquin in the woods yonder one day, when he wasn't so high, and taught him to beg for his dinner; and then thar's Polly—that's the magpie —she knows no end of tricks, and makes it quite sociable of evenings with her talk, and so I don't feel like as I was the only living being about the ranch. And Jim here," said Miggles, with her old laugh again, and coming out quite into the firelight, "Jim— why, boys, you would admire to see how much he knows for a man like him. Sometimes I bring him flowers, and he looks at 'em just as natural as if he knew 'em; and times, when we're sitting alone, I read him those things on the wall. Why, Lord!" said Miggles, with her frank laugh, "I've read him that whole side of the house this winter. There never was such a man for reading as Jim."

"Why," asked the Judge, "do you not marry this man to whom you have devoted your youthful life?"

"Well, you see," said Miggles, "it would be playing it rather low down on Jim, to take advantage of his being so helpless. And then, too, if we were man and wife, now, we'd both know that I was *bound* to do what I do now of my own accord."

"But you are young yet and attractive—"

"It's getting late," said Miggles, gravely, "and you'd better all turn in. Good-night, boys;" and, throwing the blanket over her head, Miggles laid herself down beside Jim's chair, her head pillowed on the low stool that held his feet, and spoke no more. The fire slowly faded from the hearth; we each sought our blankets in silence; and presently there was no sound in the long room but the pattering of the rain upon the roof, and the heavy breathing of the sleepers.

It was nearly morning when I awoke from a troubled dream. The storm had passed, the stars were shining, and through the shutterless window the full moon, lifting itself over the solemn pines without, looked into the room. It touched the lonely figure in the chair with an infinite compassion, and seemed to baptize with a shining flood the lowly head of the woman whose hair, as in the sweet old story, bathed the feet of him she loved. It even lent a kindly poetry to the rugged outline of Yuba Bill, half reclining on his elbow between them and his passengers, with savagely patient eyes keeping watch and ward. And then I fell asleep and only woke at broad day, with Yuba Bill standing over me, and "All aboard" ringing in my ears.

Coffee was waiting for us on the table, but Miggles was gone. We wandered about the house and lingered long after the horses were harnessed, but she did not return. It was evident that she wished to avoid a formal leave-taking, and had so left us to depart as we had come. After we had helped the ladies into the coach, we returned to the house and solemnly shook hands with the paralytic Jim, as solemnly settling him back into position after each hand-shake. Then we looked for the last time around the long low room, at the stool where Miggles had sat, and slowly took our seats in the waiting coach. The whip cracked, and we were off!

But as we reached the high-road, Bill's dexterous hand laid the six horses back on their haunches, and the stage stopped with a jerk. For there, on a little eminence beside the road, stood Miggles, her hair flying, her eyes sparkling, her white handkerchief waving, and her white teeth flashing a last "good-by." We waved our hats in return. And then Yuba Bill, as if fearful of further fascination, madly lashed his horses forward, and we sank back in our seats. We exchanged not a word until we reached the North Fork, and the stage drew up at the Independence House. Then, the Judge leading, we walked into the bar-room and took our places gravely at the bar.

"Are your glasses charged, gentlemen?" said the Judge, solemnly taking off his white hat.

They were.

"Well, then, here's to *Miggles*, GOD BLESS HER!"

Perhaps He had. Who knows?

TENNESSEE'S PARTNER.

I DO not think that we ever knew his real name. Our ignorance of it certainly never gave us any social inconvenience, for at Sandy Bar in 1854 most men were christened anew. Sometimes these appellatives were derived from some distinctiveness of dress, as in the case of "Dungaree Jack"; or from some peculiarity of habit, as shown in "Saleratus Bill," so called from an undue proportion of that chemical in his daily bread; or from some unlucky slip, as exhibited in "The Iron Pirate," a mild, inoffensive man, who earned that baleful title by his unfortunate mispronunciation of the term "iron pyrites." Perhaps this may have been the beginning of a rude heraldry; but I am constrained to think that it was because a man's real name in that day rested solely upon his own unsupported statement. "Call yourself Clifford, do you?" said Boston, addressing a timid new-comer with infinite scorn; "hell is full of such Cliffords!" He then introduced the unfortunate man, whose name happened to be really Clifford, as "Jay-bird Charley,"—an unhallowed inspiration of the moment that clung to him ever after.

But to return to Tennessee's Partner, whom we never knew by any other than this relative title; that he had ever existed as a separate and distinct individuality we only learned later. It seems that in 1853 he left Poker Flat to go to San Francisco, ostensibly to procure a wife. He never got any farther than Stockton. At that place he was attracted by a young person who waited upon the table at the hotel where he took his meals. One morning he said something to her which caused her to smile not unkindly, to somewhat coquettishly break a plate of toast over his upturned, serious, simple face, and to retreat to the kitchen. He followed her, and emerged a few moments later, covered, with more toast and victory. That day week they were married by a Justice of the Peace, and returned to Poker Flat. I am aware that something more might be made of this episode, but I prefer to tell it as it was current at Sandy Bar,—in the gulches and bar-rooms,—where all sentiment was modified by a strong sense of humor.

Of their married felicity but little is known, perhaps for the reason that Tennessee, then living with his partner, one day took occasion to say something to the bride on his own account, at which, it is said, she smiled not unkindly and chastely retreated,—this time as far as Marysville, where Tennessee followed her, and where they went to housekeeping without the aid of a Justice of the Peace. Tennessee's Partner took the loss of his wife simply and seriously, as was his fashion. But to everybody's surprise, when Tennessee one day returned from Marysville, without his partner's wife,—she having smiled and retreated with somebody else,—Tennessee's Partner was the first man to shake his hand and greet him with affection. The boys who had gathered in the cañon to see the shooting were naturally indignant. Their indignation might have found vent in sarcasm but for a certain look in Tennessee's Partner's eye that indicated a lack of humorous appreciation. In fact, he was a grave man, with a steady application to practical detail which was unpleasant in a difficulty.

Meanwhile a popular feeling against Tennessee had grown up on the Bar. He was known to be a gambler; he was suspected to be a thief. In these suspicions Tennessee's Partner was equally compromised; his continued intimacy with Tennessee after the affair above quoted could only be accounted for on the hypothesis of a copartnership of crime. At last Tennessee's guilt became flagrant. One day he overtook a stranger on his way to Red Dog. The stranger afterward related that Tennessee beguiled the time with interesting anecdote and reminiscence, but illogically concluded the interview in the following words: "And now, young man, I'll trouble you for your knife, your pistols, and your money. You see your weppings might get you into trouble at Red Dog, and your money's a temptation to the evilly disposed. I think you said your address was San Francisco. I shall endeavor to call." It may be stated here that Tennessee had a fine flow of humor, which no business preoccupation could wholly subdue.

This exploit was his last. Red Dog and Sandy Bar made common cause against the highwayman. Tennessee was hunted in very much the same fashion as his prototype, the grizzly. As the toils closed around him, he made a desperate dash through the Bar, emptying his revolver at the crowd before the Arcade Saloon, and so on up Grizzly Cañon; but at its farther extremity he was stopped by a small man on a gray horse. The men looked at each other a moment in silence. Both were fearless, both self-possessed and independent; and both types of a civilization that in the seventeenth century would have been called heroic, but, in the nineteenth, simply "reckless." "What have you got there?—I call," said Tennessee, quietly. "Two bowers and an ace," said the stranger, as quietly, showing two revolvers and a bowie-knife. "That takes me," returned Tennessee; and with this gamblers' epigram, he threw away his useless pistol, and rode back with his captor.

It was a warm night. The cool breeze which usually sprang up with the going down of the sun behind the *chaparral*-crested mountain was that evening withheld from Sandy Bar. The little cañon was stifling with heated resinous odors, and the decaying driftwood on the Bar sent forth faint, sickening exhalations. The feverishness of day, and its fierce passions, still filled the camp. Lights moved restlessly along the bank of the river, striking no answering reflection from its tawny current. Against the blackness of the pines the windows of the old loft above the express-office stood out staringly bright; and through their curtainless panes the loungers below could see the forms of those who were even then deciding the fate of Tennessee. And above all this, etched on the dark firmament, rose the Sierra, remote and passionless, crowned with remoter passionless stars.

The trial of Tennessee was conducted as fairly as was consistent with a judge and jury who felt themselves to some extent obliged to justify, in their verdict, the previous irregularities of arrest and indictment. The law of Sandy Bar was implacable, but not vengeful. The excitement and personal feeling of the chase were over; with Tennessee safe in their hands they were ready to listen patiently to any defence, which they were already satisfied was insufficient. There being no doubt in their own minds, they were willing to give the prisoner the benefit of any that might exist. Secure in the hypothesis that he ought to be hanged, on general principles, they indulged him with more latitude of defence than his reckless hardihood seemed to ask. The Judge appeared to be more anxious than the prisoner, who, otherwise unconcerned, evidently took a grim pleasure in the responsibility he had created. "I don't take any hand in this yer game," had been his invariable, but good-humored reply to all questions. The Judge—who was also his captor—for a moment vaguely regretted that he had not shot him "on sight," that morning, but presently dismissed this human weakness as unworthy of the judicial mind. Nevertheless, when there was a tap at the door, and it was said that Tennessee's Partner was there on behalf of the prisoner, he was admitted at once without question. Perhaps the younger members of the jury, to whom the proceedings were becoming irksomely thoughtful, hailed him as a relief.

For he was not, certainly, an imposing figure. Short and stout, with a square face, sunburned into a preternatural redness, clad in a loose duck "jumper," and trousers streaked and splashed with red soil, his aspect under any circumstances would have been quaint, and was now even ridiculous. As he stooped to deposit at his feet a heavy carpet-bag he was carrying, it became obvious, from partially developed legends and inscriptions, that the material with which his trousers had been patched had been originally intended for a less ambitious covering. Yet he advanced with great gravity, and after having shaken the hand of each person in the room with labored cordiality, he wiped his serious, perplexed face on a red bandanna handkerchief, a shade lighter than his complexion, laid his powerful hand upon the table to steady himself, and thus addressed the Judge:—

"I was passin' by," he began, by way of apology, "and I thought I'd just step in and see how things was gittin' on with Tennessee thar,—my pardner. It's a hot night. I disremember any sich weather before on the Bar."

He paused a moment, but nobody volunteering any other meteorological recollection, he again had recourse to his pocket-handkerchief, and for some moments mopped his face diligently.

"Have you anything to say in behalf of the prisoner?" said the Judge, finally.

"Thet's it," said Tennessee's Partner, in a tone of relief. "I come yar as Tennessee's pardner,—knowing him nigh on four year, off and on, wet and dry, in luck and out o' luck. His ways ain't allers my ways, but thar ain't any p'ints in that young man, thar ain't any liveliness as he's been up to, as I don't know. And you sez to me, sez you,—confidential-like, and between man and man,—sez you, 'Do you know anything in his behalf?' and I sez to you, sez I—confidential-like, as between man and man,—'What should a man know of his pardner?'"

"Is this all you have to say?" asked the Judge, impatiently, feeling, perhaps, that a dangerous sympathy of humor was beginning to humanize the Court.

"Thet's so," continued Tennessee's Partner. "It

ain't for me to say anything agin' him. And now, what's the case? Here's Tennessee wants money, wants it bad, and doesn't like to ask it of his old pardner. Well, what does Tennessee do? He lays for a stranger, and he fetches that stranger. And you lays for *him*, and you fetches *him;* and the honors is easy. And I put it to you, bein' a far-minded man, and to you, gentlemen, all, as far-minded men, ef this isn't so."

"Prisoner," said the Judge, interrupting, "have you any questions to ask this man?"

"No! no!" continued Tennessee's Partner, hastily. "I play this yer hand alone. To come down to the bed-rock, it's just this: Tennessee, thar, has played it pretty rough and expensive-like on a stranger, and on this yer camp. And now, what's the fair thing? Some would say more; some would say less. Here's seventeen hundred dollars in coarse gold and a watch, —it's about all my pile,—and call it square!" And before a hand could be raised to prevent him, he had emptied the contents of the carpet-bag upon the table.

For a moment his life was in jeopardy. One or two men sprang to their feet, several hands groped for hidden weapons, and a suggestion to "throw him from the window" was only overridden by a gesture from the Judge. Tennessee laughed. And apparently oblivious of the excitement, Tennessee's Partner improved the opportunity to mop his face again with his handkerchief.

When order was restored, and the man was made to understand, by the use of forcible figures and rhetoric, that Tennessee's offence could not be condoned by money, his face took a more serious and sanguinary hue, and those who were nearest to him noticed that his rough hand trembled slightly on the table. He hesitated a moment as he slowly returned the gold to the carpet-bag, as if he had not yet entirely caught the elevated sense of justice which swayed the tribunal, and was perplexed with the belief that he had not offered enough. Then he turned to the Judge, and saying, "This yer is a lone hand, played alone, and without my pardner," he bowed to the jury and was about to withdraw, when the Judge called him back. "If you have anything to say to Tennessee, you had better say it now." For the first time that evening the eyes of the prisoner and his strange advocate met. Tennessee smiled, showed his white teeth, and, saying, "Euchred, old man!" held out his hand. Tennessee's Partner took it in his own, and saying, "I just dropped in as I was passin' to see how things was gettin' on," let the hand passively fall, and adding that "it was a warm night," again mopped his face with his handkerchief, and without another word withdrew.

The two men never again met each other alive. For the unparalleled insult of a bribe offered to Judge Lynch—who, whether bigoted, weak, or narrow, was at least incorruptible—firmly fixed in the mind of that mythical personage any wavering determination of Tennessee's fate; and at the break of day he was marched, closely guarded, to meet it at the top of Marley's Hill.

How he met it, how cool he was, how he refused to say anything, how perfect were the arrangements of the committee, were all duly reported, with the addition of a warning moral and example to all future evildoers, in the Red Dog Clarion, by its editor, who was present, and to whose vigorous English I cheerfully refer the reader. But the beauty of that midsummer morning, the blessed amity of earth and air and sky, the awakened life of the free woods and hills, the joyous renewal and promise of Nature, and above all, the infinite Serenity that thrilled through each, was not reported, as not being a part of the social lesson. And yet, when the weak and foolish deed was done, and a life, with its possibilities and responsibilities, had passed out of the misshapen thing that dangled between earth and sky, the birds sang, the flowers bloomed, the sun shone, as cheerily as before; and possibly the Red Dog Clarion was right.

Tennessee's Partner was not in the group that surrounded the ominous tree. But as they turned to disperse attention was drawn to the singular appearance of a motionless donkey-cart halted at the side of the road. As they approached, they at once recognized the venerable "Jenny" and the two-wheeled cart as the property of Tennessee's Partner,—used by him in carrying dirt from his claim; and a few paces distant the owner of the equipage himself, sitting under a buckeye-tree, wiping the perspiration from his glowing face. In answer to an inquiry, he said he had come for the body of the "diseased," "if it was all the same to the committee." He didn't wish to "hurry anything"; he could "wait." He was not working that day; and when the gentlemen were done with the "diseased," he would take him. "Ef thar is any present," he added, in his simple, serious way, "as would care to jine in the fun'l, they kin come." Perhaps it was from a sense of humor, which I have already intimated was a feature of Sandy Bar,—perhaps it was from something even better than that; but two thirds of the loungers accepted the invitation at once.

It was noon when the body of Tennessee was delivered into the hands of his partner. As the cart drew up to the fatal tree, we noticed that it contained a rough, oblong box,—apparently made from a section of sluicing,—and half filled with bark and the tassels of pine. The cart was further decorated with slips of willow, and made fragrant with buckeye-blossoms. When the body was deposited in the box, Tennessee's Partner drew over it a piece of tarred canvas, and gravely mounting the narrow seat in front, with his feet upon the shafts, urged the little donkey forward. The equipage moved slowly on, at that decorous pace which was habitual with "Jenny" even under less solemn circumstances. The men—half curiously, half jestingly, but all good-humoredly—strolled along beside the cart; some in advance, some a little in the rear of the homely catafalque. But, whether from the narrowing of the road or some present sense of decorum, as the cart passed on, the company fell to the rear in couples, keeping step, and otherwise assuming the external show of a formal procession. Jack Folinsbee, who had at the outset played a funeral march in dumb show upon an imaginary trombone, desisted, from a lack of sympathy and appreciation,—not having, perhaps, your true humorist's capacity to be content with the enjoyment of his own fun.

The way led through Grizzly Cañon,—by this time clothed in funereal drapery and shadows. The redwoods, burying their moccasoned feet in the red soil, stood in Indian-file along the track, trailing an uncouth benediction from their bending boughs upon the passing bier. A hare, surprised into helpless inactivity, sat upright and pulsating in the ferns by the roadside, as the *cortège* went by. Squirrels hastened to gain a secure outlook from higher boughs; and the blue-jays, spreading their wings, fluttered before them like outriders, until the outskirts of Sandy Bar were reached, and the solitary cabin of Tennessee's Partner.

Viewed under more favorable circumstances, it would not have been a cheerful place. The unpicturesque site, the rude and unlovely outlines, the unsavory details, which distinguish the nest-building of the California miner, were all here with the dreariness of decay superadded. A few paces from the cabin there was a rough enclosure, which, in the brief days of Tennessee's Partner's matrimonial felicity, had been used as a garden, but was now overgrown with fern. As we approached it we were surprised to find that what we had taken for a recent attempt at cultivation was the broken soil about an open grave.

The cart was halted before the enclosure; and rejecting the offers of assistance with the same air of simple self-reliance he had displayed throughout, Tennessee's Partner lifted the rough coffin on his back, and deposited it, unaided, within the shallow grave. He then nailed down the board which served as a lid; and mounting the little mound of earth beside it, took off his hat, and slowly mopped his face with his handkerchief. This the crowd felt was a preliminary to speech; and they disposed themselves variously on stumps and boulders, and sat expectant.

"When a man," began Tennessee's Partner, slowly,

"has been running free all day, what's the natural thing for him to do? Why, to come home. And if he ain't in a condition to go home, what can his best friend do? Why, bring him home! And here's Tennessee has been running free, and we brings him home from his wandering." He paused, and picked up a fragment of quartz, rubbed it thoughtfully on his sleeve, and went on: "It ain't the first time that I've packed him on my back, as you see'd me now. It ain't the first time that I brought him to this yer cabin when he couldn't help himself; it ain't the first time that I and 'Jinny' have waited for him on yon hill, and picked him up and so fetched him home, when he couldn't speak and didn't know me. And now that it's the last time, why—" he paused, and rubbed the quartz gently on his sleeve—"you see it's sort of rough on his pardner. And now, gentlemen," he added, abruptly, picking up his long-handled shovel, "the fun'l's over; and my thanks, and Tennessee's thanks, to you for your trouble."

Resisting any proffers of assistance, he began to fill in the grave, turning his back upon the crowd, that after a few moments' hesitation gradually withdrew. As they crossed the little ridge that hid Sandy Bar from view, some, looking back, thought they could see Tennessee's Partner, his work done, sitting upon the grave, his shovel between his knees, and his face buried in his red bandanna handkerchief. But it was argued by others that you couldn't tell his face from his handkerchief at that distance; and this point remained undecided.

In the reaction that followed the feverish excitement of that day, Tennessee's Partner was not forgotten. A secret investigation had cleared him of any complicity in Tennessee's guilt, and left only a suspicion of his general sanity. Sandy Bar made a point of calling on him, and proffering various uncouth, but well-meant kindnesses. But from that day his rude health and great strength seemed visibly to decline; and when the rainy season fairly set in, and the tiny grass-blades were beginning to peep from the rocky mound above Tennessee's grave, he took to his bed.

One night, when the pines beside the cabin were swaying in the storm, and trailing their slender fingers over the roof, and the roar and rush of the swollen river were heard below, Tennessee's Partner lifted his head from the pillow, saying, "It is time to go for Tennessee; I must put 'Jinny' in the cart"; and would have risen from his bed but for the restraint of his attendant. Struggling, he still pursued his singular fancy: "There, now, steady, 'Jinny,'—steady, old girl. How dark it is! Look out for the ruts,—and look out for him, too, old gal. Sometimes, you know, when he's blind drunk, he drops down right in the trail. Keep on straight up to the pine on the top of the hill. Thar—I told you so!—thar he is,—coming this way, too,—all by himself, sober, and his face a-shining. Tennessee! Pardner!"

And so they met.

THE IDYL OF RED GULCH.

SANDY was very drunk. He was lying under an azalea-bush, in pretty much the same attitude in which he had fallen some hours before. How long he had been lying there he could not tell, and didn't care; how long he should lie there was a matter equally indefinite and unconsidered. A tranquil philosophy, born of his physical condition, suffused and saturated his moral being.

The spectacle of a drunken man, and of this drunken man in particular, was not, I grieve to say, of sufficient novelty in Red Gulch to attract attention. Earlier in the day some local satirist had erected a temporary tombstone at Sandy's head, bearing the inscription, "Effects of McCorkle's whiskey,—kills at forty rods," with a hand pointing to McCorkle's saloon. But this, I imagine, was, like most local satire, personal; and was a reflection upon the unfairness of the process rather than a commentary upon the impropriety of the result. With this facetious exception, Sandy had been undisturbed. A wandering mule, released from his pack, had cropped the scant herbage beside him, and sniffed curiously at the prostrate man; a vagabond dog, with that deep sympathy which the species have for drunken men, had licked his dusty boots, and curled himself up at his feet, and lay there, blinking one eye in the sunlight, with a simulation of dissipation that was ingenious and dog-like in its implied flattery of the unconscious man beside him.

Meanwhile the shadows of the pine-trees had slowly swung around until they crossed the road, and their trunks barred the open meadow with gigantic parallels of black and yellow. Little puffs of red dust, lifted by the plunging hoofs of passing teams, dispersed in a grimy shower upon the recumbent man. The sun sank lower and lower; and still Sandy stirred not. And then the repose of this philosopher was disturbed, as other philosophers have been, by the intrusion of an unphilosophical sex.

"Miss Mary," as she was known to the little flock that she had just dismissed from the log school-house beyond the pines, was taking her afternoon walk. Observing an unusually fine cluster of blossoms on the azalea-bush opposite, she crossed the road to pluck it, — picking her way through the red dust, not without certain fierce little shivers of disgust, and some feline circumlocution. And then she came suddenly upon Sandy!

Of course she uttered the little *staccato* cry of her sex. But when she had paid that tribute to her physical weakness she became overbold, and halted for a moment,— at least six feet from this prostrate monster,— with her white skirts gathered in her hand, ready for flight. But neither sound nor motion came from the bush. With one little foot she then overturned the satirical head-board, and muttered "Beasts!"— an epithet which probably, at that moment, conveniently classified in her mind the entire male population of Red Gulch. For Miss Mary, being possessed of certain rigid notions of her own, had not, perhaps, properly appreciated the demonstrative gallantry for which the Californian has been so justly celebrated by his brother Californians, and had, as a new-comer, perhaps, fairly earned the reputation of being "stuck up."

As she stood there she noticed, also, that the slant sunbeams were heating Sandy's head to what she judged to be an unhealthy temperature, and that his hat was lying uselessly at his side. To pick it up and to place it over his face was a work requiring some courage, particularly as his eyes were open. Yet she did it and made good her retreat. But she was somewhat concerned, on looking back, to see that the hat was removed, and that Sandy was sitting up and saying something.

The truth was, that in the calm depths of Sandy's mind he was satisfied that the rays of the sun were beneficial and healthful; that from childhood he had objected to lying down in a hat; that no people but condemned fools, past redemption, ever wore hats; and that his right to dispense with them when he pleased was inalienable. This was the statement of his inner consciousness. Unfortunately, its outward expression was vague, being limited to a repetition of the following formula, — "Su'shine all ri'! Wasser maär, eh? Wass up, su'shine?"

Miss Mary stopped, and, taking fresh courage from her vantage of distance, asked him if there was anything that he wanted.

"Wass up? Wasser maär?" continued Sandy, in a very high key.

"Get up, you horrid man!" said Miss Mary, now thoroughly incensed; "get up, and go home."

Sandy staggered to his feet. He was six feet high, and Miss Mary trembled. He started forward a few paces and then stopped.

"Wass I go home for?" he suddenly asked, with great gravity.

"Go and take a bath," replied Miss Mary, eying his grimy person with great disfavor.

To her infinite dismay, Sandy suddenly pulled off his coat and vest, threw them on the ground, kicked off his boots, and, plunging wildly forward, darted headlong over the hill, in the direction of the river.

"Goodness Heavens!—the man will be drowned!" said Miss Mary; and then, with feminine inconsistency, she ran back to the school-house, and locked herself in.

That night, while seated at supper with her hostess, the blacksmith's wife, it came to Miss Mary to ask, demurely, if her husband ever got drunk. "Abner," responded Mrs. Stidger, reflectively, "let's see: Abner hasn't been tight since last 'lection." Miss Mary would have liked to ask if he preferred lying in the sun on these occasions, and if a cold bath would have hurt him; but this would have involved an explanation, which she did not then care to give. So she contented herself with opening her gray eyes widely at the red-cheeked Mrs. Stidger, — a fine specimen of Southwestern efflorescence,—and then dismissed the subject altogether. The next day she wrote to her dearest friend, in Boston: "I think I find the intoxicated portion of this community the least objectionable. I refer, my dear, to the men, of course. I do not know anything that could make the women tolerable."

In less than a week Miss Mary had forgotten this episode, except that her afternoon walks took thereafter, almost unconsciously, another direction. She noticed, however, that every morning a fresh cluster of azalea-blossoms appeared among the flowers on her desk. This was not strange, as her little flock were aware of her fondness for flowers, and invariably kept her desk bright with anemones, syringas, and lupines; but, on questioning them, they, one and all, professed ignorance of the azaleas. A few days later, Master Johnny Stidger, whose desk was nearest to the window, was suddenly taken with spasms of apparently gratuitous laughter, that threatened the discipline of the school. All that Miss Mary could get from him was, that some one had been "looking in the winder." Irate and indignant, she sallied from her hive to do battle with the intruder. As she turned the corner of the school-house she came plump upon the quondam drunkard,— now perfectly sober, and inexpressibly sheepish and guilty-looking.

These facts Miss Mary was not slow to take a feminine advantage of, in her present humor. But it was somewhat confusing to observe, also, that the beast, despite some faint signs of past dissipation, was amiable-looking,— in fact, a kind of blond Samson, whose corn-colored, silken beard apparently had never yet known the touch of barber's razor or Delilah's shears. So that the cutting speech which quivered on her ready tongue died upon her lips, and she contented herself with receiving his stammering apology with supercilious eyelids and the gathered skirts of uncontamination. When she re-entered the school-room, her eyes fell upon the azaleas with a new sense of revelation. And then she laughed, and the little people all laughed, and they were all unconsciously very happy.

It was on a hot day—and not long after this—that two short-legged boys came to grief on the threshold of the school with a pail of water, which they had laboriously brought from the spring, and that Miss Mary compassionately seized the pail and started for the spring herself. At the foot of the hill a shadow crossed her path, and a blue-shirted arm dexterously, but gently relieved her of her burden. Miss Mary was both embarrassed and angry. "If you carried more of that for yourself," she said, spitefully, to the blue arm, without deigning to raise her lashes to its owner, "you'd do better." In the submissive silence that followed she regretted the speech, and thanked him so sweetly at the door that he stumbled. Which caused the children to laugh again,—a laugh in which Miss Mary joined, until the color came faintly into her pale cheek. The next day a barrel was mysteriously placed beside the door, and as mysteriously filled with fresh spring-water every morning.

Nor was this superior young person without other quiet attentions. "Profane Bill," driver of the Slumgullion Stage, widely known in the newspapers for his "gallantry" in invariably offering the box-seat to the fair sex, had excepted Miss Mary from this attention, on the ground that he had a habit of "cussin' on up grades," and gave her half the coach to herself. Jack Hamlin, a gambler, having once silently ridden with her in the same coach, afterward threw a decanter at the head of a confederate for mentioning her name in a bar-room. The over-dressed mother of a pupil whose paternity was doubtful had often lingered near this astute Vestal's temple, never daring to enter its sacred precincts, but content to worship the priestess from afar.

With such unconscious intervals the monotonous procession of blue skies, glittering sunshine, brief twilights, and starlit nights passed over Red Gulch. Miss Mary grew fond of walking in the sedate and proper woods. Perhaps she believed, with Mrs. Stidger, that the balsamic odors of the firs "did her chest good," for certainly her slight cough was less frequent and her step was firmer; perhaps she had learned the unending lesson which the patient pines are never weary of repeating to heedful or listless ears. And so, one day, she planned a picnic on Buckeye Hill, and took the children with her. Away from the dusty road, the straggling shanties, the yellow ditches, the clamor of restless engines, the cheap finery of shop-windows, the deeper glitter of paint and colored glass, and the thin veneering which barbarism takes upon itself in such localities,—what infinite relief was theirs! The last heap of ragged rock and clay passed, the last unsightly chasm crossed,—how the waiting woods opened their long files to receive them! How the children—perhaps because they had not yet grown quite away from the breast of the bounteous Mother—threw themselves face downward on her brown bosom with uncouth caresses, filling the air with their laughter; and how Miss Mary herself—felinely fastidious and intrenched as she was in the purity of spotless skirts, collar, and cuffs—forgot all, and ran like a crested quail at the head of her brood, until, romping, laughing, and panting, with a loosened braid of brown hair, a hat hanging by a knotted ribbon from her throat, she came suddenly and violently, in the heart of the forest, upon—the luckless Sandy!

The explanations, apologies, and not overwise conversation that ensued, need not be indicated here. It would seem, however, that Miss Mary had already established some acquaintance with this ex-drunkard. Enough that he was soon accepted as one of the party; that the children, with that quick intelligence which Providence gives the helpless, recognized a friend, and played with his blond beard, and long silken moustache, and took other liberties,—as the helpless are apt to do. And when he had built a fire against a tree, and had shown them other mysteries of wood-craft, their admiration knew no bounds. At the close of two such foolish, idle, happy hours he found himself lying at the feet of the schoolmistress, gazing dreamily in her face, as she sat upon the sloping hillside, weaving wreaths of laurel and syringa, in very much the same attitude as he had lain when first they met. Nor was the similitude greatly forced. The weakness of an easy, sensuous nature, that had found a dreamy exaltation in liquor, it is to be feared was now finding an equal intoxication in love.

I think that Sandy was dimly conscious of this himself. I know that he longed to be doing something,—slaying a grizzly, scalping a savage, or sacrificing himself in some way for the sake of this sallow-faced, gray-eyed schoolmistress. As I should like to present him in a heroic attitude, I stay my hand with great difficulty at this moment, being only withheld from introducing such an episode by a strong conviction that it does not usually occur at such times.

And I trust that my fairest reader, who remembers that, in a real crisis, it is always some uninteresting stranger or unromantic policeman, and not Adolphus, who rescues, will forgive the omission.

So they sat there, undisturbed,—the woodpeckers chattering overhead, and the voices of the children coming pleasantly from the hollow below. What they said matters little. What they thought—which might have been interesting—did not transpire. The woodpeckers only learned how Miss Mary was an orphan; how she left her uncle's house, to come to California, for the sake of health and independence; how Sandy was an orphan, too; how he came to California for excitement; how he had lived a wild life, and how he was trying to reform; and other details, which, from a woodpecker's view-point, undoubtedly must have seemed stupid, and a waste of time. But even in such trifles was the afternoon spent; and when the children were again gathered, and Sandy, with a delicacy which the schoolmistress well understood, took leave of them quietly at the outskirts of the settlement, it had seemed the shortest day of her weary life.

As the long, dry summer withered to its roots, the school term of Red Gulch—to use a local euphuism—"dried up" also. In another day Miss Mary would be free; and for a season, at least, Red Gulch would know her no more. She was seated alone in the school-house, her cheek resting on her hand, her eyes half closed in one of those day-dreams in which Miss Mary—I fear, to the danger of school discipline—was lately in the habit of indulging. Her lap was full of mosses, ferns, and other woodland memories. She was so preoccupied with these and her own thoughts that a gentle tapping at the door passed unheard, or translated itself into the remembrance of far-off woodpeckers. When at last it asserted itself more distinctly, she started up with a flushed cheek and opened the door. On the threshold stood a woman, the self-assertion and audacity of whose dress were in singular contrast to her timid, irresolute bearing.

Miss Mary recognized at a glance the dubious mother of her anonymous pupil. Perhaps she was disappointed, perhaps she was only fastidious; but as she coldly invited her to enter, she half unconsciously settled her white cuffs and collar, and gathered closer her own chaste skirts. It was, perhaps, for this reason that the embarrassed stranger, after a moment's hesitation, left her gorgeous parasol open and sticking in the dust beside the door, and then sat down at the farther end of a long bench. Her voice was husky as she began:—

"I heerd tell that you were goin' down to the Bay to-morrow, and I couldn't let you go until I came to thank you for your kindness to my Tommy."

Tommy, Miss Mary said, was a good boy, and deserved more than the poor attention she could give him.

"Thank you, miss; thank ye!" cried the stranger, brightening even through the color which Red Gulch knew facetiously as her "war paint," and striving, in her embarrassment, to drag the long bench nearer the schoolmistress. "I thank you, miss, for that! and if I am his mother, there ain't a sweeter, dearer, better boy lives than him. And if I ain't much as says it, thar ain't a sweeter, dearer, angeler teacher lives than he's got."

Miss Mary, sitting primly behind her desk, with a ruler over her shoulder, opened her gray eyes widely at this, but said nothing.

"It ain't for you to be complimented by the like of me, I know," she went on, hurriedly. "It ain't for me to be comin' here, in broad day, to do it, either; but I come to ask a favor,—not for me, miss,—not for me, but for the darling boy."

Encouraged by a look in the young schoolmistress's eye, and putting her lilac-gloved hands together, the fingers downward, between her knees, she went on, in a low voice:—

"You see, miss, there's no one the boy has any claim on but me, and I ain't the proper person to bring him up. I thought some, last year, of sending him away to 'Frisco to school, but when they talked of bringing a schoolma'am here, I waited till I saw you, and then I knew it was all right, and I could keep my boy a little longer. And O, miss, he loves you so much; and if you could hear him talk about you, in his pretty way, and if he could ask you what I ask you now, you couldn't refuse him.

"It is natural," she went on, rapidly, in a voice that trembled strangely between pride and humility,— "it's natural that he should take to you, miss, for his father, when I first knew him, was a gentleman,—and the boy must forget me, sooner or later,—and so I ain't a goin' to cry about that. For I come to ask you to take my Tommy,—God bless him for the bestest, sweetest boy that lives,—to—to—take him with you."

She had risen and caught the young girl's hand in her own, and had fallen on her knees beside her.

"I've money plenty, and it's all yours and his.

Put him in some good school, where you can go and see him, and help him to—to—to forget his mother. Do with him what you like. The worst you can do will be kindness to what he will learn with me. Only take him out of this wicked life, this cruel place, this home of shame and sorrow. You will; I know you will,—won't you? You will,—you must not, you cannot say no! You will make him as pure, as gentle as yourself; and when he has grown up, you will tell him his father's name,—the name that hasn't passed my lips for years,—the name of Alexander Morton, whom they call here Sandy! Miss Mary!—do not take your hand away! Miss Mary, speak to me! You will take my boy? Do not put your face from me. I know it ought not to look on such as me. Miss Mary!—my God, be merciful!—she is leaving me!"

Miss Mary had risen, and, in the gathering twilight, had felt her way to the open window. She stood there, leaning against the casement, her eyes fixed on the last rosy tints that were fading from the western sky. There was still some of its light on her pure young forehead, on her white collar, on her clasped white hands, but all fading slowly away. The suppliant had dragged herself, still on her knees, beside her.

"I know it takes time to consider. I will wait here all night; but I cannot go until you speak. Do not deny me now. You will!—I see it in your sweet face,—such a face as I have seen in my dreams. I see it in your eyes, Miss Mary!—you will take my boy!"

The last red beam crept higher, suffused Miss Mary's eyes with something of its glory, flickered, and faded, and went out. The sun had set on Red Gulch. In the twilight and silence Miss Mary's voice sounded pleasantly.

"I will take the boy. Send him to me to-night."

The happy mother raised the hem of Miss Mary's skirts to her lips. She would have buried her hot face in its virgin folds, but she dared not. She rose to her feet.

"Does—this man—know of your intention?" asked Miss Mary, suddenly.

"No, nor cares. He has never even seen the child to know it."

"Go to him at once,—to-night,—now! Tell him what you have done. Tell him I have taken his child, and tell him—he must never see—see—the child again. Wherever it may be, he must not come; wherever I may take it, he must not follow! There, go now, please,—I'm weary, and—have much yet to do!"

They walked together to the door. On the threshold the woman turned.

"Good night."

She would have fallen at Miss Mary's feet. But at the same moment the young girl reached out her arms, caught the sinful woman to her own pure breast for one brief moment, and then closed and locked the door.

It was with a sudden sense of great responsibility that Profane Bill took the reins of the Slumgullion Stage the next morning, for the schoolmistress was one of his passengers. As he entered the high-road, in obedience to a pleasant voice from the "inside," he suddenly reined up his horses and respectfully waited, as "Tommy" hopped out at the command of Miss Mary.

"Not that bush, Tommy,—the next."

Tommy whipped out his new pocket-knife, and, cutting a branch from a tall azalea-bush, returned with it to Miss Mary.

"All right now?"

"All right."

And the stage-door closed on the Idyl of Red Gulch.

BROWN OF CALAVERAS.

A SUBDUED tone of conversation, and the absence of cigar-smoke and boot-heels at the windows of the Wingdam stage-coach, made it evident that one of the inside passengers was a woman. A disposition on the part of loungers at the stations to congregate before the window, and some concern in regard to the appearance of coats, hats, and collars, further indicated that she was lovely. All of which Mr. Jack Hamlin, on the box-seat, noted with the smile of cynical philosophy. Not that he depreciated the sex, but that he recognized therein a deceitful element, the pursuit of which sometimes drew mankind away from the equally uncertain blandishments of poker,—of which it may be remarked that Mr. Hamlin was a professional exponent.

So that, when he placed his narrow boot on the wheel and leaped down, he did not even glance at the window from which a green veil was fluttering, but lounged up and down with that listless and grave indifference of his class, which was, perhaps, the next thing to good-breeding. With his closely buttoned figure and self-contained air he was a marked contrast to the other passengers, with their feverish restlessness, and boisterous emotion; and even Bill Masters, a graduate of Harvard, with his slovenly dress, his overflowing vitality, his intense appreciation of lawlessness and barbarism, and his mouth filled with crackers and cheese, I fear cut but an unromantic figure beside this lonely calculator of chances, with his pale Greek face and Homeric gravity.

The driver called "All aboard!" and Mr. Hamlin returned to the coach. His foot was upon the wheel, and his face raised to the level of the open window, when, at the same moment, what appeared to him to be the finest eyes in the world suddenly met his. He quietly dropped down again, addressed a few words to one of the inside passengers, effected an exchange of seats, and as quietly took his place inside. Mr. Hamlin never allowed his philosophy to interfere with decisive and prompt action.

I fear that this irruption of Jack cast some restraint upon the other passengers,—particularly those who were making themselves most agreeable to the lady. One of them leaned forward, and apparently conveyed to her information regarding Mr. Hamlin's profession in a single epithet. Whether Mr. Hamlin heard it, or whether he recognized in the informant a distinguished jurist, from whom, but a few evenings before, he had won several thousand dollars, I cannot say. His colorless face betrayed no sign; his black eyes, quietly observant, glanced indifferently past the legal gentleman, and rested on the much more pleasing features of his neighbor. An Indian stoicism—said to be an inheritance from his maternal ancestor—stood him in good service, until the rolling wheels rattled upon the river-gravel at Scott's Ferry, and the stage drew up at the International Hotel for dinner. The legal gentleman and a member of Congress leaped out, and stood ready to assist the descending goddess, while Colonel Starbottle, of Siskiyou, took charge of her parasol and shawl. In this multiplicity of attention there was a momentary confusion and delay. Jack Hamlin quietly opened the *opposite* door of the coach, took the lady's hand,—with that decision and positiveness which a hesitating and undecided sex know how to admire,— and in an instant had dexterously and gracefully swung her to the ground, and again lifted her to the platform. An audible chuckle on the box, I fear, came from that other cynic, "Yuba Bill," the driver. "Look keerfully arter that baggage, Kernel," said the expressman, with affected concern, as he looked after Colonel Starbottle, gloomily bringing up the rear of the triumphant procession to the waiting-room.

Mr. Hamlin did not stay for dinner. His horse was already saddled, and awaiting him. He dashed over the ford, up the gravelly hill, and out into the dusty perspective of the Wingdam road, like one leaving an unpleasant fancy behind him. The inmates of dusty cabins by the roadside shaded their eyes with their hands, and looked after him, recognizing the man by his horse, and speculating what "was up with Comanche Jack." Yet much of this interest centred in the horse, in a community where the time made by "French Pete's" mare, in his run from the Sheriff of Calaveras, eclipsed all concern in the ultimate fate of that worthy.

The sweating flanks of his gray at length recalled him to himself. He checked his speed, and, turning into a by-road, sometimes used as a cut-off, trotted leisurely along, the reins hanging listlessly from his fingers. As he rode on, the character of the landscape changed, and became more pastoral. Openings in groves of pine and sycamore disclosed some rude attempts at cultivation,—a flowering vine trailed over the porch of one cabin, and a woman rocked her cradled babe under the roses of another. A little farther on Mr. Hamlin came upon some barelegged children, wading in the willowy creek, and so wrought upon them with a badinage peculiar to himself, that they were emboldened to climb up his horse's legs and over his saddle, until he was fain to develop an exaggerated ferocity of demeanor, and to escape, leaving behind some kisses and coin. And then, advancing deeper into the woods, where all signs of habitation failed, he began to sing,—uplifting a tenor so singularly sweet, and shaded by a pathos so subduing and tender, that I wot the robins and linnets stopped to listen. Mr. Hamlin's voice was not cultivated; the subject of his song was some sentimental lunacy, borrowed from the negro minstrels; but there thrilled through all some occult quality of tone and expression that was unspeakably touching. Indeed, it was a wonderful sight to see this sentimental blackleg, with a pack of cards in his pocket and a revolver at his back, sending his voice before him through the dim woods with a plaint about his "Nelly's grave," in a way that overflowed the eyes of the listener. A sparrow-hawk, fresh from his sixth victim, possibly recognizing in Mr. Hamlin a kindred spirit, stared at him in surprise, and was fain to confess the superiority of man. With a superior predatory capacity, *he* couldn't sing.

But Mr. Hamlin presently found himself again on the high-road, and at his former pace. Ditches and banks of gravel, denuded hillsides, stumps, and decayed trunks of trees, took the place of woodland and ravine, and indicated his approach to civilization. Then a church-steeple came in sight, and he knew that he had reached home. In a few moments he was clattering down the single narrow street, that lost itself in a chaotic ruin of races, ditches, and tailings at the foot of the hill, and dismounted before the gilded windows of the "Magnolia" saloon. Passing through the long bar-room, he pushed open a green-baize door, entered a dark passage, opened another door with a pass-key, and found himself in a dimly lighted room, whose furniture, though elegant and costly for the locality, showed signs of abuse. The inlaid centre-table was overlaid with stained disks that were not contemplated in the original design. The embroidered arm-chairs were discolored, and the green velvet lounge, on which Mr. Hamlin threw himself, was soiled at the foot with the red soil of Wingdam.

Mr. Hamlin did not sing in his cage. He lay still, looking at a highly colored painting above him, representing a young creature of opulent charms. It occurred to him then, for the first time, that he had never seen exactly that kind of a woman, and that, if he should, he would not, probably, fall in love with her. Perhaps he was thinking of another style of beauty. But just then some one knocked at the door. Without rising, he pulled a cord that apparently shot back a bolt, for the door swung open, and a man entered.

The new-comer was broad-shouldered and robust, — a vigor not borne out in the face, which, though handsome, was singularly weak, and disfigured by dissipation. He appeared to be also under the influence of liquor, for he started on seeing Mr. Hamlin, and said, "I thought Kate was here;" stammered, and seemed confused and embarrassed.

Mr. Hamlin smiled the smile which he had before worn on the Wingdam coach, and sat up, quite refreshed and ready for business.

"You didn't come up on the stage," continued the new-comer, "did you?"

"No," replied Hamlin; "I left it at Scott's Ferry. It isn't due for half an hour yet. But how's luck, Brown?"

"D—— bad," said Brown, his face suddenly assuming an expression of weak despair; "I'm cleaned out again. Jack," he continued, in a whining tone, that formed a pitiable contrast to his bulky figure, "can't you help me with a hundred till to-morrow's clean-up? You see I've got to send money home to the old woman, and—you've won twenty times that amount from me."

The conclusion was, perhaps, not entirely logical, but Jack overlooked it, and handed the sum to his visitor. "The old woman business is about played out, Brown," he added, by way of commentary; "why don't you say you want to buck agin' faro? You know you ain't married!"

"Fact, sir," said Brown, with a sudden gravity, as if the mere contact of the gold with the palm of the hand had imparted some dignity to his frame. "I've got a wife—a d—— good one, too, if I do say it—in the States. It's three year since I've seen her, and a year since I've writ to her. When things is about straight, and we get down to the lead, I'm going to send for her."

"And Kate?" queried Mr. Hamlin, with his previous smile.

Mr. Brown, of Calaveras, essayed an archness of glance, to cover his confusion, which his weak face and whiskey-muddled intellect but poorly carried out, and said,—

"D—— it, Jack, a man must have a little liberty, you know. But come, what do you say to a little game? Give us a show to double this hundred."

Jack Hamlin looked curiously at his fatuous friend. Perhaps he knew that the man was predestined to lose the money, and preferred that it should flow back into his own coffers rather than any other. He nodded his head, and drew his chair toward the table. At the same moment there came a rap upon the door.

"It's Kate," said Mr. Brown.

Mr. Hamlin shot back the bolt, and the door opened. But, for the first time in his life, he staggered to his feet, utterly unnerved and abashed, and for the first time in his life the hot blood crimsoned his colorless cheeks to his forehead. For before him stood the lady he had lifted from the Wingdam coach, whom Brown—dropping his cards with a hysterical laugh—greeted as

"My old woman, by thunder!"

They say that Mrs. Brown burst into tears, and reproaches of her husband. I saw her, in 1857, at Marysville, and disbelieve the story. And the Wingdam Chronicle, of the next week, under the head of "Touching Reunion," said: "One of those beautiful and touching incidents, peculiar to California life, occurred last week in our city. The wife of one of Wingdam's eminent pioneers, tired of the effete civilization of the East and its inhospitable climate, resolved to join her noble husband upon these golden shores. Without informing him of her intention, she undertook the long journey, and arrived last week. The joy of the husband may be easier imagined than described. The meeting is said to have been indescribably affecting. We trust her example may be followed."

Whether owing to Mrs. Brown's influence, or to some more successful speculations, Mr. Brown's financial fortune from that day steadily improved. He bought out his partners in the "Nip and Tuck" lead, with money which was said to have been won at poker, a week or two after his wife's arrival, but which rumor, adopting Mrs. Brown's theory that Brown had forsworn the gaming-table, declared to have been furnished by Mr. Jack Hamlin. He built and furnished the "Wingdam House," which pretty Mrs. Brown's great popularity kept overflowing with guests. He was elected to the Assembly, and gave largess to churches. A street in Wingdam was named in his honor.

Yet it was noted that in proportion as he waxed wealthy and fortunate, he grew pale, thin, and anxious. As his wife's popularity increased, he became fretful and impatient. The most uxorious of husbands, he was absurdly jealous. If he did not interfere with his wife's social liberty, it was because it was maliciously whispered that his first and only attempt was met by an outburst from Mrs. Brown that terrified him into silence. Much of this kind of gossip came from those of her own sex whom she had supplanted in the chivalrous attentions of Wingdam, which, like most popular chivalry, was devoted to an admiration of power, whether of masculine force or feminine beauty. It should be remembered, too, in her extenuation, that, since her arrival, she had been the unconscious priestess of a mythological worship, perhaps not more ennobling to her womanhood than that which distinguished an older Greek democracy. I think that Brown was dimly conscious of this. But his only confidant was Jack Hamlin, whose *infelix* reputation naturally precluded any open intimacy with the family, and whose visits were infrequent.

It was midsummer, and a moonlit night; and Mrs. Brown, very rosy, large-eyed, and pretty, sat upon the piazza, enjoying the fresh incense of the mountain breeze, and, it is to be feared, another incense which was not so fresh, nor quite as innocent. Beside her sat Colonel Starbottle and Judge Boompointer, and a later addition to her court, in the shape of a foreign tourist. She was in good spirits.

"What do you see down the road?" inquired the gallant Colonel, who had been conscious, for the last few minutes, that Mrs. Brown's attention was diverted.

"Dust," said Mrs. Brown, with a sigh. "Only Sister Anne's 'flock of sheep.'"

The Colonel, whose literary recollections did not extend farther back than last week's paper, took a more practical view. "It ain't sheep," he continued; "it's a horseman. Judge, ain't that Jack Hamlin's gray?"

But the Judge didn't know; and, as Mrs. Brown suggested the air was growing too cold for further investigations, they retired to the parlor.

Mr. Brown was in the stable, where he generally retired after dinner. Perhaps it was to show his contempt for his wife's companions; perhaps, like other weak natures, he found pleasure in the exercise of absolute power over inferior animals. He had a certain gratification in the training of a chestnut mare, whom he could beat or caress as pleased him, which he couldn't do with Mrs. Brown. It was here that he recognized a certain gray horse which had just come in, and, looking a little farther on, found his rider. Brown's greeting was cordial and hearty; Mr. Hamlin's somewhat restrained. But at Brown's urgent request, he followed him up the back stairs to a narrow corridor, and thence to a small room looking out upon the stable-yard. It was plainly furnished with a bed, a table, a few chairs, and a rack for guns and whips.

"This yer's my home, Jack," said Brown, with a sigh, as he threw himself upon the bed, and motioned his companion to a chair. "Her room's t' other end of the hall. It's more 'n six months since we've lived together, or met, except at meals. It's mighty rough papers on the head of the house, ain't it?" he said, with a forced laugh. "But I'm glad to see you, Jack, d—— glad," and he reached from the bed, and again shook the unresponsive hand of Jack Hamlin.

"I brought ye up here, for I didn't want to talk in the stable; though, for the matter of that, it's all round town. Don't strike a light. We can talk here in the moonshine. Put up your feet on that winder, and sit here beside me. Thar's whiskey in that jug."

Mr. Hamlin did not avail himself of the information. Brown, of Calaveras, turned his face to the wall, and continued:—

"If I didn't love the woman, Jack, I wouldn't mind. But it's loving her, and seeing her, day arter day, goin' on at this rate, and no one to put down the brake; that's what gits me! But I'm glad to see ye, Jack, d—— glad."

In the darkness he groped about until he had found and wrung his companion's hand again. He would have detained it, but Jack slipped it into the buttoned breast of his coat, and asked, listlessly, "How long has this been going on?"

"Ever since she came here; ever since the day she walked into the Magnolia. I was a fool then; Jack, I'm a fool now; but I didn't know how much I loved her till then. And she hasn't been the same woman since.

"But that ain't all, Jack; and it's what I wanted to see you about, and I'm glad you've come. It ain't that she doesn't love me any more; it ain't that she fools with every chap that comes along, for, perhaps, I staked her love and lost it, as I did everything else at the Magnolia; and, perhaps, foolin' is nateral to some women, and thar ain't no great harm done, 'cept to the fools. But, Jack, I think,—I think she loves somebody else. Don't move, Jack; don't move; if your pistol hurts ye, take it off.

"It's been more 'n six months now that she's seemed unhappy and lonesome, and kinder nervous and scared like. And sometimes I've ketched her lookin' at me sort of timid and pitying. And she writes to somebody. And for the last week she's been gathering her own things,—trinkets, and furbelows, and jew'lry,—and, Jack, I think she's goin' off. I could stand all but that. To have her steal away like a thief—" He put his face downward to the pillow, and for a few moments there was no sound but the ticking of a clock on the mantel. Mr. Hamlin lit a cigar, and moved to the open window. The moon no longer shone into the room, and the bed and its occupant were in shadow. "What shall I do, Jack?" said the voice from the darkness.

The answer came promptly and clearly from the window-side,—"Spot the man, and kill him on sight."

"But, Jack?"

"He's took the risk!"

"But will that bring *her* back?"

Jack did not reply, but moved from the window towards the door.

"Don't go yet, Jack; light the candle, and sit by the table. It's a comfort to see ye, if nothin' else."

Jack hesitated, and then complied. He drew a pack of cards from his pocket and shuffled them, glancing at the bed. But Brown's face was turned to the wall. When Mr. Hamlin had shuffled the cards, he cut them, and dealt one card on the opposite side of the table and towards the bed, and another on his side of the table for himself. The first was a deuce; his own card, a king. He then shuffled and cut again. This time "dummy" had a queen, and himself a four-spot. Jack brightened up for the third deal. It brought his adversary a deuce, and himself a king again. "Two out of three," said Jack, audibly.

"What's that, Jack?" said Brown.

"Nothing."

Then Jack tried his hand with dice; but he always

threw sixes, and his imaginary opponent aces. The force of habit is sometimes confusing.

Meanwhile, some magnetic influence in Mr. Hamlin's presence, or the anodyne of liquor, or both, brought surcease of sorrow, and Brown slept. Mr. Hamlin moved his chair to the window, and looked out on the town of Wingdam, now sleeping peacefully, — its harsh outlines softened and subdued, its glaring colors mellowed and sobered in the moonlight that flowed over all. In the hush he could hear the gurgling of water in the ditches, and the sighing of the pines beyond the hill. Then he looked up at the firmament, and as he did so a star shot across the twinkling field. Presently another, and then another. The phenomenon suggested to Mr. Hamlin a fresh augury. If in another fifteen minutes another star should fall— He sat there, watch in hand, for twice that time, but the phenomenon was not repeated.

The clock struck two, and Brown still slept. Mr. Hamlin approached the table, and took from his pocket a letter, which he read by the flickering candle-light. It contained only a single line, written in pencil, in a woman's hand,—

"Be at the corral, with the buggy, at three."

The sleeper moved uneasily, and then awoke. "Are you there, Jack?"

"Yes."

"Don't go yet. I dreamed just now, Jack,—dreamed of old times. I thought that Sue and me was being married agin, and that the parson, Jack, was—who do you think?—you!"

The gambler laughed, and seated himself on the bed,—the paper still in his hand.

"It's a good sign, ain't it?" queried Brown.

"I reckon. Say, old man, hadn't you better get up?"

The "old man," thus affectionately appealed to, rose, with the assistance of Hamlin's outstretched hand.

"Smoke?"

Brown mechanically took the proffered cigar.

"Light?"

Jack had twisted the letter into a spiral, lit it, and held it for his companion. He continued to hold it until it was consumed, and dropped the fragment—a fiery star—from the open window. He watched it as it fell, and then returned to his friend.

"Old man," he said, placing his hands upon Brown's shoulders, "in ten minutes I'll be on the road, and gone like that spark. We won't see each other agin; but, before I go, take a fool's advice: sell out all you've got, take your wife with you, and quit the country. It ain't no place for you, nor her. Tell her she must go; make her go, if she won't. Don't whine because you can't be a saint, and she ain't an angel. Be a man,—and treat her like a woman. Don't be a d—— fool. Good by."

He tore himself from Brown's grasp, and leaped down the stairs like a deer. At the stable-door he collared the half-sleeping hostler, and backed him against the wall. "Saddle my horse in two minutes, or I'll—" The ellipsis was frightfully suggestive.

"The missis said you was to have the buggy," stammered the man.

"D——n the buggy!"

The horse was saddled as fast as the nervous hands of the astounded hostler could manipulate buckle and strap.

"Is anything up, Mr. Hamlin?" said the man, who, like all his class, admired the *élan* of his fiery patron, and was really concerned in his welfare.

"Stand aside!"

The man fell back. With an oath, a bound, and clatter, Jack was into the road. In another moment, to the man's half-awakened eyes, he was but a moving cloud of dust in the distance, towards which a star just loosed from its brethren was trailing a stream of fire.

But early that morning the dwellers by the Wing-dam turnpike, miles away, heard a voice, pure as a sky-lark's, singing afield. They who were asleep turned over on their rude couches to dream of youth and love and olden days. Hard-faced men and anxious gold-seekers, already at work, ceased their labors and leaned upon their picks, to listen to a romantic vagabond ambling away against the rosy sunrise.

MLISS.

CHAPTER I.

Just where the Sierra Nevada begins to subside in gentler undulations, and the rivers grow less rapid and yellow, on the side of a great red mountain, stands "Smith's Pocket." Seen from the red road at sunset, in the red light and the red dust, its white houses look like the outcroppings of quartz on the mountain-side. The red stage topped with red-shirted passengers is lost to view half a dozen times in the tortuous descent, turning up unexpectedly in out-of-the-way places, and vanishing altogether within a hundred yards of the town. It is probably owing to this sudden twist in the road that the advent of a stranger at Smith's Pocket is usually attended with a peculiar circumstance. Dismounting from the vehicle at the stage-office, the too confident traveller is apt to walk straight out of town under the impression that it lies in quite another direction. It is related that one of the tunnel-men, two miles from town, met one of these self-reliant passengers with a carpet-bag, umbrella, Harper's Magazine, and other evidences of "Civilization and Refinement," plodding along over the road he had just ridden, vainly endeavoring to find the settlement of Smith's Pocket.

An observant traveller might have found some compensation for his disappointment in the weird aspect of that vicinity. There were huge fissures on the hillside, and displacements of the red soil, resembling more the chaos of some primary elemental upheaval than the work of man; while, half-way down, a long flume straddled its narrow body and disproportionate legs over the chasm, like an enormous fossil of some forgotten antediluvian. At every step smaller ditches crossed the road, hiding in their sallow depths unlovely streams that crept away to a clandestine union with the great yellow torrent below, and here and there were the ruins of some cabin with the chimney alone left intact and the hearthstone open to the skies.

The settlement of Smith's Pocket owed its origin to the finding of a "pocket" on its site by a veritable Smith. Five thousand dollars were taken out of it in one half-hour by Smith. Three thousand dollars were expended by Smith and others in erecting a flume and in tunnelling. And then Smith's Pocket was found to be only a pocket, and subject like other pockets to depletion. Although Smith pierced the bowels of the great red mountain, that five thousand dollars was the first and last return of his labor. The mountain grew reticent of its golden secrets, and the flume steadily ebbed away the remainder of Smith's fortune. Then Smith went into quartz-mining; then into quartz-milling; then into hydraulics and ditching, and then by easy degrees into saloon-keeping. Presently it was whispered that Smith was drinking a great deal; then it was known that Smith was a habitual drunkard, and then people began to think, as they are apt to, that he had never been anything else. But the settlement of Smith's Pocket, like that of most discoveries, was happily not dependent on the fortune of its pioneer, and other parties projected tunnels and found pockets. So Smith's Pocket became a settlement with its two fancy stores, its two hotels, its one express-office, and its two first families. Occasionally its one long straggling street was overawed by the assumption of the latest San Francisco fashions, imported per express, exclusively to the first families; making outraged Nature, in the ragged outline of her furrowed surface, look still more homely, and putting personal insult on that greater portion of the population to whom the Sabbath, with a change of linen, brought merely the necessity of cleanliness, without the luxury of adornment. Then there was a Methodist Church, and hard by a Monte Bank, and a little beyond, on the mountain-side, a graveyard; and then a little school-house.

"The Master," as he was known to his little flock, sat alone one night in the school-house, with some open copy-books before him, carefully making those bold and full characters which are supposed to combine the extremes of chirographical and moral excellence, and had got as far as "Riches are deceitful," and was elaborating the noun with an insincerity of flourish that was quite in the spirit of his text, when he heard a gentle tapping. The woodpeckers had been busy about the roof during the day, and the noise did not disturb his work. But the opening of the door, and the tapping continuing from the inside, caused him to look up. He was slightly startled by the figure of a young girl, dirty and shabbily clad. Still, her great black eyes, her coarse, uncombed, lustreless black hair falling over her sun-burned face, her red arms and feet streaked with the red soil, were all familiar to him. It was Melissa Smith,—Smith's motherless child.

"What can she want here?" thought the master. Everybody knew "Mliss," as she was called, throughout the length and height of Red Mountain. Everybody knew her as an incorrigible girl. Her fierce, ungovernable disposition, her mad freaks and lawless character, were in their way as proverbial as the story of her father's weaknesses, and as philosophically accepted by the townsfolk. She wrangled with and fought the school-boys with keener invective and quite as powerful arm. She followed the trails with a woodman's craft, and the master had met her before, miles away, shoeless, stockingless, and bareheaded on the mountain road. The miners' camps along the stream supplied her with subsistence during these voluntary pilgrimages, in freely offered alms. Not but that a larger protection had been previously extended to Mliss. The Rev. Joshua McSnagley, "stated" preacher, had placed her in the hotel as servant, by way of preliminary refinement, and had introduced her to his scholars at Sunday school. But she threw plates occasionally at the landlord, and quickly retorted to the cheap witticisms of the guests, and created in the Sabbath school a sensation that was so inimical to the orthodox dulness and placidity of that institution, that, with a decent regard for the starched frocks and unblemished morals of the two pink-and-white-faced children of the first families, the reverend gentleman had her ignominiously expelled. Such were the antecedents, and such the character of Mliss, as she stood before the master. It was shown in the ragged dress, the unkempt hair, and bleeding feet, and asked his pity. It flashed from her black, fearless eyes, and commanded his respect.

"I come here to-night," she said rapidly and boldly, keeping her hard glance on his, "because I knew you was alone. I wouldn't come here when them gals was here. I hate 'em and they hates me. That's why. You keep school, don't you? I want to be teached!"

If to the shabbiness of her apparel and uncomeliness of her tangled hair and dirty face she had added the humility of tears, the master would have extended to her the usual moiety of pity, and nothing more. But with the natural, though illogical instincts of his species, her boldness awakened in him something of that respect which all original natures pay unconsciously to one another in any grade. And he gazed at her the more fixedly as she went on still rapidly, her hand on that door-latch and her eyes on his:—

"My name's Mliss,—Mliss Smith! You can bet your life on that. My father's Old Smith,—Old Bummer Smith,—that's what's the matter with him. Mliss Smith, —and I'm coming to school!"

"Well?" said the master.

Accustomed to be thwarted and opposed, often wantonly and cruelly, for no other purpose than to excite the violent impulses of her nature, the master's phlegm evidently took her by surprise. She stopped; she began to twist a lock of her hair between her fingers; and the rigid line of upper lip, drawn over the wicked little teeth, relaxed and quivered slightly. Then her eyes dropped, and something like a blush struggled up to her cheek, and tried to assert itself through the splashes of redder soil, and the sunburn of years. Suddenly she threw herself forward, calling on God to strike her dead, and fell quite weak and helpless, with her face on the master's desk, crying and sobbing as if her heart would break.

The master lifted her gently and waited for the paroxysm to pass. When with face still averted, she was repeating between her sobs the *mea culpa* of childish penitence,—that "she'd be good, she didn't mean to," etc., it came to him to ask her why she had left Sabbath school.

Why had she left the Sabbath school?—why? O yes. What did he (McSnagley) want to tell her she was wicked for? What did he tell her that God hated her for? If God hated her, what did she want to go to Sabbath school for? *She* didn't want to be "beholden" to anybody who hated her.

Had she told McSnagley this?

Yes, she had.

The master laughed. It was a hearty laugh, and echoed so oddly in the little school-house, and seemed so inconsistent and discordant with the sighing of the pines without, that he shortly corrected himself with a sigh. The sigh was quite as sincere in its way, however, and after a moment of serious silence he asked about her father.

Her father? What father? Whose father? What had he ever done for her? Why did the girls hate her? Come now! what made the folks say, "Old Bummer Smith's Mliss!" when she passed? Yes; O yes. She wished he was dead,—she was dead,—everybody was dead; and her sobs broke forth anew.

The master then, leaning over her, told her as well as he could what you or I might have said after hearing such unnatural theories from childish lips;

only bearing in mind perhaps better than you or I the unnatural facts of her ragged dress, her bleeding feet, and the omnipresent shadow of her drunken father. Then, raising her to her feet, he wrapped his shawl around her, and, bidding her come early in the morning, he walked with her down the road. There he bade her "good night." The moon shone brightly on the narrow path before them. He stood and watched the bent little figure as it staggered down the road, and waited until it had passed the little graveyard and reached the curve of the hill, where it turned and stood for a moment, a mere atom of suffering outlined against the far-off patient stars. Then he went back to his work. But the lines of the copy-book thereafter faded into long parallels of never-ending road, over which childish figures seemed to pass sobbing and crying into the night. Then, the little school-house seeming lonelier than before, he shut the door and went home.

The next morning Mliss came to school. Her face had been washed, and her coarse black hair bore evidence of recent struggles with the comb, in which both had evidently suffered. The old defiant look shone occasionally in her eyes, but her manner was tamer and more subdued. Then began a series of little trials and self-sacrifices, in which master and pupil bore an equal part, and which increased the confidence and sympathy between them. Although obedient under the master's eye, at times during recess, if thwarted or stung by a fancied slight, Mliss would rage in ungovernable fury, and many a palpitating young savage, finding himself matched with his own weapons of torment, would seek the master with torn jacket and scratched face, and complaints of the dreadful Mliss. There was a serious division among the townspeople on the subject; some threatening to withdraw their children from such evil companionship, and others as warmly upholding the course of the master in his work of reclamation. Meanwhile, with a steady persistence that seemed quite astonishing to him on looking back afterward, the master drew Mliss gradually out of the shadow of her past life, as though it were but her natural progress down the narrow path on which he had set her feet the moonlit night of their first meeting. Remembering the experience of the evangelical McSnagley, he carefully avoided that Rock of Ages on which that unskilful pilot had shipwrecked her young faith. But if, in the course of her reading, she chanced to stumble upon those few words which have lifted such as she above the level of the older, the wiser, and the more prudent,—if she learned something of a faith that is symbolized by suffering, and the old light softened in her eyes, it did not take the shape of a lesson. A few of the plainer people had made up a little sum by which the ragged Mliss was enabled to assume the garments of respect and civilization; and often a rough shake of the hand, and words of homely commendation from a red-shirted and burly figure, sent a glow to the cheek of the young master, and set him to thinking if it was altogether deserved.

Three months had passed from the time of their first meeting, and the master was sitting late one evening over the moral and sententious copies, when there came a tap at the door, and again Mliss stood before him. She was neatly clad and clean-faced, and there was nothing perhaps but the long black hair and bright black eyes to remind him of his former apparition. "Are you busy?" she asked. "Can you come with me?"—and on his signifying his readiness, in her old wilful way she said, "Come, then, quick!"

They passed out of the door together and into the dark road. As they entered the town the master asked her whither she was going. She replied, "To see my father."

It was the first time he had heard her call him by that filial title, or indeed anything more than "Old Smith" or the "Old Man." It was the first time in three months that she had spoken of him at all, and the master knew she had kept resolutely aloof from him since her great change. Satisfied from her manner that it was fruitless to question her purpose, he passively followed. In out-of-the-way places, low groggeries, restaurants, and saloons; in gambling-hells and dance-houses, the master, preceded by Mliss, came and went. In the reeking smoke and blasphemous outcries of low dens, the child, holding the master's hand, stood and anxiously gazed, seemingly unconscious of all in the one absorbing nature of her pursuit. Some of the revellers, recognizing Mliss, called to the child to sing and dance for them, and would have forced liquor upon her but for the interference of the master. Others, recognizing him mutely, made way for them to pass. So an hour slipped by. Then the child whispered in his ear that there was a cabin on the other side of the creek crossed by the long flume, where she thought he still might be. Thither they crossed,—a toilsome half-hour's walk,—but in vain. They were returning by the ditch at the abutment of the flume, gazing at the lights of the town on the opposite bank, when, suddenly, sharply, a quick report rang out on the clear night air. The echoes caught it, and carried it round and round Red Mountain, and set the dogs to barking all along the streams. Lights seemed to dance and move quickly on the outskirts of the town for a few moments, the stream rippled quite audibly beside them, a few stones loosened themselves from the hillside and splashed into the stream, a heavy wind seemed to surge the branches of the funereal pines, and then the silence seemed to fall thicker, heavier, and deadlier. The master turned towards Mliss with an unconscious gesture of protection, but the child had gone. Oppressed by a strange fear, he ran quickly down the trail to the river's bed, and, jumping from boulder to boulder, reached the base of Red Mountain and the outskirts of the village. Midway of the crossing he looked up and held his breath in awe. For high above him on the narrow flume he saw the fluttering little figure of his late companion crossing swiftly in the darkness.

He climbed the bank, and, guided by a few lights moving about a central point on the mountain, soon found himself breathless among a crowd of awe-stricken and sorrowful men. Out from among them the child appeared, and, taking the master's hand, led him silently before what seemed a ragged hole in the mountain. Her face was quite white, but her excited manner gone, and her look that of one to whom some long-expected event had at last happened,—an expression that to the master in his bewilderment seemed almost like relief. The walls of the cavern were partly propped by decaying timbers. The child pointed to what appeared to be some ragged, cast-off clothes left in the hole by the late occupant. The master approached nearer with his flaming dip, and bent over them. It was Smith, already cold, with a pistol in his hand and a bullet in his heart, lying beside his empty pocket.

CHAPTER II.

THE opinion which McSnagley expressed in reference to a "change of heart" supposed to be experienced by Mliss was more forcibly described in the gulches and tunnels. It was thought there that Mliss had "struck a good lead." So when there was a new grave added to the little enclosure, and at the expense of the master a little board and inscription put above it, the Red Mountain Banner came out quite handsomely, and did the fair thing to the memory of one of "our oldest Pioneers," alluding gracefully to that "bane of noble intellects," and otherwise genteelly shelving our dear brother with the past. "He leaves an only child to mourn his loss," says the Banner, "who is now an exemplary scholar, thanks to the efforts of the Rev. Mr. McSnagley." The Rev. McSnagley, in fact, made a strong point of Mliss's conversion, and, indirectly attributing to the unfortunate child the suicide of her father, made affecting allusions in Sunday school to the beneficial effects of the "silent tomb," and in this cheerful contemplation drove most of the children into speechless horror, and caused the pink-and-white scions of the first families to howl dismally and refuse to be comforted.

The long dry summer came. As each fierce day

burned itself out in little whiffs of pearl-gray smoke on the mountain summits, and the upspringing breeze scattered its red embers over the landscape, the green wave which in early spring upheaved above Smith's grave grew sere and dry and hard. In those days the master, strolling in the little churchyard of a Sabbath afternoon, was sometimes surprised to find a few wild-flowers plucked from the damp pine-forests scattered there, and oftener rude wreaths hung upon the little pine cross. Most of these wreaths were formed of a sweet-scented grass, which the children loved to keep in their desks, intertwined with the plumes of the buckeye, the syringa, and the wood-anemone; and here and there the master noticed the dark blue cowl of the monk's-hood, or deadly aconite. There was something in the odd association of this noxious plant with these memorials which occasioned a painful sensation to the master deeper than his esthetic sense. One day, during a long walk, in crossing a wooded ridge he came upon Mliss in the heart of the forest, perched upon a prostrate pine, on a fantastic throne formed by the hanging plumes of lifeless branches, her lap full of grasses and pine-burrs, and crooning to herself one of the negro melodies of her younger life. Recognizing him at a distance, she made room for him on her elevated throne, and with a grave assumption of hospitality and patronage that would have been ridiculous had it not been so terribly earnest, she fed him with pine-nuts and crab-apples. The master took that opportunity to point out to her the noxious and deadly qualities of the monk's-hood, whose dark blossoms he saw in her lap, and extorted from her a promise not to meddle with it as long as she remained his pupil. This done,—as the master had tested her integrity before,—he rested satisfied, and the strange feeling which had overcome him on seeing them died away.

Of the homes that were offered Mliss when her conversion became known, the master preferred that of Mrs. Morpher, a womanly and kind-hearted specimen of Southwestern efflorescence, known in her maidenhood as the "Per-rairie Rose." Being one of those who contend resolutely against their own natures, Mrs. Morpher, by a long series of self-sacrifices and struggles, had at last subjugated her naturally careless disposition to principles of "order," which she considered, in common with Mr. Pope, as "Heaven's first law." But she could not entirely govern the orbits of her satellites, however regular her own movements, and even her own "Jeemes" sometimes collided with her. Again her old nature asserted itself in her children. Lycurgus dipped into the cupboard "between meals," and Aristides came home from school without shoes, leaving those important articles on the threshold, for the delight of a barefooted walk down the ditches. Octavia and Cassandra were "keerless" of their clothes. So with but one exception, however much the "Prairie Rose" might have trimmed and pruned and trained her own matured luxuriance, the little shoots came up defiantly wild and straggling. That one exception was Clytemnestra Morpher, aged fifteen. She was the realization of her mother's immaculate conception,—neat, orderly, and dull.

It was an amiable weakness of Mrs. Morpher to imagine that "Clytie" was a consolation and model for Mliss. Following this fallacy, Mrs. Morpher threw Clytie at the head of Mliss when she was "bad," and set her up before the child for adoration in her penitential moments. It was not, therefore, surprising to the master to hear that Clytie was coming to school, obviously as a favor to the master and as an example for Mliss and others. For "Clytie" was quite a young lady. Inheriting her mother's physical peculiarities, and in obedience to the climatic laws of the Red Mountain region, she was an early bloomer. The youth of Smith's Pocket, to whom this kind of flower was rare, sighed for her in April and languished in May. Enamored swains haunted the school-house at the hour of dismissal. A few were jealous of the master.

Perhaps it was this latter circumstance that opened the master's eyes to another. He could not help noticing that Clytie was romantic; that in school she required a great deal of attention; that her pens were uniformly bad and wanted fixing; that she usually accompanied the request with a certain expectation in her eye that was somewhat disproportionate to the quality of service she verbally required; that she sometimes allowed the curves of a round, plump white arm to rest on his when he was writing her copies; that she always blushed and flung back her blond curls when she did so. I don't remember whether I have stated that the master was a young man,—it's of little consequence, however; he had been severely educated in the school in which Clytie was taking her first lesson, and, on the whole, withstood the flexible curves and factitious glance like the fine young Spartan that he was. Perhaps an insufficient quality of food may have tended to this asceticism. He generally avoided Clytie; but one evening, when she returned to the school-house after something she had forgotten, and did not find it until the master walked home with her, I hear that he endeavored to make himself particularly agreeable,—partly from the fact, I imagine, that his conduct was adding gall and bitterness to the already overcharged hearts of Clytemnestra's admirers.

The morning after this affecting episode Mliss did not come to school. Noon came, but not Mliss. Questioning Clytie on the subject, it appeared that they had left the school together, but the wilful Mliss had taken another road. The afternoon brought her not. In the evening he called on Mrs. Morpher, whose motherly heart was really alarmed. Mr. Morpher had spent all day in search of her, without discovering a trace that might lead to her discovery. Aristides was summoned as a probable accomplice, but that equitable infant succeeded in impressing the household with his innocence. Mrs. Morpher entertained a vivid impression that the child would yet be found drowned in a ditch, or, what was almost as terrible, muddied and soiled beyond the redemption of soap and water. Sick at heart, the master returned to the school-house. As he lit his lamp and seated himself at his desk, he found a note lying before him addressed to himself, in Mliss's handwriting. It seemed to be written on a leaf torn from some old memorandum-book, and, to prevent sacrilegious trifling, had been sealed with six broken wafers. Opening it almost tenderly, the master read as follows:—

RESPECTED SIR,—When you read this, I am run

away. Never to come back. *Never*, NEVER, NEVER. You can give my beeds to Mary Jennings, and my Amerika's Pride [a highly colored lithograph from a tobacco-box] to Sally Flanders. But don't you give anything to Clytie Morpher. Don't you dare to. Do you know what my oppinion is of her, it is this, she is perfckly disgustin. That is all and no more at present from

      Yours respectfully,
        MELISSA SMITH.

 The master sat pondering on this strange epistle till the moon lifted its bright face above the distant hills, and illuminated the trail that led to the school-house, beaten quite hard with the coming and going of little feet. Then, more satisfied in mind, he tore the missive into fragments and scattered them along the road.

 At sunrise the next morning he was picking his way through the palm-like fern and thick underbrush of the pine-forest, starting the hare from its form, and awakening a querulous protest from a few dissipated crows, who had evidently been making a night of it, and so came to the wooded ridge where he had once found Mliss. There he found the prostrate pine and tasselled branches, but the throne was vacant. As he drew nearer, what might have been some frightened animal started through the crackling limbs. It ran up the tossed arms of the fallen monarch, and sheltered itself in some friendly foliage. The master, reaching the old seat, found the nest still warm; looking up in the intertwining branches, he met the black eyes of the errant Mliss. They gazed at each other without speaking. She was first to break the silence.

"What do you want?" she asked curtly.

The master had decided on a course of action. "I want some crab-apples," he said humbly.

"Sha' n't have 'em! go away. Why don't you get 'em of Clytemnerestera?" (It seemed to be a relief to Mliss to express her contempt in additional syllables to that classical young woman's already long-drawn title.) "O you wicked thing!"

"I am hungry, Lissy. I have eaten nothing since dinner yesterday. I am famished!" and the young man in a state of remarkable exhaustion leaned against the tree.

Melissa's heart was touched. In the bitter days of her gypsy life she had known the sensation he so artfully simulated. Overcome by his heart-broken tone, but not entirely divested of suspicion, she said,—

"Dig under the tree near the roots, and you'll find lots; but mind you don't tell," for Mliss had *her* hoards as well as the rats and squirrels.

But the master, of course, was unable to find them; the effects of hunger probably blinding his senses. Mliss grew uneasy. At length she peered at him through the leaves in an elfish way, and questioned,—

"If I come down and give you some, you'll promise you won't touch me?"

The master promised.

"Hope you'll die if you do!"

The master accepted instant dissolution as a forfeit. Mliss slid down the tree. For a few moments nothing transpired but the munching of the pine-nuts. "Do you feel better?" she asked, with some solicitude. The master confessed to a recuperated feeling, and then, gravely thanking her, proceeded to retrace his steps. As he expected, he had not gone far before she called him. He turned. She was standing there quite white, with tears in her widely opened orbs. The master felt that the right moment had come. Going up to her, he took both her hands, and, looking in her tearful eyes, said, gravely, "Lissy, do you remember the first evening you came to see me?"

Lissy remembered.

"You asked me if you might come to school, for you wanted to learn something and be better, and I said—"

"Come," responded the child, promptly.

"What would *you* say if the master now came to you and said that he was lonely without his little scholar, and that he wanted her to come and teach him to be better?"

The child hung her head for a few moments in silence. The master waited patiently. Tempted by the quiet, a hare ran close to the couple, and raising her bright eyes and velvet forepaws, sat and gazed at them. A squirrel ran half-way down the furrowed bark of the fallen tree, and there stopped.

"We are waiting, Lissy," said the master, in a whisper, and the child smiled. Stirred by a passing breeze, the tree-tops rocked, and a long pencil of light stole through their interlaced boughs full on the doubting face and irresolute little figure. Suddenly she took the master's hand in her quick way. What she said was scarcely audible, but the master, putting the black hair back from her forehead, kissed her; and so, hand in hand, they passed out of the damp aisles and forest odors into the open sunlit road.

CHAPTER III.

SOMEWHAT less spiteful in her intercourse with other scholars, Mliss still retained an offensive attitude in regard to Clytemnestra. Perhaps the jealous element was not entirely lulled in her passionate little breast. Perhaps it was only that the round curves and plump outline offered more extended pinching surface. But while such ebullitions were under the master's control, her enmity occasionally took a new and irrepressible form.

The master in his first estimate of the child's character could not conceive that she had ever possessed a doll. But the master, like many other professed readers of character, was safer in *a posteriori* than *a priori* reasoning. Mliss had a doll, but then it was emphatically Mliss's doll,—a smaller copy of herself. Its unhappy existence had been a secret discovered accidentally by Mrs. Morpher. It had been the old-time companion of Mliss's wanderings, and bore evident marks of suffering. Its original complexion was long since washed away by the weather and anointed by the slime of ditches. It looked very much as Mliss had in days past. Its one gown of faded stuff was dirty and ragged as hers had been. Mliss had never been known to apply to it any childish term of endearment. She never exhibited it in the presence of other children. It was put severely to bed in a hollow tree near the school-house, and only allowed exercise during Mliss's rambles. Fulfilling a stern duty to her doll, as she would to herself, it knew no luxuries.

Now Mrs. Morpher, obeying a commendable impulse, bought another doll and gave it to Mliss. The child received it gravely and curiously. The master on looking at it one day fancied he saw a slight resemblance in its round red cheeks and mild blue eyes to Clytemnestra. It became evident before long that Mliss had also noticed the same resemblance. Accordingly she hammered its waxen head on the rocks when she was alone, and sometimes dragged it with a string round its neck to and from school. At other times, setting it up on her desk, she made a pincushion of its patient and inoffensive body. Whether this was done in revenge of what she considered a second figurative obtrusion of Clytie's excellences upon her, or whether she had an intuitive appreciation of the rites of certain other heathens, and, indulging in that "Fetish" ceremony, imagined that the original of her wax model would pine away and finally die, is a metaphysical question I shall not now consider.

In spite of these moral vagaries, the master could not help noticing in her different tasks the working of a quick, restless, and vigorous perception. She knew neither the hesitancy nor the doubts of childhood. Her answers in class were always slightly dashed with audacity. Of course she was not infallible. But her courage and daring in passing beyond her own depth and that of the floundering little swimmers around her, in their minds outweighed all errors of judgment. Children are not better than grown people in this respect, I fancy; and whenever the little red hand flashed above her desk, there was a wondering silence, and even the master was sometimes oppressed with a doubt of his own experience and judgment.

Nevertheless, certain attributes which at first amused

and entertained his fancy began to afflict him with grave doubts. He could not but see that Mliss was revengeful, irreverent, and wilful. That there was but one better quality which pertained to her semi-savage disposition,—the faculty of physical fortitude and self-sacrifice, and another, though not always an attribute of the noble savage,—Truth. Mliss was both fearless and sincere; perhaps in such a character the adjectives were synonymous.

The master had been doing some hard thinking on this subject, and had arrived at that conclusion quite common to all who think sincerely, that he was generally the slave of his own prejudices, when he determined to call on the Rev. McSnagley for advice. This decision was somewhat humiliating to his pride, as he and McSnagley were not friends. But he thought of Mliss, and the evening of their first meeting; and perhaps with a pardonable superstition that it was not chance alone that had guided her wilful feet to the school-house, and perhaps with a complacent consciousness of the rare magnanimity of the act, he choked back his dislike and went to McSnagley.

The reverend gentleman was glad to see him. Moreover, he observed that the master was looking "peartish," and hoped he had got over the "neuralgy" and "rheumatiz." He himself had been troubled with a dumb "ager" since last conference. But he had learned to "rastle and pray."

Pausing a moment to enable the master to write his certain method of curing the dumb "ager" upon the book and volume of his brain, Mr. McSnagley proceeded to inquire after Sister Morpher. "She is an adornment to Chris/ewanity, and has a likely growin' young family," added Mr. McSnagley; "and there's that mannerly young gal,—so well behaved,—Miss Clytie." In fact, Clytie's perfections seemed to affect him to such an extent that he dwelt for several minutes upon them. The master was doubly embarrassed. In the first place, there was an enforced contrast with poor Mliss in all this praise of Clytie. Secondly, there was something unpleasantly confidential in his tone of speaking of Mrs. Morpher's earliest born. So that the master, after a few futile efforts to say something natural, found it convenient to recall another engagement, and left without asking the information required, but in his after reflections somewhat unjustly giving the Rev. Mr. McSnagley the full benefit of having refused it.

Perhaps this rebuff placed the master and pupil once more in the close communion of old. The child seemed to notice the change in the master's manner, which had of late been constrained, and in one of their long post-prandial walks she stopped suddenly, and, mounting a stump, looked full in his face with big, searching eyes. "You ain't mad?" said she, with an interrogative shake of the black braids. "No." "Nor bothered?" "No." "Nor hungry?" (Hunger was to Mliss a sickness that might attack a person at any moment.) "No." "Nor thinking of her?" "Of whom, Lissy?" "That white girl." (This was the latest epithet invented by Mliss, who was a very dark brunette, to express Clytemnestra.) "No." "Upon your word?" (A substitute for "Hope you'll die!" proposed by the master.) "Yes." "And sacred honor?" "Yes." Then Mliss gave him a fierce little kiss, and, hopping down, fluttered off. For two or three days after that she condescended to appear more like other children, and be, as she expressed it, "good."

Two years had passed since the master's advent at Smith's Pocket, and as his salary was not large, and the prospects of Smith's Pocket eventually becoming the capital of the State not entirely definite, he contemplated a change. He had informed the school trustees privately of his intentions, but, educated young men of unblemished moral character being scarce at that time, he consented to continue his school term through the winter to early spring. None else knew of his intention except his one friend, a Dr. Duchesne, a young Creole physician known to the people of Wingdam as "Duchesny." He never mentioned it to Mrs. Morpher, Clytie, or any of his scholars. His reticence was partly the result of a constitutional indisposition to fuss, partly a desire to be spared the questions and surmises of vulgar curiosity, and partly that he never really believed he was going to do anything before it was done.

He did not like to think of Mliss. It was a selfish instinct, perhaps, which made him try to fancy his feeling for the child was foolish, romantic, and unpractical. He even tried to imagine that she would do better under the control of an older and sterner teacher. Then she was nearly eleven, and in a few years, by the rules of Red Mountain, would be a woman. He had done his duty. After Smith's death he addressed letters to Smith's relatives, and received one answer from a sister of Melissa's mother. Thanking the master, she stated her intention of leaving the Atlantic States for California with her husband in a few months. This was a slight superstructure for the airy castle which the master pictured for Mliss's home, but it was easy to fancy that some loving, sympathetic woman, with the claims of kindred, might better guide her wayward nature. Yet, when the master had read the letter, Mliss listened to it carelessly, received it submissively, and afterwards cut figures out of it with her scissors, supposed to represent Clytemnestra, labelled "the white girl," to prevent mistakes, and impaled them upon the outer walls of the school-house.

When the summer was about spent, and the last harvest had been gathered in the valleys, the master bethought him of gathering in a few ripened shoots of the young idea, and of having his Harvest-Home, or Examination. So the savans and professionals of Smith's Pocket were gathered to witness that time-honored custom of placing timid children in a constrained position, and bullying them as in a witness-box. As usual in such cases, the most audacious and self-possessed were the lucky recipients of the honors. The reader will imagine that in the present instance Mliss and Clytie were pre-eminent, and divided public attention; Mliss with her clearness of material perception and self-reliance, Clytie with her placid self-esteem and saint-like correctness of deportment. The other little ones were timid and blundering. Mliss's readiness and brilliancy, of course, captivated the greatest number and provoked the greatest applause. Mliss's antecedents had unconsciously awakened the strongest sympathies of a class whose athletic forms were ranged against the walls, or whose handsome bearded faces looked in at the windows. But Mliss's popularity was overthrown by an unexpected circumstance.

McSnagley had invited himself, and had been going

through the pleasing entertainment of frightening the more timid pupils by the vaguest and most ambiguous questions delivered in an impressive funereal tone; and Mliss had soared into Astronomy, and was tracking the course of our spotted ball through space, and keeping time with the music of the spheres, and defining the tethered orbits of the planets, when McSnagley impressively arose. "Meelissy! ye were speaking of the revolutions of this yere yearth and the move-*ments* of the sun, and I think ye said it had been a doing of it since the creashun, eh?" Mliss nodded a scornful affirmative. "Well, war that the truth?" said McSnagley, folding his arms. "Yes," said Mliss, shutting up her little red lips tightly. The handsome outlines at the windows peered further in the school-room, and a saintly Raphael-face, with blond beard and soft blue eyes, belonging to the biggest scamp in the diggings, turned toward the child and whispered, "Stick to it, Mliss!" The reverend gentleman heaved a deep sigh, and cast a compassionate glance at the master, then at the children, and then rested his look on Clytie. That young woman softly elevated her round, white arm. Its seductive curves were enhanced by a gorgeous and massive specimen bracelet, the gift of one of her humblest worshippers, worn in honor of the occasion. There was a momentary silence. Clytie's round cheeks were very pink and soft. Clytie's big eyes were very bright and blue. Clytie's low-necked white book-muslin rested softly on Clytie's white, plump shoulders. Clytie looked at the master, and the master nodded. Then Clytie spoke softly:—

"Joshua commanded the sun to stand still, and it obeyed him!" There was a low hum of applause in the school-room, a triumphant expression on McSnagley's face, a grave shadow on the master's, and a comical look of disappointment reflected from the windows. Mliss skimmed rapidly over her Astronomy, and then shut the book with a loud snap. A groan burst from McSnagley, an expression of astonishment from the school-room, a yell from the windows, as Mliss brought her red fist down on the desk, with the emphatic declaration,—

"It's a d—n lie. I don't believe it!"

CHAPTER IV.

THE long wet season had drawn near its close. Signs of spring were visible in the swelling buds and rushing torrents. The pine-forests exhaled the fresher spicery. The azaleas were already budding, the Ceanothus getting ready its lilac livery for spring. On the green upland which climbed Red Mountain at its southern aspect the long spike of the monk's-hood shot up from its broad-leaved stool, and once more shook its dark-blue bells. Again the billow above Smith's grave was soft and green, its crest just tossed with the foam of daisies and buttercups. The little graveyard had gathered a few new dwellers in the past year, and the mounds were placed two by two by the little paling until they reached Smith's grave, and there there was but one. General superstition had shunned it, and the plot beside Smith was vacant.

There had been several placards posted about the town, intimating that, at a certain period, a celebrated dramatic company would perform, for a few days, a series of "side splitting" and "screaming farces"; that, alternating pleasantly with this, there would be some melodrama and a grand divertisement, which would include singing, dancing, etc. These announcements occasioned a great fluttering among the little folk, and were the theme of much excitement and great speculation among the master's scholars. The master had promised Mliss, to whom this sort of thing was sacred and rare, that she should go, and on that momentous evening the master and Mliss "assisted."

The performance was the prevalent style of heavy mediocrity; the melodrama was not bad enough to laugh at nor good enough to excite. But the master, turning wearily to the child, was astonished, and felt something like self-accusation in noticing the peculiar effect upon her excitable nature. The red blood flushed in her cheeks at each stroke of her panting little heart. Her small passionate lips were slightly parted to give vent to her hurried breath. Her widely opened lids threw up and arched her black eyebrows. She did not laugh at the dismal comicalities of the funny man, for Mliss seldom laughed. Nor was she discreetly affected to the delicate extremes of the corner of a white handkerchief, as was the tender-hearted "Clytie," who was talking with her "feller" and ogling the master at the same moment. But when the performance was over, and the green curtain fell on the little stage, Mliss drew a long deep breath, and turned to the master's grave face with a half-apologetic smile and wearied gesture. Then she said, "Now take me home!" and dropped the lids of her black eyes, as if to dwell once more in fancy on the mimic stage.

On their way to Mrs. Morpher's the master thought

proper to ridicule the whole performance. Now he shouldn't wonder if Mliss thought that the young lady who acted so beautifully was really in earnest, and in love with the gentleman who wore such fine clothes. Well, if she were in love with him it was a very unfortunate thing! "Why?" said Mliss, with an upward sweep of the drooping lid. "Oh! well, he couldn't support his wife at his present salary, and pay so much a week for his fine clothes, and then they wouldn't receive as much wages if they were married as if they were merely lovers,—that is," added the master, "if they are not already married to somebody else; but I think the husband of the pretty young countess takes the tickets at the door, or pulls up the curtain, or snuffs the candles, or does something equally refined and elegant. As to the young man with nice clothes, which are really nice now, and must cost at least two and a half or three dollars, not to speak of that mantle of red drugget which I happen to know the price of, for I bought some of it for my room once,—as to this young man, Lissy, he is a pretty good fellow, and if he does drink occasionally, I don't think people ought to take advantage of it and give him black eyes and throw him in the mud. Do you? I am sure he might owe me two dollars and a half a long time, before I would throw it up in his face, as the fellow did the other night at Wingdam."

Mliss had taken his hand in both of hers and was trying to look in his eyes, which the young man kept as resolutely averted. Mliss had a faint idea of irony, indulging herself sometimes in a species of sardonic humor, which was equally visible in her actions and her speech. But the young man continued in this strain until they had reached Mrs. Morpher's, and he had deposited Mliss in her maternal charge. Waiving the invitation of Mrs. Morpher to refreshment and rest, and shading his eyes with his hand to keep out the blue-eyed Clytemnestra's siren glances, he excused himself, and went home.

For two or three days after the advent of the dramatic company, Mliss was late at school, and the master's usual Friday afternoon ramble was for once omitted, owing to the absence of his trustworthy guide. As he was putting away his books and preparing to leave the school-house, a small voice piped at his side, "Please, sir?" The master turned and there stood Aristides Morpher.

"Well, my little man," said the master, impatiently, "what is it? quick!"

"Please, sir, me and 'Kerg' thinks that Mliss is going to run away agin."

"What's that, sir?" said the master, with that unjust testiness with which we always receive disagreeable news.

"Why, sir, she don't stay home any more, and 'Kerg' and me see her talking with one of those actor fellers, and she's with him now; and please, sir, yesterday she told 'Kerg' and me she could make a speech as well as Miss Cellerstina Montmoressy, and she spouted right off by heart," and the little fellow paused in a collapsed condition.

"What actor?" asked the master.

"Him as wears the shiny hat. And hair. And gold pin. And gold chain," said the just Aristides, putting periods for commas to eke out his breath.

The master put on his gloves and hat, feeling an

unpleasant tightness in his chest and thorax, and walked out in the road. Aristides trotted along by his side, endeavoring to keep pace with his short legs to the master's strides, when the master stopped suddenly, and Aristides bumped up against him. "Where were they talking?" asked the master, as if continuing the conversation.

"At the Arcade," said Aristides.

When they reached the main street the master paused. "Run down home," said he to the boy. "If Mliss is there, come to the Arcade and tell me. If she isn't there, stay home; run!" And off trotted the short-legged Aristides.

The Arcade was just across the way,—a long, rambling building containing a bar-room, billiard-room, and restaurant. As the young man crossed the plaza he noticed that two or three of the passers-by turned and looked after him. He looked at his clothes, took out his handkerchief and wiped his face, before he entered the bar-room. It contained the usual number of loungers, who stared at him as he entered. One of them looked at him so fixedly and with such a strange expression that the master stopped and looked again, and then saw it was only his own reflection in a large mirror. This made the master think that perhaps he was a little excited, and so he took up a copy of the Red Mountain Banner from one of the tables, and tried to recover his composure by reading the column of advertisements.

He then walked through the bar-room, through the restaurant, and into the billiard-room. The child was not there. In the latter apartment a person was standing by one of the tables with a broad-brimmed glazed hat on his head. The master recognized him as the agent of the dramatic company; he had taken a dislike to him at their first meeting, from the peculiar fashion of wearing his beard and hair. Satisfied that the object of his search was not there, he turned to the man with a glazed hat. He had noticed the master, but tried that common trick of unconsciousness, in which vulgar natures always fail. Balancing a billiard-cue in his hand, he pretended to play with a ball in the centre of the table. The master stood opposite to him until he raised his eyes; when their glances met, the master walked up to him.

He had intended to avoid a scene or quarrel, but when he began to speak, something kept rising in his throat and retarded his utterance, and his own voice frightened him, it sounded so distant, low, and resonant. "I understand," he began, "that Melissa Smith, an orphan, and one of my scholars, has talked with you about adopting your profession. Is that so?"

The man with the glazed hat leaned over the table, and made an imaginary shot, that sent the ball spinning round the cushions. Then walking round the table he recovered the ball and placed it upon the spot. This duty discharged, getting ready for another shot, he said,—

"S'pose she has?"

The master choked up again, but, squeezing the cushion of the table in his gloved hand, he went on:—

"If you are a gentleman, I have only to tell you that I am her guardian, and responsible for her career. You know as well as I do the kind of life you offer her. As you may learn of any one here, I have already brought her out of an existence worse than death,—out of the streets and the contamination of vice. I am trying to do so again. Let us talk like men. She has neither father, mother, sister, or brother. Are you seeking to give her an equivalent for these?"

The man with the glazed hat examined the point of his cue, and then looked around for somebody to enjoy the joke with him.

"I know that she is a strange, wilful girl," continued the master, "but she is better than she was. I believe that I have some influence over her still. I beg and hope, therefore, that you will take no further steps in this matter, but as a man, as a gentleman, leave her to me. I am willing—" But here something rose again in the master's throat, and the sentence remained unfinished.

The man with the glazed hat, mistaking the master's silence, raised his head with a coarse, brutal laugh, and said in a loud voice,—

"Want her yourself, do you? That cock won't fight here, young man!"

The insult was more in the tone than the words, more in the glance than tone, and more in the man's instinctive nature than all these. The best appreciable rhetoric to this kind of animal is a blow. The master felt this, and, with his pent-up, nervous energy finding expression in the one act, he struck the brute full in his grinning face. The blow sent the glazed hat one way and the cue another, and tore the glove and skin from the master's hand from knuckle to joint. It opened up the corners of the fellow's mouth, and spoilt the peculiar shape of his beard for some time to come.

There was a shout, an imprecation, a scuffle, and the trampling of many feet. Then the crowd parted right and left, and two sharp quick reports followed each other in rapid succession. Then they closed again about his opponent, and the master was standing alone. He remembered picking bits of burning wadding from his coat-sleeve with his left hand. Some one was holding his other hand. Looking at it, he saw it was still bleeding from the blow, but his fingers were clenched around the handle of a glittering knife. He could not remember when or how he got it.

The man who was holding his hand was Mr. Morpher. He hurried the master to the door, but the master held back, and tried to tell him as well as he could with his parched throat about "Mliss." "It's all right, my boy," said Mr. Morpher. "She's home!" And they passed out into the street together. As they walked along Mr. Morpher said that Mliss had come running into the house a few moments before, and had dragged him out, saying that somebody was trying to kill the master at the Arcade. Wishing to be alone, the master promised Mr. Morpher that he would not seek the Agent again that night, and parted from him, taking the road toward the school-house. He was surprised in nearing it to find the door open,— still more surprised to find Mliss sitting there.

The master's nature, as I have hinted before, had like most sensitive organizations, a selfish basis. The brutal taunt thrown out by his late adversary still rankled in his heart. It was possible, he thought, that such a construction might be put upon his affection for the child, which at best was foolish and Quixotic. Besides, had she not voluntarily abnegated his authority and affection? And what had everybody else said about her? Why should he alone combat the opinion of all, and be at last obliged tacitly to confess the truth of all they had predicted? And he had been a participant in a low bar-room fight with a common boor, and risked his life, to prove what? What had he proved? Nothing? What would the people say? What would his friends say? What would McSnagley say?

In his self-accusation the last person he should have wished to meet was Mliss. He entered the door, and, going up to his desk, told the child, in a few cold words, that he was busy, and wished to be alone. As she rose he took her vacant seat, and, sitting down, buried his head in his hands. When he looked up again she was still standing there. She was looking at his face with an anxious expression.

"Did you kill him?" she asked.

"No!" said the master.

"That's what I gave you the knife for!" said the child, quickly.

"Gave me the knife?" repeated the master, in bewilderment.

"Yes, gave you the knife. I was there under the bar. Saw you hit him. Saw you both fall. He dropped his old knife. I gave it to you. Why didn't you stick him?" said Mliss rapidly, with an expressive twinkle of the black eyes and a gesture of the little red hand.

The master could only look his astonishment.

"Yes," said Mliss. "If you'd asked me, I'd told you I was off with the play-actors. Why was I off with the play-actors? Because you wouldn't tell me you was going away. I knew it. I heard you tell the Doctor so. I wasn't a goin' to stay here alone with those Morphers. I'd rather die first."

With a dramatic gesture which was perfectly consistent with her character, she drew from her bosom a few limp green leaves, and, holding them out at arm's-length, said in her quick vivid way, and in the queer pronunciation of her old life, which she fell into when unduly excited,—

"That's the poison plant you said would kill me. I'll go with the play-actors, or I'll eat this and die here. I don't care which. I won't stay here, where they hate and despise me! Neither would you let me, if you didn't hate and despise me too!"

The passionate little breast heaved, and two big tears peeped over the edge of Mliss's eyelids, but she whisked them away with the corner of her apron as if they had been wasps.

"If you lock me up in jail," said Mliss, fiercely, "to keep me from the play-actors, I'll poison myself. Father killed himself,—why shouldn't I? You said a mouthful of that root would kill me, and I always carry it here," and she struck her breast with her clenched fist.

The master thought of the vacant plot beside Smith's grave, and of the passionate little figure before him. Seizing her hands in his and looking full into her truthful eyes, he said,—

"Lissy, will you go with *me?*"

The child put her arms around his neck, and said joyfully, "Yes."

"But now—to-night?"

"To-night."

And, hand in hand, they passed into the road,— the narrow road that had once brought her weary feet to the master's door, and which it seemed she should not tread again alone. The stars glittered brightly above them. For good or ill the lesson had been learned, and behind them the school of Red Mountain closed upon them forever.

NIGHT AT WINGDAM.

As I stepped into the Slumgullion stage I saw that it was a dark night, a lonely road, and that I was the only passenger. Let me assure the reader that I have no ulterior design in making this assertion. A long course of light reading has forewarned me what every experienced intelligence must confidently look for from such a statement. The story-teller who wilfully tempts Fate by such obvious beginnings; who is to the expectant reader in danger of being robbed or half murdered, or frightened by an escaped lunatic, or introduced to his lady-love for the first time, deserves to be detected. I am relieved to say that none of these things occurred to me. The road from Wingdam to Slumgullion knew no other banditti than the regularly licensed hotel-keepers; lunatics had not yet reached such depth of imbecility as to ride of their own freewill in California stages; and my Laura, amiable and long-suffering as she always is, could not, I fear, have borne up against these depressing circumstances long enough to have made the slightest impression on me.

I stood with my shawl and carpet-bag in hand, gazing doubtingly on the vehicle. Even in the darkness the red dust of Wingdam was visible on its roof and sides, and the red slime of Slumgullion clung tenaciously to its wheels. I opened the door; the stage creaked uneasily, and in the gloomy abyss the swaying straps beckoned me, like ghostly hands, to come in now, and have my sufferings out at once.

I must not omit to mention the occurrence of a circumstance which struck me as appalling and mysterious. A lounger on the steps of the hotel, whom I had reason to suppose was not in any way connected with the stage company, gravely descended, and, walking toward the conveyance, tried the handle of the door, opened it, expectorated in the carriage, and returned to the hotel with a serious demeanor. Hardly had he resumed his position, when another individual, equally disinterested, impassively walked down the steps, proceeded to the back of the stage, lifted it, expectorated carefully on the axle, and returned slowly and pensively to the hotel. A third spectator wearily disengaged himself from one of the Ionic columns of the portico and walked to the box, remained for a moment in serious and expectorative contemplation of the boot, and then returned to his column. There was something so weird in this baptism that I grew quite nervous.

Perhaps I was out of spirits. A number of infinitesimal annoyances, winding up with the resolute persistency of the clerk at the stage-office to enter my name misspelt on the way-bill, had not predisposed me to cheerfulness. The inmates of the Eureka House, from a social view-point, were not attractive. There was the prevailing opinion—so common to many honest people—that a serious style of deportment and conduct toward a stranger indicates high gentility and elevated station. Obeying this principle, all hilarity ceased on my entrance to supper, and general remark merged into the safer and uncompromising chronicle of several bad cases of diphtheria, then epidemic at Wingdam. When I left the dining-room, with an odd feeling that I had been supping exclusively on mustard and tea-leaves, I stopped a moment at the parlor door. A piano, harmoniously related to the dinner-bell, tinkled responsive to a diffident and uncertain touch. On the white wall the shadow of an old and sharp profile was bending over several symmetrical and shadowy curls. "I sez to Mariar, Mariar, sez I, 'Praise to the face is open disgrace.'" I heard no more. Dreading some susceptibility to sincere expression on the subject of female loveliness, I walked away, checking the compliment that otherwise might have risen unbidden to my lips, and have brought shame and sorrow to the household.

It was with the memory of these experiences resting heavily upon me, that I stood hesitatingly before the stage door. The driver, about to mount, was for a moment illuminated by the open door of the hotel. He had the wearied look which was the distinguishing expression of Wingdam. Satisfied that I was properly way-billed and receipted for, he took no further notice of me. I looked longingly at the box-seat, but he did not respond to the appeal. I flung my carpet-bag into the chasm, dived recklessly after it, and—before I was fairly seated—with a great sigh, a creaking of unwilling springs, complaining bolts, and harshly expostulating axle, we moved away. Rather the hotel door slipped behind, the sound of the piano sank to rest, and the night and its shadows moved solemnly upon us.

To say it was dark expressed but faintly the pitchy obscurity that encompassed the vehicle. The roadside trees were scarcely distinguishable as deeper masses of shadow; I knew them only by the peculiar sodden odor that from time to time sluggishly flowed in at the open window as we rolled by. We proceeded slowly; so leisurely that, leaning from the carriage, I more than once detected the fragrant sigh of some astonished cow, whose ruminating repose upon the highway we had ruthlessly disturbed. But in the darkness our progress, more the guidance of some mysterious instinct than any apparent volition of our own, gave an indefinable charm of security to our journey, that a moment's hesitation or indecision on the part of the driver would have destroyed.

I had indulged a hope that in the empty vehicle I might obtain that rest so often denied me in its crowded condition. It was a weak delusion. When I stretched out my limbs it was only to find that the ordinary conveniences for making several people distinctly uncomfortable were distributed throughout my individual frame. At last, resting my arms on the straps, by dint of much gymnastic effort I became sufficiently composed to be aware of a more refined species of torture. The springs of the stage, rising and falling regularly, produced a rhythmical beat, which began to painfully absorb my attention. Slowly this thumping merged into a senseless echo of the mysterious female of the hotel parlor, and shaped itself into this awful and benumbing axiom,—"Praise-to-the-face-is-open-disgrace. Praise-to-the-face-is-open-disgrace." Inequalities of the road only quickened its utterance or drawled it to an exasperating length.

It was of no use to seriously consider the statement. It was of no use to except to it indignantly.

It was of no use to recall the many instances where praise to the face had redounded to the everlasting honor of praiser and bepraised; of no use to dwell sentimentally on modest genius and courage lifted up and strengthened by open commendation; of no use to except to the mysterious female,—to picture her as rearing a thin-blooded generation on selfish and mechanically repeated axioms,—all this failed to counteract the monotonous repetition of this sentence. There was nothing to do but to give in,—and I was about to accept it weakly, as we too often treat other illusions of darkness and necessity, for the time being,—when I became aware of some other annoyance that had been forcing itself upon me for the last few moments. How quiet the driver was!

Was there any driver? Had I any reason to suppose that he was not lying, gagged and bound on the roadside, and the highwayman, with blackened face who did the thing so quietly, driving me—whither? The thing is perfectly feasible. And what is this fancy now being jolted out of me. A story? It's of no use to keep it back,—particularly in this abysmal vehicle, and here it comes: I am a Marquis,—a French Marquis; French, because the peerage is not so well known, and the country is better adapted to romantic incident, —a Marquis, because the democratic reader delights in the nobility. My name is something *ligny*. I am coming from Paris to my country-seat at St. Germain. It is a dark night, and I fall asleep and tell my honest coachman, André, not to disturb me, and dream of an angel. The carriage at last stops at the chateau. It is so dark that when I alight I do not recognize the face of the footman who holds the carriage door. But what of that?—*peste!* I am heavy with sleep. The same obscurity also hides the old familiar indecencies of the statues on the terrace; but there is a door, and it opens and shuts behind me smartly. Then I find myself in a trap, in the presence of the brigand who has quietly gagged poor André and conducted the carriage thither. There is nothing for me to do, as a gallant French Marquis, but to say, "*Parbleu!*" draw my rapier, and die valorously! I am found a week or two after, outside a deserted *cabaret* near the barrier, with a hole through my ruffled linen and my pockets stripped. No; on second thoughts, I am rescued,— rescued by the angel I have been dreaming of, who is the assumed daughter of the brigand, but the real daughter of an intimate friend.

Looking from the window again, in the vain hope of distinguishing the driver, I found my eyes were growing accustomed to the darkness. I could see the distant horizon, defined by India-inky woods, relieving a lighter sky. A few stars widely spaced in this picture glimmered sadly. I noticed again the infinite depth of patient sorrow in their serene faces; and I hope that the Vandal who first applied the flippant "twinkle" to them may not be driven melancholy mad by their reproachful eyes I noticed again the mystic charm of space that imparts a sense of individual solitude to each integer of the densest constellation, involving the smallest star with immeasurable loneliness. Something of this calm and solitude crept over me, and I dozed in my gloomy cavern. When I awoke the full moon was rising. Seen from my window, it had an indescribably unreal and theatrical effect. It was the full moon of Norma,—that remarkable celestial phenomenon which rises so palpably to a hushed audience and a sublime *andante* chorus, until the *Casta Diva* is sung,—the "inconstant moon" that then and thereafter remains fixed in the heavens as though it were a part of the solar system inaugurated by Joshua. Again the white-robed Druids filed past me, again I saw that improbable mistletoe cut from that impossible oak, and again cold chills ran down my back with the first strain of the recitative. The thumping springs essayed to beat time, and the private-box-like obscurity of the vehicle lent a cheap enchantment to the view. But it was a vast improvement upon my past experience, and I hugged the fond delusion.

My fears for the driver were dissipated with the rising moon. A familiar sound had assured me of his presence in the full possession of at least one of his most important functions. Frequent and full expectoration convinced me that his lips were as yet not sealed by the gag of highwaymen, and soothed my anxious ear. With this load lifted from my mind, and assisted by the mild presence of Diana, who left, as when she visited Endymion, much of her splendor outside my cavern,—I looked around the empty vehicle. On the forward seat lay a woman's hair-pin. I picked it up with an interest that, however, soon abated. There was no scent of the roses to cling to it still, not even of hair-oil. No bend or twist in its rigid angles betrayed any trait of its wearer's character. I tried to think that it might have been "Mariar's." I tried to imagine that, confining the symmetrical curls of that girl, it might have heard the soft compliments whispered in her ears, which provoked the wrath of the aged female. But in vain. It was reticent and unswerving in its upright fidelity, and at last slipped listlessly through my fingers.

I had dozed repeatedly,—waked on the threshold of oblivion by contact with some of the angles of the coach, and feeling that I was unconsciously assuming, in imitation of a humble insect of my childish recollection, that spherical shape which could best resist those impressions, when I perceived that the moon, riding high in the heavens, had begun to separate the formless masses of the shadowy landscape. Trees isolated, in clumps and assemblages, changed places before my window. The sharp outlines of the distant hills came back, as in daylight, but little softened in the dry, cold, dewless air of a California summer night. I was wondering how late it was, and thinking that if the horses of the night travelled as slowly as the team before us, Faustus might have been spared his agonizing prayer, when a sudden spasm of activity attacked my driver. A succession of whip-snappings, like a pack of Chinese crackers, broke from the box before me. The stage leaped forward, and when I could pick myself from under the seat, a long white building had in some mysterious way rolled before my window. It must be Slumgullion! As I descended from the stage I addressed the driver:—

"I thought you changed horses on the road?"

"So we did. Two hours ago."

"That's odd. I didn't notice it."

"Must have been asleep, sir. Hope you had a pleasant nap. Bully place for a nice quiet snooze,— empty stage, sir!"

HIGH-WATER MARK.

WHEN the tide was out on the Dedlow Marsh, its extended dreariness was patent. Its spongy, low-lying surface, sluggish, inky pools, and tortuous sloughs, twisting their slimy way, eel-like, toward the open bay, were all hard facts. So were the few green tussocks, with their scant blades, their amphibious flavor, and unpleasant dampness. And if you choose to indulge your fancy,—although the flat monotony of the Dedlow Marsh was not inspiring,—the wavy line of scattered drift gave an unpleasant consciousness of the spent waters, and made the dead certainty of the returning tide a gloomy reflection, which no present sunshine could dissipate. The greener meadow-land seemed oppressed with this idea, and made no positive attempt at vegetation until the work of reclamation should be complete. In the bitter fruit of the low cranberry-bushes one might fancy he detected a naturally sweet disposition curdled and soured by an injudicious course of too much regular cold water.

The vocal expression of the Dedlow Marsh was also melancholy and depressing. The sepulchral boom of the bittern, the shriek of the curlew, the scream of passing brent, the wrangling of quarrelsome teal, the sharp, querulous protest of the startled crane, and syllabled complaint of the "killdeer" plover were beyond the power of written expression. Nor was the aspect of these mournful fowls at all cheerful and inspiring.

Certainly not the blue peron standing midleg deep in the water, obviously catching cold in a reckless disregard of wet feet and consequences; nor the mournful curlew, the dejected plover, or the low-spirited snipe, who saw fit to join him in his suicidal contemplation; nor the impassive kingfisher—an ornithological Marius—reviewing the desolate expanse; nor the black raven that went to and fro over the face of the marsh continually, but evidently couldn't make up his mind whether the waters had subsided, and felt low-spirited in the reflection that, after all this trouble, he wouldn't be able to give a definite answer. On the contrary, it was evident at a glance that the dreary expanse of Dedlow Marsh told unpleasantly on the birds, and that the season of migration was looked forward to with a feeling of relief and satisfaction by the full-grown, and of extravagant anticipation by the callow, brood. But if Dedlow Marsh was cheerless at the slack of the low tide, you should have seen it when the tide was strong and full. When the damp air blew chilly over the cold, glittering expanse, and came to the faces of those who looked seaward like another tide; when a steel-like glint marked the low hollows and the sinuous line of slough; when the great shell-incrusted trunks of fallen trees arose again, and went forth on their dreary, purposeless wanderings, drifting hither and thither, but getting no farther toward any goal at the falling tide or the day's decline than the cursed Hebrew in the legend; when the glossy ducks swung silently, making neither ripple nor furrow on the shimmering surface; when the fog came in with the tide and shut out the blue above, even as the green below had been obliterated; when boatmen, lost in that fog, paddling about in a hopeless way, started at what seemed the brushing of mermen's fingers on the boat's keel, or shrank from the tufts of grass spreading around like the floating hair of a corpse, and knew by these signs that they were lost upon Dedlow Marsh, and must make a night of it, and a gloomy one at that,—then you might know something of Dedlow Marsh at high water.

Let me recall a story connected with this latter view which never failed to recur to my mind in my long gunning excursions upon Dedlow Marsh. Although the event was briefly recorded in the county paper, I had the story, in all its eloquent detail, from the lips of the principal actor. I cannot hope to catch the varying emphasis and peculiar coloring of feminine delineation, for my narrator was a woman; but I'll try to give at least its substance.

She lived midway of the great slough of Dedlow Marsh and a good-sized river, which debouched four miles beyond into an estuary formed by the Pacific Ocean, on the long sandy peninsula which constituted the southwestern boundary of a noble bay. The house in which she lived was a small frame cabin raised from the marsh a few feet by stout piles, and was three miles distant from the settlements upon the river. Her husband was a logger,—a profitable business in a county where the principal occupation was the manufacture of lumber.

It was the season of early spring, when her husband left on the ebb of a high tide, with a raft of logs for the usual transportation to the lower end of the bay. As she stood by the door of the little cabin when the voyagers departed she noticed a cold look in the southeastern sky, and she remembered hearing her husband say to his companions that they must endeavor to complete their voyage before the coming of the southwesterly gale which he saw brewing. And that night it began to storm and blow harder than she had ever before experienced, and some great trees fell in the forest by the river, and the house rocked like her baby's cradle.

But however the storm might roar about the little cabin, she knew that one she trusted had driven bolt and bar with his own strong hand, and that had he feared for her he would not have left her. This, and her domestic duties, and the care of her little sickly baby, helped to keep her mind from dwelling on the weather, except, of course, to hope that he was safely harbored with the logs at Utopia in the dreary distance. But she noticed that day, when she went out to feed the chickens and look after the cow, that the tide was up to the little fence of their garden-patch, and the roar of the surf on the south beach, though miles away, she could hear distinctly. And she began to think that she would like to have some one to talk with about matters, and she believed that if it had not been so far and so stormy, and the trail so impassable she would have taken the baby and have gone over to Ryckman's, her nearest neighbor. But then, you see, he might have returned in the storm, all wet, with no one to see to him; and it was a long exposure for baby, who was croupy and ailing.

But that night, she never could tell why, she didn't feel like sleeping or even lying down. The storm had somewhat abated, but she still "sat and sat," and even tried to read. I don't know whether it was a Bible or some profane magazine that this poor woman read, but most probably the latter, for the words all ran together and made such sad nonsense that she was forced at last to put the book down and turn to that dearer volume which lay before her in the cradle, with its white initial leaf as yet unsoiled, and try to look forward to its mysterious future. And, rocking the cradle, she thought of everything and everybody, but still was wide awake as ever.

It was nearly twelve o'clock when she at last laid down in her clothes. How long she slept she could not remember, but she awoke with a dreadful choking in her throat, and found herself standing, trembling all over, in the middle of the room, with her baby clasped to her breast, and she was "saying something." The baby cried and sobbed, and she walked up and down trying to hush it, when she heard a scratching at the door. She opened it fearfully, and was glad to see it was only old Pete, their dog, who crawled, dripping with water, into the room. She would like to have looked out, not in the faint hope of her husband's coming, but to see how things looked; but the wind shook the door so savagely that she could hardly hold it. Then she sat down a little while, and then walked up and down a little while, and then she lay down again a little while. Lying close by the wall of the little cabin, she thought she heard once or twice something scrape slowly against the clapboards, like the scraping of branches. Then there was a little gurgling sound, "like the baby made when it was swallowing"; then something went "click-click" and "cluck-cluck," so that she sat up in bed. When she did so she was attracted by something else that seemed creeping from the back door towards the centre of the room. It wasn't much wider than her little finger, but soon it swelled to the width of her hand, and began spreading all over the floor. It was water.

She ran to the front door and threw it wide open, and saw nothing but water. She ran to the back door and threw it open, and saw nothing but water. She ran to the side window, and, throwing that open, she saw nothing but water. Then she remembered hearing her husband once say that there was no danger in the tide, for that fell regularly, and people could calculate on it, and that he would rather live near the bay than the river, whose banks might overflow at any time. But was it the tide? So she ran again to the back door, and threw out a stick of wood. It drifted away towards the bay. She scooped up some of the water and put it eagerly to her lips. It was fresh and sweet. It was the river, and not the tide!

It was then—O, God be praised for his goodness! she did neither faint nor fall; it was then—blessed be the Saviour, for it was his merciful hand that touched and strengthened her in this awful moment—that fear dropped from her like a garment, and her trembling ceased. It was then and thereafter that she never lost her self-command, through all the trials of that gloomy night.

She drew the bedstead towards the middle of the room, and placed a table upon it and on that she put the cradle. The water on the floor was already over her ankles, and the house once or twice moved so perceptibly, and seemed to be racked so, that the closet doors all flew open. Then she heard the same rasping and thumping against the wall, and, looking out, saw that a large uprooted tree, which had lain near the road at the upper end of the pasture, had floated down to the house. Luckily its long roots dragged in the soil and kept it from moving as rapidly as the current, for had it struck the house in its full career, even the strong nails and bolts in the piles could not have withstood the shock. The hound had leaped upon its knotty surface, and crouched near the roots shivering and whining. A ray of hope flashed across her mind. She drew a heavy blanket from the bed, and, wrapping it about the babe, waded in the deepening waters to the door. As the tree swung again, broadside on, making the little cabin creak and tremble, she leaped on to its trunk. By God's mercy she succeeded in obtaining a footing on its slippery surface, and, twining an arm about its roots, she held in the other her moaning child. Then something cracked near the front porch, and the whole front of the house she had just quitted fell forward,—just as cattle fall on their knees before they lie down,—and at the same moment the great redwood-tree swung round and drifted away with its living cargo into the black night.

For all the excitement and danger, for all her soothing of her crying babe, for all the whistling of the wind, for all the uncertainty of her situation, she still turned to look at the deserted and water-swept cabin. She remembered even then, and she wonders how foolish she was to think of it at that time, that she wished she had put on another dress and the baby's best clothes; and she kept praying that the house would be spared so that he, when he returned, would have something to come to, and it wouldn't be quite so desolate, and—how could he ever know what had become of her and baby? And at the thought she grew sick and faint. But she had something else to do besides worrying, for whenever the long roots of her ark struck an obstacle, the whole trunk made half a revolution, and twice dipped her in the black water. The hound, who kept distracting her by running up and down the tree and howling, at last fell off at one of these collisions. He swam for some time beside her, and she tried to get the poor beast upon the tree, but he "acted silly" and wild, and at last she lost sight of him forever. Then she and her baby were left alone. The light which had burned for a few minutes in the deserted cabin was quenched suddenly. She could not then tell whither she was drifting. The outline of the white dunes on the peninsula showed dimly ahead, and she judged the tree was moving in a line with the river. It must be about slack water, and she had probably reached the eddy formed by the confluence of the tide and the overflowing waters of the river. Unless the tide fell soon, there was present danger of her drifting to its channel, and being carried out to sea or crushed in the floating drift. That peril averted, if she were carried out on the ebb toward the bay, she might hope to strike one of the wooded promontories of the peninsula, and rest till daylight. Sometimes she thought she heard voices and shouts from the river, and the bellowing of cattle and bleating of sheep. Then again it was only the ringing in her ears and throbbing of her heart. She found at about this time that she was so chilled and stiffened in her cramped position that she could scarcely move, and the baby cried so when she put it to her breast that she noticed the milk refused to flow; and she was so frightened at that, that she put her head under her shawl, and for the first time cried bitterly.

When she raised her head again, the boom of the surf was behind her, and she knew that her ark had again swung round. She dipped up the water to cool her parched throat, and found that it was salt as her tears. There was a relief, though, for by this sign she knew that she was drifting with the tide. It was then the wind went down, and the great and awful silence oppressed her. There was scarcely a ripple against the furrowed sides of the great trunk on which she rested, and around her all was black gloom and quiet. She spoke to the baby just to hear herself speak, and to know that she had not lost her voice. She thought then,—it was queer, but she could not help thinking it,—how awful must have been the night when the great ship swung over the Asiatic peak, and the sounds of creation were blotted out from the world. She thought, too, of mariners clinging to spars, and of poor women who were lashed to rafts, and beaten to death by the cruel sea. She tried to thank God that she was thus spared, and lifted her eyes from the baby who had fallen into a fretful sleep. Suddenly, away to the southward, a great light lifted itself out of the gloom, and flashed and flickered, and flickered and flashed again. Her heart fluttered quickly against the baby's cold cheek. It was the lighthouse at the entrance of the bay. As she was yet wondering, the tree suddenly rolled a little, dragged a little, and then seemed to lie quiet and still. She put out her hand and the current gurgled against it. The tree was aground, and, by the position of the light and the noise of the surf, aground upon the Dedlow Marsh.

Had it not been for her baby, who was ailing and croupy, had it not been for the sudden drying up of that sensitive fountain, she would have felt safe and relieved. Perhaps it was this which tended to make all her impressions mournful and gloomy. As the tide rapidly fell, a great flock of black brent fluttered by her, screaming and crying. Then the plover flew up and piped mournfully, as they wheeled around the trunk, and at last fearlessly lit upon it like a gray cloud. Then the heron flew over and around her, shrieking and protesting, and at last dropped its gaunt legs only a few yards from her. But, strangest of all, a pretty white bird, larger than a dove,—like a pelican, but not a pelican,—circled around and around her. At last it lit upon a rootlet of the tree, quite over her shoulder. She put out her hand and stroked its beautiful white neck, and it never appeared to move. It stayed there so long that she thought she would lift up the baby to see it, and try to attract her attention. But when she did so, the child was so chilled and cold, and had such a blue look under the little lashes which it didn't raise at all, that she screamed aloud, and the bird flew away, and she fainted.

Well, that was the worst of it, and perhaps it was not so much, after all, to any but herself. For when she recovered her senses it was bright sunlight, and dead low water. There was a confused noise of guttural voices about her, and an old squaw, singing an Indian "hushaby," and rocking herself from side to side before a fire built on the marsh, before which she, the recovered wife and mother, lay weak and weary. Her first thought was for her baby, and she was about to speak, when a young squaw, who must have been a mother herself, fathomed her thought and brought her the "mowitch," pale but living, in such a queer little willow cradle all bound up, just like the squaw's own young one, that she laughed and cried together, and the young squaw and the old squaw showed their big white teeth and glinted their black eyes and said, "Plenty get well, skeena mowitch," "wagee man come plenty soon," and she could have kissed their brown faces in her joy. And then she found that they had been gathering berries on the marsh in their queer, comical baskets, and saw the skirt of her gown fluttering on the tree from afar, and the old squaw couldn't resist the temptation of procuring a new garment, and came down and discovered the "wagee" woman and child. And of course she gave the garment to the old squaw, as you may imagine, and when *he* came at last and rushed up to her, looking about ten years older in his anxiety, she felt so faint again that they had to carry her to the canoe. For, you see, he knew nothing about the flood until he met the Indians at Utopia, and knew by the signs that the poor woman was his wife. And at the next high-tide he towed the tree away back home, although it wasn't worth the trouble, and built another house, using the old tree for the foundation and props, and called it after her, "Mary's Ark!" But you may guess the next house was built above High-water mark. And that's all.

Not much, perhaps, considering the malevolent capacity of the Dedlow Marsh. But you must tramp over it at low water, or paddle over it at high tide, or get lost upon it once or twice in the fog, as I have, to understand properly Mary's adventure, or to appreciate duly the blessings of living beyond High-Water Mark.

THE MAN OF NO ACCOUNT.

His name was Fagg,—David Fagg. He came to California in '52 with us, in the "Skyscraper." I don't think he did it in an adventurous way. He probably had no other place to go to. When a knot of us young fellows would recite what splendid opportunities we resigned to go, and how sorry our friends were to have us leave, and show daguerreotypes and locks of hair, and talk of Mary and Susan, the man of no account used to sit by and listen with a pained, mortified expression on his plain face, and say nothing. I think he had nothing to say. He had no associates except when we patronized him; and, in point of fact, he was a good deal of sport to us. He was always sea-sick whenever we had a capful of wind. He never got his sea-legs on either. And I never shall forget how we all laughed when Rattler took him the piece of pork on a string, and— But you know that time-honored joke. And then we had such a splendid lark with him. Miss Fanny Twinkler couldn't bear the sight of him, and we used to make Fagg think that she had taken a fancy to him, and send him little delicacies and books from the cabin. You ought to have witnessed the rich scene that took place when he came up, stammering and very sick, to thank her! Didn't she flash up grandly and beautifully and scornfully? So like "Medora," Rattler said,—Rattler knew Byron by heart,—and wasn't old Fagg awfully cut up? But he got over it, and when Rattler fell sick at Valparaiso, old Fagg used to nurse him. You see he was a good sort of fellow, but he lacked manliness and spirit.

He had absolutely no idea of poetry. I've seen him sit stolidly by, mending his old clothes, when Rattler delivered that stirring apostrophe of Byron's to the ocean. He asked Rattler once, quite seriously, if he thought Byron was ever sea-sick. I don't remember Rattler's reply, but I know we all laughed very much, and I have no doubt it was something good, for Rattler was smart.

When the "Skyscraper" arrived at San Francisco we had a grand "feed." We agreed to meet every year and perpetuate the occasion. Of course we didn't invite Fagg. Fagg was a steerage-passenger, and it was necessary, you see, now we were ashore, to exercise a little discretion. But Old Fagg, as we called him,—he was only about twenty-five years old, by the way,—was the source of immense amusement to us that day. It appeared that he had conceived the idea that he could walk to Sacramento, and actually started off afoot. We had a good time, and shook hands with one another all around, and so parted. Ah me! only eight years ago, and yet some of those hands then clasped in amity have been clenched at each other, or have dipped furtively in one another's pockets. I know that we didn't dine together the next year, because young Barker swore he wouldn't put his feet under the same mahogany with such a very contemptible scoundrel as that Mixer; and Nibbles, who borrowed money at Valparaiso of young Stubbs, who was then a waiter in a restaurant, didn't like to meet such people.

When I bought a number of shares in the Coyote Tunnel at Mugginsville, in '54, I thought I'd take a run up there and see it. I stopped at the Empire Hotel, and after dinner I got a horse and rode round the town and out to the claim. One of those individuals whom newspaper correspondents call "our intelligent informant," and to whom in all small communities the right of answering questions is tacitly yielded, was quietly pointed out to me. Habit had enabled him to work and talk at the same time, and he never pretermitted either. He gave me a history of the claim, and added: "You see, stranger" (he addressed the bank before him), "gold is sure to come out'er that theer claim (he put in a comma with his pick), but the old pro-pri-e-tor (he wriggled out the word and the point of his pick) warn't of much account (a long stroke of the pick for a period). He was green, and let the boys about here jump him,"—and the rest of his sentence was confided to his hat, which he had removed to wipe his manly brow with his red bandanna.

I asked him who was the original proprietor.

"His name war Fagg."

I went to see him. He looked a little older and plainer. He had worked hard, he said, and was getting on "so, so." I took quite a liking to him and patronized him to some extent. Whether I did so because I was beginning to have a distrust for such fellows as Rattler and Mixer is not necessary for me to state.

You remember how the Coyote Tunnel went in,

and how awfully we shareholders were done! Well, the next thing I heard was that Rattler, who was one of the heaviest shareholders, was up at Mugginsville keeping bar for the proprietor of the Mugginsville Hotel, and that old Fagg had struck it rich, and didn't know what to do with his money. All this was told me by Mixer, who had been there, settling up matters, and likewise that Fagg was sweet upon the daughter of the proprietor of the aforesaid hotel. And so by hearsay and letter I eventually gathered that old Robins, the hotel man, was trying to get up a match between Nellie Robins and Fagg. Nellie was a pretty, plump, and foolish little thing, and would do just as her father wished. I thought it would be a good thing for Fagg if he should marry and settle down; that as a married man he might be of some account. So I ran up to Mugginsville one day to look after things.

It did me an immense deal of good to make Rattler mix my drinks for me,—Rattler! the gay, brilliant, and unconquerable Rattler, who had tried to snub me two years ago. I talked to him about old Fagg and Nellie, particularly as I thought the subject was distasteful. He never liked Fagg, and he was sure, he said, that Nellie didn't. Did Nellie like anybody else? He turned around to the mirror behind the bar and brushed up his hair! I understood the conceited wretch. I thought I'd put Fagg on his guard and get him to hurry up matters. I had a long talk with him. You could see by the way the poor fellow acted that he was badly stuck. He sighed, and promised to pluck up courage to hurry matters to a crisis. Nellie was a good girl, and I think had a sort of quiet respect for old Fagg's unobtrusiveness. But her fancy was already taken captive by Rattler's superficial qualities, which were obvious and pleasing. I don't think Nellie was any worse than you or I. We are more apt to take acquaintances at their apparent value than their intrinsic worth. It's less trouble, and, except when we want to trust them, quite as convenient. The difficulty with women is that their feelings are apt to get interested sooner than ours, and then, you know, reasoning is out of the question. This is what old Fagg would have known had he been of any account. But he wasn't. So much the worse for him.

It was a few months afterward, and I was sitting in my office when in walked old Fagg. I was surprised to see him down, but we talked over the current topics in that mechanical manner of people who know that they have something else to say, but are obliged to get at it in that formal way. After an interval Fagg in his natural manner said,—

"I'm going home!"

"Going home?"

"Yes,—that is, I think I'll take a trip to the Atlantic States. I came to see you, as you know I have some little property, and I have executed a power of attorney for you to manage my affairs. I have some papers I'd like to leave with you. Will you take charge of them?"

"Yes," I said. "But what of Nellie?"

His face fell. He tried to smile, and the combination resulted in one of the most startling and grotesque effects I ever beheld. At length he said,—

"I shall not marry Nellie,—that is,"—he seemed to apologize internally for the positive form of expression,—"I think that I had better not."

"David Fagg," I said with sudden severity, "you're of no account!"

To my astonishment his face brightened. "Yes," said he, "that's it!—I'm of no account! But I always knew it. You see I thought Rattler loved that girl as well as I did, and I knew she liked him better than she did me, and would be happier I dare say with him. But then I knew that old Robins would have preferred me to him, as I was better off,—and the girl would do as he said,—and, you see, I thought I was kinder in the way,—and so I left. But," he continued, as I was about to interrupt him, "for fear the old man might object to Rattler, I've lent him enough to set him up in business for himself in Dogtown. A pushing, active, brilliant fellow, you know, like Rattler can get along, and will soon be in his old position again, —and you needn't be hard on him, you know, if he doesn't. Good by."

I was too much disgusted with his treatment of that Rattler to be at all amiable, but as his business was profitable, I promised to attend to it, and he left. A few weeks passed. The return steamer arrived, and a terrible incident occupied the papers for days afterward. People in all parts of the State conned eagerly the details of an awful shipwreck, and those who had friends aboard went away by themselves, and read the long list of the lost under their breath. I read of the gifted, the gallant, the noble, and loved ones who had perished, and among them I think I was the first to read the name of David Fagg. For the "man of no account" had "gone home!"

NOTES BY FLOOD AND FIELD.

PART I.—IN THE FIELD.

It was near the close of an October day that I began to be disagreeably conscious of the Sacramento Valley. I had been riding since sunrise, and my course through the depressing monotony of the long level landscape affected me more like a dull dyspeptic dream than a business journey, performed under that sincerest of natural phenomena,—a California sky. The recurring stretches of brown and baked fields, the gaping fissures in the dusty trail, the hard outline of the distant hills, and the herds of slowly moving cattle, seemed like features of some glittering stereoscopic picture that never changed. Active exercise might have removed this feeling, but my horse by some subtle instinct had long since given up all ambitious effort, and had lapsed into a dogged trot.

It was autumn, but not the season suggested to the Atlantic reader under that title. The sharply defined boundaries of the wet and dry seasons were prefigured in the clear outlines of the distant hills. In the dry atmosphere the decay of vegetation was too rapid for the slow hectic which overtakes an Eastern landscape, or else Nature was too practical for such thin disguises. She merely turned the Hippocratic face to the spectator, with the old diagnosis of Death in her sharp, contracted features.

In the contemplation of such a prospect there was little to excite any but a morbid fancy. There were no clouds in the flinty blue heavens, and the setting of the sun was accompanied with as little ostentation as was consistent with the dryly practical atmosphere. Darkness soon followed, with a rising wind, which increased as the shadows deepened on the plain. The fringe of alder by the watercourse began to loom up as I urged my horse forward. A half-hour's active spurring brought me to a *corral*, and a little beyond a house, so low and broad it seemed at first sight to be half buried in the earth.

My second impression was that it had grown out of the soil, like some monstrous vegetable, its dreary proportions were so in keeping with the vast prospect. There were no recesses along its roughly boarded walls for vagrant and unprofitable shadows to lurk in the daily sunshine. No projection for the wind by night to grow musical over, to wail, whistle, or whisper to; only a long wooden shelf containing a chilly-looking tin basin, and a bar of soap. Its uncurtained windows were red with the sinking sun, as though bloodshot and inflamed from a too long unlidded existence. The tracks of cattle led to its front door, firmly closed against the rattling wind.

To avoid being confounded with this familiar element, I walked to the rear of the house, which was connected with a smaller building by a slight platform. A grizzled, hard-faced old man was standing there, and met my salutation with a look of inquiry, and, without speaking, led the way to the principal room. As I entered, four young men who were reclining by the fire, slightly altered their attitudes of perfect repose, but beyond that betrayed neither curiosity nor interest. A hound started from a dark corner with a growl, but was immediately kicked by the old man into obscurity, and silenced again. I can't tell why, but I instantly received the impression that for a long time the group by the fire had not uttered a word or moved a muscle. Taking a seat, I briefly stated my business.

Was a United States surveyor. Had come on account of the Espíritu Santo Rancho. Wanted to correct the exterior boundaries of township lines, so as to connect with the near exteriors of private grants. There had been some intervention to the old survey by a Mr. Tryan who had pre-empted adjacent— "settled land warrants," interrupted the old man. "Ah, yes! Land Warrants,—and then this was Mr. Tryan?"

I had spoken mechanically, for I was preoccupied in connecting other public lines with private surveys, as I looked in his face. It was certainly a hard face, and reminded me of the singular effect of that mining operation known as "ground sluicing"; the harder lines of underlying character were exposed, and what were once plastic curves and soft outlines were obliterated by some powerful agency.

There was a dryness in his voice not unlike the prevailing atmosphere of the valley, as he launched into an *ex parte* statement of the contest, with a fluency, which, like the wind without, showed frequent and unrestrained expression. He told me—what I had already learned—that the boundary line of the old Spanish grant was a creek, described in the loose phraseology of the *deseño* as beginning in the *valda* or skirt of the hill, its precise location long the subject of litigation. I listened and answered with little interest, for my mind was still distracted by the wind which swept violently by the house, as well as by his odd face, which was again reflected in the resemblance that the silent group by the fire bore toward him. He was still talking, and the wind was yet blowing, when my confused attention was aroused by a remark addressed to the recumbent figures.

"Now, then, which on ye'll see the stranger up the creek to Altascar's, to-morrow?"

There was a general movement of opposition in the group, but no decided answer.

"Kin you go, Kerg?"

"Who's to look up stock in Strarberry per-ar-ie?"

This seemed to imply a negative, and the old man turned to another hopeful, who was pulling the fur from a mangy bear-skin on which he was lying, with an expression as though it were somebody's hair.

"Well, Tom, wot's to hinder you from goin'?"

"Mam 's goin' to Brown's store at sun-up, and I s'pose I've got to pack her and the baby agin."

I think the expression of scorn this unfortunate youth exhibited for the filial duty into which he had been evidently beguiled, was one of the finest things I had ever seen.

"Wise?"

Wise deigned no verbal reply, but figuratively thrust a worn and patched boot into the discourse. The old man flushed quickly.

"I told ye to get Brown to give you a pair the last time you war down the river."

"Said he wouldn't without'en order. Said it was

like pulling gum-teeth to get the money from you even then."

There was a grim smile at this local hit at the old man's parsimony, and Wise, who was clearly the privileged wit of the family, sank back in honorable retirement.

"Well, Joe, ef your boots are new, and you aren't pestered with wimmin and children, p'r'aps you'll go," said Tryan, with a nervous twitching, intended for a smile, about a mouth not remarkably mirthful.

Tom lifted a pair of bushy eyebrows, and said shortly,—

"Got no saddle."

"Wot's gone of your saddle?"

"Kerg, there,"—indicating his brother with a look such as Cain might have worn at the sacrifice.

"You lie!" returned Kerg, cheerfully.

Tryan sprang to his feet, seizing the chair, flourishing it around his head and gazing furiously in the hard young faces which fearlessly met his own. But it was only for a moment; his arm soon dropped by his side, and a look of hopeless fatality crossed his face. He allowed me to take the chair from his hand, and I was trying to pacify him by the assurance that I required no guide, when the irrepressible Wise again lifted his voice:—

"Theer's George comin'! why don't ye ask him? He'll go and introduce you to Don Fernandy's darter, too, ef you ain't pertickler."

The laugh which followed this joke, which evidently had some domestic allusion (the general tendency of rural pleasantry), was followed by a light step on the platform, and the young man entered. Seeing a stranger present, he stopped and colored; made a shy salute and colored again, and then, drawing a box from the corner, sat down, his hands clasped lightly together and his very handsome bright blue eyes turned frankly on mine.

Perhaps I was in a condition to receive the romantic impression he made upon me, and I took it upon myself to ask his company as guide, and he cheerfully assented. But some domestic duty called him presently away.

The fire gleamed brightly on the hearth, and, no longer resisting the prevailing influence, I silently watched the spirting flame, listening to the wind which continually shook the tenement. Besides the one chair which had acquired a new importance in my eyes, I presently discovered a crazy table in one corner, with an ink-bottle and pen; the latter in that greasy state of decomposition peculiar to country taverns and farm-houses. A goodly array of rifles and double-barrelled guns stocked the corner; half a dozen saddles and blankets lay near, with a mild flavor of the horse about them. Some deer and bear skins completed the inventory. As I sat there, with the silent group around me, the shadowy gloom within and the dominant wind without, I found it difficult to believe I had ever known a different existence. My profession had often led me to wilder scenes, but rarely among those whose unrestrained habits and easy unconsciousness made me feel so lonely and uncomfortable. I shrank closer to myself, not without grave doubts—which I think occur naturally to people in like situations—that this was the general rule of humanity, and I was a solitary and somewhat gratuitous exception.

It was a relief when a laconic announcement of supper by a weak-eyed girl caused a general movement in the family. We walked across the dark platform, which led to another low-ceiled room. Its entire length was occupied by a table, at the farther end of which a weak-eyed woman was already taking her repast, as she, at the same time, gave nourishment to a weak-eyed baby. As the formalities of introduction had been dispensed with, and as she took no notice of me, I was enabled to slip into a seat without discomposing or interrupting her. Tryan extemporized a grace, and the attention of the family became absorbed in bacon, potatoes, and dried apples.

The meal was a sincere one. Gentle gurglings at the upper end of the table often betrayed the presence of the "wellspring of pleasure." The conversation generally referred to the labors of the day, and comparing notes as to the whereabouts of missing stock. Yet the supper was such a vast improvement upon the previous intellectual feast, that when a chance allusion of mine to the business of my visit brought out the elder Tryan, the interest grew quite exciting. I remember he inveighed bitterly against the system of ranch-holding by the "greasers," as he was pleased to term the native Californians. As the same ideas have been sometimes advanced under more pretentious circumstances, they may be worthy of record.

"Look at 'em holdin' the finest grazin' land that ever lay outer doors? Whar's the papers for it? Was it grants? Mighty fine grants,—most of 'em made arter the 'Merrikans got possession. More fools the 'Merrikans for lettin' 'em hold 'em. Wat paid for 'em? 'Merrikan blood and money.

"Didn't they oughter have suthin out of their native country? Wot for? Did they ever improve? Got a lot of yaller-skinned diggers, not so sensible as niggers to look arter stock, and they a sittin' home and smokin'. With their gold and silver candlesticks, and missions, and crucifixens, priests and graven idols, and sich? Them sort things wurent allowed in Mizzoori."

At the mention of improvements, I involuntarily lifted my eyes, and met the half-laughing, half-embarrassed look of George. The act did not escape detection, and I had at once the satisfaction of seeing that the rest of the family had formed an offensive alliance against us.

"It was agin Nater, and agin God," added Tryan. "God never intended gold in the rocks to be made into heathen candlesticks and crucifixens. That's why he sent 'Merrikins here. Nater never intended such a climate for lazy lopers. She never gin six months' sunshine to be slept and smoked away."

How long he continued, and with what further illustration I could not say, for I took an early opportunity to escape to the sitting-room. I was soon followed by George, who called me to an open door leading to a smaller room, and pointed to a bed.

"You'd better sleep there to-night," he said; "you'll be more comfortable, and I'll call you early."

I thanked him, and would have asked him several questions which were then troubling me, but he shyly slipped to the door and vanished.

A shadow seemed to fall on the room when he had gone. The "boys" returned, one by one, and shuffled to their old places. A larger log was thrown on the fire, and the huge chimney glowed like a furnace, but it did not seem to melt or subdue a single line of the hard faces that it lit. In half an hour later, the furs which had served as chairs by day undertook the nightly office of mattresses, and each received its owner's full-length figure. Mr. Tryan had not returned, and I missed George. I sat there, until, wakeful and nervous, I saw the fire fall and shadows mount the wall. There was no sound but the rushing of the wind and the snoring of the sleepers. At last, feeling the place insupportable, I seized my hat and, opening the door, ran out briskly into the night.

The acceleration of my torpid pulse in the keen fight with the wind, whose violence was almost equal to that of a tornado, and the familiar faces of the bright stars above me, I felt as a blessed relief. I ran not knowing whither, and when I halted, the square outline of the house was lost in the alder-bushes. An uninterrupted plain stretched before me, like a vast sea beaten flat by the force of the gale. As I kept on I noticed a slight elevation toward the horizon, and presently my progress was impeded by the ascent of an Indian mound. It struck me forcibly as resembling an island in the sea. Its height gave me a better view of the expanding plain. But even here I found no rest. The ridiculous interpretation Tryan had given the climate was somehow sung in my ears, and echoed in my throbbing pulse, as, guided by the star, I sought the house again.

But I felt fresher and more natural as I stepped upon the platform. The door of the lower building was open, and the old man was sitting beside the table, thumbing the leaves of a Bible with a look in his face as though he were hunting up prophecies against the "Greaser." I turned to enter, but my attention was attracted by a blanketed figure lying beside the house, on the platform. The broad chest heaving with healthy slumber, and the open, honest face were familiar. It was George, who had given up his bed to the stranger among his people. I was about to wake him, but he lay so peaceful and quiet, I felt awed and hushed. And I went to bed with a pleasant impression of his handsome face and tranquil figure soothing me to sleep.

I was awakened the next morning from a sense of lulled repose and grateful silence by the cheery voice of George, who stood beside my bed, ostentatiously twirling a "riata," as if to recall the duties of the day to my sleep-bewildered eyes. I looked around me. The wind had been magically laid, and the sun shone warmly through the windows. A dash of cold water, with an extra chill on from the tin basin, helped to brighten me. It was still early, but the family had already breakfasted and dispersed, and a wagon winding far in the distance showed that the unfortunate Tom had already "packed" his relatives away. I felt more cheerful,—there are few troubles Youth cannot distance with the start of a good night's rest. After a substantial breakfast, prepared by George, in a few moments we were mounted and dashing down the plain.

We followed the line of alder that defined the creek, now dry and baked with summer's heat, but which in winter, George told me, overflowed its banks. I still retain a vivid impression of that morning's ride, the far-off mountains, like *silhouettes*, against the steel-blue sky, the crisp dry air, and the expanding track before me, animated often by the well-knit figure of George Tryan, musical with jingling spurs, and picturesque with flying "riata." He rode a powerful native roan, wild-eyed, untiring in stride and unbroken in nature. Alas! the curves of beauty were concealed by the cumbrous *machillas* of the Spanish saddle, which levels all equine distinctions. The single rein lay loosely on the cruel bit that can gripe, and, if need be, crush the jaw it controls.

Again the illimitable freedom of the valley rises before me, as we again bear down into sunlit space. Can this be "Chu-Chu," staid and respectable filly of American pedigree,—"Chu-Chu," forgetful of plank-roads and cobble-stones, wild with excitement, twinkling her small white feet beneath me? George laughs out of a cloud of dust, "Give her her head; don't you see she likes it?" and "Chu-Chu" seems to like it, and, whether bitten by native tarantula into native barbarism or emulous of the roan, "blood" asserts itself, and in a moment the peaceful servitude of years is beaten out in the music of her clattering hoofs. The creek widens to a deep gully. We dive into it and up on the opposite side, carrying a moving cloud of impalpable powder with us. Cattle are scattered over the plain, grazing quietly, or banded together in vast restless herds. George makes a wide, indefinite sweep with the "riata," as if to include them all in his *vaquero's* loop, and says, "Ours!"

"About how many, George?"

"Don't know."

"How many?"

"Well, p'r'aps three thousand head," says George,

reflecting. "We don't know, takes five men to look 'em up and keep run."

"What are they worth?"

"About thirty dollars a head."

I make a rapid calculation, and look my astonishment at the laughing George. Perhaps a recollection of the domestic economy of the Tryan household is expressed in that look, for George averts his eye and says, apologetically,—

"I've tried to get the old man to sell and build, but you know he says it ain't no use to settle down, just yet. We must keep movin'. In fact, he built the shanty for that purpose, lest titles should fall through, and we'd have to get up and move stakes further down."

Suddenly his quick eye detects some unusual sight in a herd we are passing, and with an exclamation he puts his roan into the centre of the mass. I follow, or rather "Chu-Chu" darts after the roan, and in a few moments we are in the midst of apparently inextricable horns and hoofs. "Toro!" shouts George, with vaquero enthusiasm, and the band opens a way for the swinging "riata." I can feel their steaming breaths, and their spume is cast on "Chu-Chu's" quivering flank.

Wild, devilish-looking beasts are they; not such shapes as Jove might have chosen to woo a goddess, nor such as peacefully range the downs of Devon, but lean and hungry Cassius-like bovines, economically got up to meet the exigencies of a six months' rainless climate, and accustomed to wrestle with the distracting wind and the blinding dust.

"That's not our brand," says George; "they're strange stock," and he points to what my scientific eye recognizes as the astrological sign of Venus deeply seared in the brown flanks of the bull he is chasing. But the herd are closing round us with low mutterings, and George has again recourse to the authoritative "Toro," and with swinging "riata" divides the "bossy bucklers" on either side. When we are free, and breathing somewhat more easily, I venture to ask George if they ever attack any one.

"Never horsemen,"—sometimes footmen. Not through rage, you know, but curiosity. They think a man and his horse are one, and if they meet a chap afoot, they run him down and trample him under hoof, in the pursuit of knowledge. But," adds George, "here's the lower bench of the foothills, and here's Altascar's corral, and that white building you see yonder is the *casa*."

A whitewashed wall enclosed a court containing another adobe building, baked with the solar beams of many summers. Leaving our horses in the charge of a few peons in the courtyard, who were basking lazily in the sun, we entered a low doorway, where a deep shadow and an agreeable coolness fell upon us, as sudden and grateful as a plunge in cool water, from its contrast with the external glare and heat. In the centre of a low-ceiled apartment sat an old man with a black silk handkerchief tied about his head; the few gray hairs that escaped from its folds relieving his gamboge-colored face. The odor of cigarritos was as incense added to the cathedral gloom of the building.

As Señor Altascar rose with well-bred gravity to receive us, George advanced with such a heightened color, and such a blending of tenderness and respect in his manner, that I was touched to the heart by so much devotion in the careless youth. In fact, my eyes were still dazzled by the effect of the outer sunshine, and at first I did not see the white teeth and black eyes of Pepita, who slipped into the corridor as we entered.

It was no pleasant matter to disclose particulars of business which would deprive the old Señor of the greater part of that land we had just ridden over, and I did it with great embarrassment. But he listened calmly,—not a muscle of his dark face stirring,—and the smoke curling placidly from his lips showed his regular respiration. When I had finished, he offered quietly to accompany us to the line of demarcation. George had meanwhile disappeared, but a suspicious conversation in broken Spanish and English, in the corridor, betrayed his vicinity. When he returned again, a little absent-minded, the old man, by far the coolest and most self-possessed of the party, extinguished his black silk cap beneath that stiff, uncomely *sombrero* which all native Californians affect. A *serapa* thrown over his shoulders hinted that he was waiting. Horses are always ready saddled in Spanish ranchos, and in half an hour from the time of our arrival we were again "loping" in the staring sunlight.

But not as cheerfully as before. George and myself were weighed down by restraint, and Altascar was gravely quiet. To break the silence, and by way of a consolatory essay, I hinted to him that there might be further intervention or appeal, but the proffered oil and wine were returned with a careless shrug of the shoulders and a sententious "*Que bueno?*—Your courts are always just."

The Indian mound of the previous night's discovery was a bearing monument of the new line, and there we halted. We were surprised to find the old man Tryan waiting us. For the first time during our interview the old Spaniard seemed moved, and the blood rose in his yellow cheek. I was anxious to close the scene, and pointed out the corner boundaries as clearly as my recollection served.

"The deputies will be here to-morrow to run the lines from this initial point, and there will be no further trouble, I believe, gentlemen."

Señor Altascar had dismounted and was gathering a few tufts of dried grass in his hands. George and I exchanged glances. He presently arose from his stooping posture, and, advancing to within a few paces of Joseph Tryan, said, in a voice broken with passion,—

"And I, Fernando Jesus Maria Altascar, put you in possession of my land in the fashion of my country."

He threw a sod to each of the cardinal points.

"I don't know your courts, your judges, or your *corregidores*. Take the *llano!*—and take this with it. May the drought seize your cattle till their tongues hang down as long as those of your lying lawyers! May it be the curse and torment of your old age, as you and yours have made it of mine!"

We stepped between the principal actors in this scene, which only the passion of Altascar made tragical, but Tryan, with a humility but ill concealing his triumph, interrupted:—

"Let him curse on. He'll find 'em coming home to him sooner than the cattle he has lost through his sloth and pride. The Lord is on the side of the just, as well as agin all slanderers and revilers."

Altascar but half guessed the meaning of the Missourian, yet sufficiently to drive from his mind all but the extravagant power of his native invective.

"Stealer of the Sacrament! Open not!—open not, I say, your lying, Judas lips to me! Ah! half-breed, with the soul of a cayote!—Car-r-r-ramba!"

With his passion reverberating among the consonants like distant thunder, he laid his hand upon the mane of his horse as though it had been the gray locks of his adversary, swung himself into the saddle and galloped away.

George turned to me:—

"Will you go back with us to-night?"

I thought of the cheerless walls, the silent figures by the fire, and the roaring wind, and hesitated.

"Well then, good by."

"Good by, George."

Another wring of the hands, and we parted. I had not ridden far, when I turned and looked back. The wind had risen early that afternoon, and was already sweeping across the plain. A cloud of dust travelled before it, and a picturesque figure occasionally emerging therefrom was my last indistinct impression of George Tryan.

PART II.—IN THE FLOOD.

THREE months after the survey of the Espíritu Santo Rancho, I was again in the valley of the Sacramento. But a general and terrible visitation had erased the memory of that event as completely as I supposed it had obliterated the boundary monuments I had planted. The great flood of 1861-62 was at its height, when, obeying some indefinite yearning, I took my carpet-bag and embarked for the inundated valley.

There was nothing to be seen from the bright cabin windows of the "Golden City" but night deepening over the water. The only sound was the pattering rain, and that had grown monotonous for the past two weeks, and did not disturb the national gravity of my countrymen as they silently sat around the cabin stove. Some on errands of relief to friends and relatives wore anxious faces, and conversed soberly on the one absorbing topic. Others, like myself, attracted by curiosity, listened eagerly to newer details. But with that human disposition to seize upon any circumstance that might give chance event the exaggerated importance of instinct, I was half conscious of something more than curiosity as an impelling motive.

The dripping of rain, the low gurgle of water, and a leaden sky greeted us the next morning as we lay beside the half-submerged levee of Sacramento. Here, however, the novelty of boats to convey us to the hotels was an appeal that was irresistible. I resigned myself to a dripping rubber-cased mariner called "Joe," and, wrapping myself in a shining cloak of the like material, about as suggestive of warmth as court-plaster might have been, took my seat in the stern-sheets of his boat. It was no slight inward struggle to part from the steamer, that to most of the passengers was the only visible connecting link between us and the dry and habitable earth, but we pulled away and entered the city, stemming a rapid current as we shot the levee.

We glided up the long level of K Street,—once a cheerful, busy thoroughfare, now distressing in its silent desolation. The turbid water which seemed to meet the horizon edge before us flowed at right angles in sluggish rivers through the streets. Nature had revenged herself on the local taste by disarraying the regular rectangles by huddling houses on street corners, where they presented abrupt gables to the current, or by capsizing them in compact ruin. Crafts of all kinds were gliding in and out of low-arched doorways. The water was over the top of the fences surrounding well-kept gardens, in the first stories of hotels and private dwellings, trailing its slime on velvet carpets as well as roughly boarded floors. And a silence quite as suggestive as the visible desolation was in the voiceless streets that no longer echoed to carriage-wheel or footfall. The low ripple of water, the occasional splash of oars, or the warning cry of boatmen were the few signs of life and habitation.

With such scenes before my eyes and such sounds in my ears, as I lie lazily in the boat, is mingled the song of my gondolier who sings to the music of his oars. It is not quite as romantic as his brother of the Lido might improvise, but my Yankee "Giuseppe" has the advantage of earnestness and energy, and gives a graphic description of the terrors of the past week and of noble deeds of self-sacrifice and devotion, occasionally pointing out a balcony from which some California Bianca or Laura had been snatched, half clothed and famished. Giuseppe is otherwise peculiar, and refuses the proffered fare, for—am I not a citizen of San

Francisco, which was first to respond to the suffering cry of Sacramento? and is not he, Giuseppe, a member of the Howard Society? No! Giuseppe is poor, but cannot take my money. Still, if I must spend it, there is the Howard Society, and the women and children without food and clothes at the Agricultural Hall.

I thank the generous gondolier, and we go to the Hall,—a dismal, bleak place, ghastly with the memories of last year's opulence and plenty, and here Giuseppe's fare is swelled by the stranger's mite. But here Giuseppe tells me of the "Relief Boat" which leaves for the flooded district in the interior, and here, profiting by the lesson he has taught me, I make the resolve to turn my curiosity to the account of others, and am accepted of those who go forth to succor and help the afflicted. Giuseppe takes charge of my carpet-bag, and does not part from me until I stand on the slippery deck of "Relief Boat No. 3."

An hour later I am in the pilot-house, looking down upon what was once the channel of a peaceful river. But its banks are only defined by tossing tufts of willow washed by the long swell that breaks over a vast inland sea. Stretches of "tule" land fertilized by its once regular channel and dotted by flourishing ranchos are now cleanly erased. The cultivated profile of the old landscape had faded. Dotted lines in symmetrical perspective mark orchards that are buried and chilled in the turbid flood. The roofs of a few farm-houses are visible, and here and there the smoke curling from chimneys of half-submerged tenements show an undaunted life within. Cattle and sheep are gathered on Indian mounds waiting the fate of their companions whose carcasses drift by us, or swing in eddies with the wrecks of barns and out-houses. Wagons are stranded everywhere where the tide could carry them. As I wipe the moistened glass, I see nothing but water, pattering on the deck from the lowering clouds, dashing against the window, dripping from the willows, hissing by the wheels, everywhere washing, coiling, sapping, hurrying in rapids, or swelling at last into deeper and vaster lakes, awful in their suggestive quiet and concealment.

As day fades into night the monotony of this strange prospect grows oppressive. I seek the engine-room, and in the company of some of the few half-drowned sufferers we have already picked up from temporary rafts, I forget the general aspect of desolation in their individual misery. Later we meet the San Francisco packet, and transfer a number of our passengers. From them we learn how inward-bound vessels report to having struck the well-defined channel of the Sacramento, fifty miles beyond the bar. There is a voluntary contribution taken among the generous travellers for the use of our afflicted, and we part company with a hearty "God speed" on either side. But our signal-lights are not far distant before a familiar sound comes back to us,—an indomitable Yankee cheer,—which scatters the gloom.

Our course is altered, and we are steaming over the obliterated banks far in the interior. Once or twice black objects loom up near us,—the wrecks of houses floating by. There is a slight rift in the sky towards the north, and a few bearing stars to guide us over the waste. As we penetrate into shallower water, it is deemed advisable to divide our party into smaller boats, and diverge over the submerged prairie. I borrow a pea-coat of one of the crew, and in that practical disguise am doubtfully permitted to pass into one of the boats. We give way northerly. It is quite dark yet, although the rift of cloud has widened.

It must have been about three o'clock, and we were lying upon our oars in an eddy formed by a clump of cottonwood, and the light of the steamer is a solitary, bright star in the distance, when the silence is broken by the "bow oar":—

"Light ahead."

All eyes are turned in that direction. In a few seconds a twinkling light appears, shines steadily, and again disappears as if by the shifting position of some black object apparently drifting close upon us.

"Stern, all; a steamer!"

"Hold hard there! Steamer be d—d!" is the reply of the coxswain. "It's a house, and a big one too."

It is a big one, looming in the starlight like a huge fragment of the darkness. The light comes from a single candle, which shines through a window as the great shape swings by. Some recollection is drifting back to me with it, as I listen with beating heart.

"There's some one in it, by Heavens! Give way, boys,—lay her alongside. Handsomely, now! The door's fastened; try the window; no! here's another!"

In another moment we are trampling in the water, which washes the floor to the depth of several inches. It is a large room, at the further end of which an old man is sitting wrapped in a blanket, holding a candle in one hand, and apparently absorbed in the book he holds with the other. I spring toward him with an exclamation:—

"Joseph Tryan!"

He does not move. We gather closer to him, and I lay my hand gently on his shoulder, and say:—

"Look up, old man, look up! Your wife and children, where are they? The boys,—George! Are they here? are they safe?"

He raises his head slowly, and turns his eyes to mine, and we involuntarily recoil before his look. It is a calm and quiet glance, free from fear, anger, or pain; but it somehow sends the blood curdling through our veins. He bowed his head over his book again, taking no further notice of us. The men look at me compassionately, and hold their peace. I make one more effort:—

"Joseph Tryan, don't you know me? the surveyor who surveyed your ranch,—the Espíritu Santo? Look up, old man!"

He shuddered and wrapped himself closer in his blanket. Presently he repeated to himself, "The surveyor who surveyed your ranch,—Espíritu Santo," over and over again, as though it were a lesson he was trying to fix in his memory.

I was turning sadly to the boatmen, when he suddenly caught me fearfully by the hand and said,—

"Hush!"

We were silent.

"Listen!" He puts his arm around my neck and whispers in my ear, "I'm a *moving off!*"

"Moving off?"

"Hush! Don't speak so loud. Moving off. Ah! wot's that? Don't you hear?—there! listen!"

We listen, and hear the water gurgle and click beneath the floor.

"It's them wot he sent!—Old Altascar sent. They've

been here all night. I heard 'em first in the creek, when they came to tell the old man to move farther off. They came nearer and nearer. They whispered under the door, and I saw their eyes on the step,— their cruel, hard eyes. Ah, why don't they quit?"

I tell the men to search the room and see if they can find any further traces of the family, while Tryan resumes his old attitude. It is so much like the figure I remember on the breezy night that a superstitious feeling is fast overcoming me. When they have returned, I tell them briefly what I know of him, and the old man murmurs again,—

"Why don't they quit, then? They have the stock, —all gone—gone, gone for the hides and hoofs," and he groans bitterly.

"There are other boats below us. The shanty cannot have drifted far, and perhaps the family are safe by this time," says the coxswain, hopefully.

We lift the old man up, for he is quite helpless, and carry him to the boat. He is still grasping the Bible in his right hand, though its strengthening grace is blank to his vacant eye, and he cowers in the stern as we pull slowly to the steamer, while a pale gleam in the sky shows the coming day.

I was weary with excitement, and when we reached the steamer, and I had seen Joseph Tryan comfortably bestowed, I wrapped myself in a blanket near the boiler and presently fell asleep. But even then the figure of the old man often started before me, and a sense of uneasiness about George made a strong undercurrent to my drifting dreams. I was awakened at about eight o'clock in the morning by the engineer, who told me one of the old man's sons had been picked up and was now on board.

"Is it George Tryan?" I ask quickly.

"Don't know; but he's a sweet one, whoever he is," adds the engineer, with a smile at some luscious remembrance. "You'll find him for'ard."

I hurry to the bow of the boat, and find, not George, but the irrepressible Wise, sitting on a coil of rope, a little dirtier and rather more dilapidated than I can remember having seen him.

He is examining, with apparent admiration, some rough, dry clothes that have been put out for his disposal. I cannot help thinking that circumstances have somewhat exalted his usual cheerfulness. He puts me at my ease by at once addressing me:—

"These are high old times, ain't they? I say, what do you reckon's become o' them thar bound'ry moniments you stuck? Ah!"

The pause which succeeds this outburst is the effect of a spasm of admiration at a pair of high boots, which, by great exertion, he has at last pulled on his feet.

"So you've picked up the ole man in the shanty, clean crazy? He must have been soft to have stuck there instead o' leavin' with the old woman. Didn't know me from Adam; took me for George!"

At this affecting instance of paternal forgetfulness, Wise was evidently divided between amusement and chagrin. I took advantage of the contending emotions to ask about George.

"Don't know whar he is! If he'd tended stock instead of running about the prairie, packin' off wimmin and children, he might have saved suthin. He lost every hoof and hide, I'll bet a cookey! Say you," to a passing boatman, "when are you goin' to give us some grub? I'm hungry 'nough to skin and eat a hoss. Reckon I'll turn butcher when things is dried up, and save hides, horns, and taller."

I could not but admire this indomitable energy, which under softer climatic influences might have borne such goodly fruit.

"Have you any idea what you'll do, Wise?" I ask.

"Thar ain't much to do now," says the practical young man. "I'll have to lay over a spell, I reckon, till things comes straight. The land ain't worth much now, and won't be, I dessay, for some time. Wonder whar the ole man 'll drive stakes next."

"I meant as to your father and George, Wise."

"O, the ole man and I'll go on to 'Miles's,' whar Tom packed the old woman and babies last week. George'll turn up somewhar atween this and Altascar's, ef he ain't thar now."

I ask how the Altascars have suffered.

"Well, I reckon he ain't lost much in stock. I shouldn't wonder if George helped him drive 'em up the foot-hills. And his 'casa' 's built too high. O, thar ain't any water thar, you bet. Ah," says Wise, with reflective admiration, "those greasers ain't the darned fools people thinks 'em. I'll bet thar ain't one swamped out in all 'er Californy." But the appearance of "grub," cut this rhapsody short.

"I shall keep on a little farther," I say, "and try to find George."

Wise stared a moment at this eccentricity until a new light dawned upon him.

"I don't think you'll save much. What's the percentage,—workin' on shares, eh!"

I answer that I am only curious, which I feel lessens his opinion of me, and with a sadder feeling than his assurance of George's safety might warrant, I walked away.

From others whom we picked up from time to time we heard of George's self-sacrificing devotion, with the praises of the many he had helped and rescued. But I did not feel disposed to return until I had seen him, and soon prepared myself to take a boat to the lower "valda" of the foot-hills, and visit Altascar. I soon perfected my arrangements, bade farewell to Wise, and took a last look at the old man, who was sitting by the furnace-fires quite passive and composed. Then our boat-head swung round, pulled by sturdy and willing hands.

It was again raining, and a disagreeable wind had risen. Our course lay nearly west, and we soon knew by the strong current that we were in the creek of the Espíritu Santo. From time to time the wrecks of barns were seen, and we passed many half-submerged willows hung with farming implements.

We emerge at last into a broad silent sea. It is the "llano de Espíritu Santo." As the wind whistles by me, piling the shallower fresh water into mimic waves, I go back, in fancy, to the long ride of October over that boundless plain, and recall the sharp outlines of the distant hills which are now lost in the lowering clouds. The men are rowing silently, and I find my mind, released from its tension, growing benumbed and depressed as then. The water, too, is getting more shallow as we leave the banks of the creek, and with my hand dipped listlessly over the thwarts, I detect the tops of chimisal, which shows the tide to have somewhat fallen. There is a black mound, bearing to the north of the line of alder, making an adverse current, which, as we sweep to the right to avoid, I recognize. We pull close alongside and I call to the men to stop.

There was a stake driven near its summit with the initials, "L. E. S. I." Tied half-way down was a curiously worked "riata." It was George's. It had been cut with some sharp instrument, and the loose gravelly soil of the mound was deeply dented with horse's hoofs. The stake was covered with horse-hairs. It was a record, but no clew.

The wind had grown more violent, as we still fought our way forward, resting and rowing by turns, and oftener "poling" the shallower surface, but the old "valda," or bench, is still distant. My recollection of the old survey enables me to guess the relative position of the meanderings of the creek, and an occasional simple professional experiment to determine the distance gives my crew the fullest faith in my ability. Night overtakes us in our impeded progress. Our condition looks more dangerous than it really is, but I urge the men, many of whom are still new in this mode of navigation, to greater exertion by assurance of perfect safety and speedy relief ahead. We go on in this way until about eight o'clock, and ground by the willows. We have a muddy walk for a few hundred yards before we strike a dry trail, and simultaneously the white walls of Altascar's appear like a snow-bank before us. Lights are moving in the courtyard; but otherwise the old tomb-like repose characterizes the building.

One of the peons recognized me as I entered the court, and Altascar met me on the corridor.

I was too weak to do more than beg his hospitality for the men who had dragged wearily with me. He looked at my hand, which still unconsciously held the broken "riata." I began, wearily, to tell him about George and my fears, but with a gentler courtesy than was even his wont, he gravely laid his hand on my shoulder.

"*Poco a poco* Señor,—not now. You are tired, you have hunger, you have cold. Necessary it is you should have peace."

He took us into a small room and poured out some French cognac, which he gave to the men that had accompanied me. They drank and threw themselves before the fire in the larger room. The repose of the building was intensified that night, and I even fancied that the footsteps on the corridor were lighter and softer. The old Spaniard's habitual gravity was deeper; we might have been shut out from the world as well as the whistling storm, behind those ancient walls with their time-worn inheritor.

Before I could repeat my inquiry he retired. In a few minutes two smoking dishes of "chupa" with coffee were placed before us, and my men ate ravenously. I drank the coffee, but my excitement and weariness kept down the instincts of hunger.

I was sitting sadly by the fire when he re-entered. "You have eat?"

I said, "Yes," to please him.

"*Bueno*, eat when you can,—food and appetite are not always."

He said this with that Sancho-like simplicity with which most of his countrymen utter a proverb, as though it were an experience rather than a legend, and, taking the "riata" from the floor, held it almost tenderly before him.

"It was made by me, Señor."

"I kept it as a clew to him, Don Altascar," I said. "If I could find him—"

"He is here."

"Here! and"—but I could not say, "well!" I understood the gravity of the old man's face, the hushed footfalls, the tomb-like repose of the building in an electric flash of consciousness; I held the clew to the broken riata at last. Altascar took my hand, and we crossed the corridor to a sombre apartment. A few tall candles were burning in sconces before the window.

In an alcove there was a deep bed with its counterpane, pillows, and sheets heavily edged with lace, in all that splendid luxury which the humblest of these strange people lavish upon this single item of their household. I stepped beside it and saw George lying, as I had seen him once before, peacefully at rest. But a greater sacrifice than that he had known was here, and his generous heart was stilled forever.

"He was honest and brave," said the old man, and turned away.

There was another figure in the room; a heavy shawl drawn over her graceful outline, and her long black hair hiding the hands that buried her downcast face. I did not seem to notice her, and, retiring presently, left the loving and loved together.

When we were again beside the crackling fire, in the shifting shadows of the great chamber, Altascar told me how he had that morning met the horse of George Tryan swimming on the prairie; how that, farther on, he found him lying, quite cold and dead, with no marks or bruises on his person; that he had probably become exhausted in fording the creek, and that he had as probably reached the mound only to die for want of that help he had so freely given to others; that, as a last act, he had freed his horse. These incidents were corroborated by many who collected in the great chamber that evening,—women and children,—most of them succored through the devoted energies of him who lay cold and lifeless above.

He was buried in the Indian mound,—the single spot of strange perennial greenness, which the poor aborigines had raised above the dusty plain. A little slab of sandstone with the initials "G. T." is his monument, and one of the bearings of the initial corner of the new survey of the "Espíritu Santo Rancho."

SPANISH AND AMERICAN LEGENDS.

THE LEGEND OF MONTE DEL DIABLO.

THE cautious reader will detect a lack of authenticity in the following pages. I am not a cautious reader myself, yet I confess with some concern to the absence of much documentary evidence in support of the singular incident I am about to relate. Disjointed memoranda, the proceedings of *ayuntamientos* and early departmental *juntas*, with other records of a primitive and superstitious people, have been my inadequate authorities. It is but just to state, however, that though this particular story lacks corroboration, in ransacking the Spanish archives of Upper California I have met with many more surprising and incredible stories, attested and supported to a degree that would have placed this legend beyond a cavil or doubt. I have, also, never lost faith in the legend myself, and in so doing have profited much from the examples of divers grant-claimants, who have often jostled me in their more practical researches, and who have my sincere sympathy at the scepticism of a modern hard-headed and practical world.

For many years after Father Junipero Serro first rang his bell in the wilderness of Upper California, the spirit which animated that adventurous priest did not wane. The conversion of the heathen went on rapidly in the establishment of Missions throughout the land. So sedulously did the good Fathers set about their work, that around their isolated chapels there presently arose *adobe* huts, whose mud-plastered and savage tenants partook regularly of the provisions, and occasionally of the Sacrament, of their pious hosts. Nay, so great was their progress, that one zealous Padre is reported to have administered the Lord's Supper one Sabbath morning to "over three hundred heathen Salvages." It was not to be wondered that the Enemy of Souls, being greatly incensed thereat, and alarmed at his decreasing popularity, should have grievously tempted and embarrassed these Holy Fathers, as we shall presently see.

Yet they were happy, peaceful days for California. The vagrant keels of prying Commerce had not as yet ruffled the lordly gravity of her bays. No torn and ragged gulch betrayed the suspicion of golden treasure. The wild oats drooped idly in the morning heat, or wrestled with the afternoon breezes. Deer and antelope dotted the plain. The watercourses brawled in their familiar channels, nor dreamed of ever shifting their regular tide. The wonders of the Yosemite and Calaveras were as yet unrecorded. The Holy Fathers noted little of the landscape beyond the barbaric prodigality with which the quick soil repaid the sowing. A new conversion, the advent of a Saint's day, or the baptism of an Indian baby, was at once the chronicle and marvel of their day.

At this blissful epoch there lived at the Mission of San Pablo, Father José Antonio Haro, a worthy brother of the Society of Jesus. He was of tall and cadaverous aspect. A somewhat romantic history had given a poetic interest to his lugubrious visage. While a youth, pursuing his studies at famous Salamanca, he had become enamored of the charms of Doña Cármen de Torrencevara, as that lady passed to her matutinal devotions. Untoward circumstances, hastened, perhaps, by a wealthier suitor, brought this amour to a disastrous issue; and Father José entered a monastery, taking upon himself the vows of celibacy. It was here that his natural fervor and poetic enthusiasm conceived expression as a missionary. A longing to convert the uncivilized heathen succeeded his frivolous earthly passion, and a desire to explore and develop unknown fastnesses continually possessed him. In his flashing eye and sombre exterior was detected a singular commingling of the discreet Las Casas and the impetuous Balboa.

Fired by this pious zeal, Father José went forward in the van of Christian pioneers. On reaching Mexico, he obtained authority to establish the Mission of San Pablo. Like the good Junipero, accompanied only by an acolyte and muleteer, he unsaddled his mules in a dusky cañon, and rang his bell in the wilderness. The savages—a peaceful, inoffensive, and inferior race—presently flocked around him. The nearest military post was far away, which contributed much to the security of these pious pilgrims, who found their open trustfulness and amiability better fitted to repress hostility than the presence of an armed, suspicious, and brawling soldiery. So the good Father José said matins and prime, mass and vespers, in the heart of Sin and Heathenism, taking no heed to himself, but looking only to the welfare of the Holy Church. Conversions soon followed, and, on the 7th of July, 1760, the first Indian baby was baptized,—an event which, as Father José piously records, "exceeds the richnesse of gold or precious jewels or the chancing upon the

Ophir of Solomon." I quote this incident as best
suited to show the ingenious blending of poetry and
piety which distinguished Father José's record.

The Mission of San Pablo progressed and pros-
pered until the pious founder thereof, like the infidel
Alexander, might have wept that there were no more
heathen worlds to conquer. But his ardent and enthusiastic spirit could not long brook an idleness that
seemed begotten of sin; and one pleasant August
morning, in the year of grace 1770, Father José issued
from the outer court of the Mission building, equipped
to explore the field for new missionary labors.

Nothing could exceed the quiet gravity and unpre-
tentiousness of the little cavalcade. First rode a stout
muleteer, leading a pack-mule laden with the provisions of the party, together with a few cheap crucifixes
and hawks' bells. After him came the devout Padre
José, bearing his breviary and cross, with a black *serapa* thrown around his shoulders; while on either side
trotted a dusky convert, anxious to show a proper
sense of their regeneration by acting as guides into
the wilds of their heathen brethren. Their new condition was agreeably shown by the absence of the
usual mud-plaster, which in their unconverted state
they assumed to keep away vermin and cold. The
morning was bright and propitious. Before their de-
parture, mass had been said in the chapel, and the
protection of St. Ignatius invoked against all contin-
gent evils, but especially against bears, which, like the
fiery dragons of old, seemed to cherish unconquerable
hostility to the Holy Church.

As they wound through the *cañon*, charming birds
disported upon boughs and sprays, and sober quails

piped from the alders; the willowy water-courses gave a musical utterance, and the long grass whispered on the hillside. On entering the deeper defiles, above them towered dark green masses of pine, and occasionally the *madroño* shook its bright scarlet berries. As they toiled up many a steep ascent, Father José sometimes picked up fragments of scoria, which spake to his imagination of direful volcanoes and impending earthquakes. To the less scientific mind of the muleteer Ignacio they had even a more terrifying significance; and he once or twice snuffed the air suspiciously, and declared that it smelt of sulphur. So the first day of their journey wore away, and at night they encamped without having met a single heathen face.

It was on this night that the Enemy of Souls appeared to Ignacio in an appalling form. He had retired to a secluded part of the camp and had sunk upon his knees in prayerful meditation, when he looked up and perceived the Arch-Fiend in the likeness of a monstrous bear. The Evil One was seated on his hind legs immediately before him, with his fore paws joined together just below his black muzzle. Wisely conceiving this remarkable attitude to be in mockery and derision of his devotions, the worthy muleteer was transported with fury. Seizing an arquebuse, he instantly closed his eyes and fired. When he had recovered from the effects of the terrific discharge, the apparition had disappeared. Father José, awakened by the report, reached the spot only in time to chide the muleteer for wasting powder and ball in a contest with one whom a single *ave* would have been sufficient to utterly discomfit. What further reliance he placed on Ignacio's story is not known; but, in commemoration of a worthy Californian custom, the place was called *La Cañada de la Tentacion del Pio Muletero*, or "The Glen of the Temptation of the Pious Muleteer," a name which it retains to this day.

The next morning the party, issuing from a narrow gorge, came upon a long valley, sear and burnt with the shadeless heat. Its lower extremity was lost in a fading line of low hills, which, gathering might and volume toward the upper end of the valley, upheaved a stupendous bulwark against the breezy North. The peak of this awful spur was just touched by a fleecy cloud that shifted to and fro like a banneret. Father José gazed at it with mingled awe and admiration. By a singular coincidence, the muleteer Ignacio uttered the simple ejaculation *"Diablo!"*

As they penetrated the valley, they soon began to miss the agreeable life and companionable echoes of the *cañon* they had quitted. Huge fissures in the parched soil seemed to gape as with thirsty mouths. A few squirrels darted from the earth, and disappeared as mysteriously before the jingling mules. A gray wolf trotted leisurely along just ahead. But whichever way Father José turned, the mountain always asserted itself and arrested his wandering eye. Out of the dry and arid valley, it seemed to spring into cooler and bracing life. Deep cavernous shadows dwelt along its base; rocky fastnesses appeared midway of its elevation; and on either side huge black hills diverged like massy roots from a central trunk. His lively fancy pictured these hills peopled with a majestic and intelligent race of savages; and looking into futurity, he already saw a monstrous cross crowning the dome-like summit. Far different were the sensations of the muleteer, who saw in those awful solitudes only fiery dragons, colossal bears and break-neck trails. The converts, Concepcion and Incarnacion, trotting modestly beside the Padre, recognized, perhaps, some manifestation of their former weird mythology.

At nightfall they reached the base of the mountain. Here Father José unpacked his mules, said vespers, and, formally ringing his bell, called upon the Gentiles within hearing to come and accept the Holy Faith. The echoes of the black frowning hills around him caught up the pious invitation, and repeated it at intervals; but no Gentiles appeared that night. Nor were the devotions of the muleteer again disturbed, although he afterward asserted, that, when the Father's exhortation was ended, a mocking peal of laughter came from the mountain. Nothing daunted by these intimations of the near hostility of the Evil One, Father José declared his intention to ascend the mountain at early dawn; and before the sun rose the next morning he was leading the way.

The ascent was in many places difficult and dangerous. Huge fragments of rock often lay across the trail, and after a few hours' climbing they were forced to leave their mules in a little gully, and continue the ascent afoot. Unaccustomed to such exertion, Father José often stopped to wipe the perspiration from his thin cheeks. As the day wore on, a strange silence oppressed them. Except the occasional pattering of a squirrel, or a rustling in the *chimisal* bushes, there were no signs of life. The half-human print of a bear's foot sometimes appeared before them, at which Ignacio always crossed himself piously. The eye was sometimes cheated by a dripping from the rocks, which on closer inspection proved to be a resinous oily liquid with an abominable sulphurous smell. When they were within a short distance of the summit, the discreet Ignacio, selecting a sheltered nook for the camp, slipped aside and busied himself in preparations for the evening, leaving the Holy Father to continue the ascent alone. Never was there a more thoughtless act of prudence, never a more imprûdent piece of caution. Without noticing the desertion, buried in pious reflection, Father José pushed mechanically on, and, reaching the summit, cast himself down and gazed upon the prospect.

Below him lay a succession of valleys opening into each other like gentle lakes, until they were lost to the southward. Westerly the distant range hid the bosky *cañada* which sheltered the mission of San Pablo. In the farther distance the Pacific Ocean stretched away, bearing a cloud of fog upon its bosom, which crept through the entrance of the bay, and rolled thickly between him and the north-eastward; the same fog hid the base of mountain and the view beyond. Still, from time to time the fleecy veil parted, and timidly disclosed charming glimpses of mighty rivers, mountain defiles, and rolling plains, sear with ripened oats, and bathed in the glow of the setting sun. As Father José gazed, he was penetrated with a pious longing. Already his imagination, filled with enthusiastic conceptions, beheld all that vast expanse gathered under the mild sway of the Holy Faith, and peopled with zealous converts. Each little knoll in fancy became crowned with a chapel; from each dark *cañon* gleamed the white walls of a mission building. Growing bolder in his enthusiasm, and looking farther into futurity, he beheld a new Spain rising on these savage shores. He already saw the spires of stately cathedrals, the domes of palaces, vineyards, gardens, and groves. Convents, half hid among the hills, peeping from plantations of branching limes; and long processions of chanting nuns wound through the defiles. So completely was the good Father's conception of the future confounded with the past, that even in their choral strain the well-remembered accents of Cármen struck his ear. He was busied in these fanciful imaginings, when suddenly over that extended prospect the faint, distant tolling of a bell rang sadly out and died. It was the *Angelus*. Father José listened with superstitious exaltation. The mission of San Pablo was far away, and the sound must have been some miraculous omen. But never before, to his enthusiastic sense, did the sweet seriousness of this angelic symbol come with such strange significance. With the last faint peal, his glowing fancy seemed to cool; the fog closed in below him, and the good Father remembered he had not had his supper. He had risen and was wrapping his *serapa* around him, when he perceived for the first time that he was not alone.

Nearly opposite, and where should have been the faithless Ignacio, a grave and decorous figure was seated. His appearance was that of an elderly *hidalgo*, dressed in mourning, with mustaches of iron-gray carefully waxed and twisted around a pair of lantern-jaws. The monstrous hat and prodigious feather, the enormous ruff and exaggerated trunk-hose, contrasted with a frame shrivelled and wizened, all belonged to a century previous. Yet Father José was not astonished. His adventurous life and poetic imagination, continually on the lookout for the marvellous, gave him a certain advantage over the practical and material minded. He instantly detected the diabolical quality of his visitant, and was prepared. With equal coolness and courtesy he met the cavalier's obeisance.

"I ask your pardon, Sir Priest," said the stranger, "for disturbing your meditations. Pleasant they must have been, and right fanciful, I imagine, when occasioned by so fair a prospect."

"Worldly, perhaps, Sir Devil,—for such I take you to be," said the Holy Father, as the stranger bowed his black plumes to the ground; "worldly, perhaps; for it hath pleased Heaven to retain even in our regenerated state much that pertaineth to the flesh, yet still, I trust, not without some speculation for the welfare of the Holy Church. In dwelling upon yon fair expanse, mine eyes have been graciously opened with prophetic inspiration, and the promise of the heathen as an inheritance hath marvellously recurred to me. For there can be none lack such diligence in the True Faith, but may see that even the conversion of these pitiful salvages hath a meaning. As the blessed St. Ignatius discreetly observes," continued Father José, clearing his throat and slightly elevating his voice, "'the heathen is given to the warriors of Christ, even as the pearls of rare discovery which gladden the hearts of shipmen.' Nay, I might say—"

But here the stranger, who had been wrinkling his brows and twisting his mustaches with well-bred patience, took advantage of an oratorical pause:—

"It grieves me, Sir Priest, to interrupt the current of your eloquence as discourteously as I have already broken your meditations; but the day already waneth to night. I have a matter of serious import to make with you, could I entreat your cautious consideration a few moments."

Father José hesitated. The temptation was great, and the prospect of acquiring some knowledge of the Great Enemy's plans not the least trifling object. And if the truth must be told, there was a certain decorum about the stranger that interested the Padre. Though well aware of the Protean shapes the Arch-Fiend could assume, and though free from the weaknesses of the flesh, Father José was not above the temptations of the spirit. Had the Devil appeared, as in the case of the pious St. Anthony, in the likeness of a comely damsel, the good Father, with his certain experience of the deceitful sex, would have whisked her away in the saying of a paternoster. But there was, added to the security of age, a grave sadness about the stranger, — a thoughtful consciousness as of being at a great moral disadvantage,—which at once decided him on a magnanimous course of conduct.

The stranger then proceeded to inform him, that he had been diligently observing the Holy Father's triumphs in the valley. That, far from being greatly exercised thereat, he had been only grieved to see so enthusiastic and chivalrous an antagonist wasting his zeal in a hopeless work. For, he observed, the issue of the great battle of Good and Evil had been otherwise settled, as he would presently show him. "It wants but a few moments of night," he continued, "and over this interval of twilight, as you know, I have been given complete control. Look to the West."

As the Padre turned, the stranger took his enormous hat from his head, and waved it three times before him. At each sweep of the prodigious feather, the fog grew thinner, until it melted impalpably away, and' the former landscape returned, yet warm with the glowing sun. As Father José gazed, a strain of martial music arose from the valley, and issuing from a deep *cañon*, the good Father beheld a long cavalcade of gallant cavaliers, habited like his companion. As they swept down the plain, they were joined by like processions, that slowly defiled from every ravine and *cañon* of the mysterious mountain. From time to time the peal of a trumpet swelled fitfully upon the breeze; the cross of Santiago glittered, and the royal banners of Castile and Aragon waved over the moving column. So they moved on solemnly toward the sea, where, in the distance, Father José saw stately caravels, bearing the same familiar banner, awaiting them. The good Padre gazed with conflicting emotions, and the serious voice of the stranger broke the silence.

"Thou hast beheld, Sir Priest, the fading footprints of adventurous Castile. Thou hast seen the declining glory of old Spain,—declining as yonder brilliant sun. The sceptre she hath wrested from the heathen is fast dropping from her decrepit and fleshless grasp. The children she hath fostered shall know her no longer. The soil she hath acquired shall be lost to her as irrevocably as she herself hath thrust the Moor from her own Granada."

The stranger paused, and his voice seemed broken by emotion; at the same time, Father José, whose sympathizing heart yearned toward the departing banners, cried in poignant accents,—

"Farewell, ye gallant cavaliers and Christian soldiers! Farewell, thou, Nuñes de Balboa! thou, Alonzo de Ojeda! and thou, most venerable Las Casas! Farewell, and may Heaven prosper still the seed ye left behind!"

Then turning to the stranger, Father José beheld him gravely draw his pocket-handkerchief from the basket-hilt of his rapier, and apply it decorously to his eyes.

"Pardon this weakness, Sir Priest," said the cavalier, apologetically; "but these worthy gentlemen were ancient friends of mine, and have done me many a delicate service,—much more, perchance, than these poor sables may signify," he added, with a grim gesture toward the mourning suit he wore.

Father José was too much preoccupied in reflection to notice the equivocal nature of this tribute, and, after a few moments' silence, said, as if continuing his thought,—

"But the seed they have planted shall thrive and prosper on this fruitful soil."

As if answering the interrogatory, the stranger turned to the opposite direction, and, again waving his hat, said, in the same serious tone,—

"Look to the East!"

The Father turned, and, as the fog broke away before the waving plume, he saw that the sun was rising. Issuing with its bright beams through the passes of the snowy mountains beyond, appeared a strange and motley crew. Instead of the dark and romantic visages of his last phantom train, the Father beheld with strange concern the blue eyes and flaxen hair of a Saxon race. In place of martial airs and musical utterance, there rose upon the ear a strange din of harsh gutturals and singular sibilation. Instead of the decorous tread and stately mien of the cavaliers of the former vision, they came pushing, bustling, panting, and swaggering. And as they passed, the good Father noticed that giant trees were prostrated as with the breath of a tornado, and the bowels of the earth were torn and rent as with a convulsion. And Father José looked in vain for holy cross or Christian symbol; there was but one that seemed an ensign, and he crossed himself with holy horror as he perceived it bore the effigy of a bear.

"Who are these swaggering Ishmaelites?" he asked, with something of asperity in his tone.

The stranger was gravely silent.

"What do they here, with neither cross nor holy symbol?" he again demanded.

"Have you the courage to see, Sir Priest?" responded the stranger, quietly.

Father José felt his crucifix, as a lonely traveller might his rapier, and assented.

"Step under the shadow of my plume," said the stranger.

Father José stepped beside him, and they instantly sank through the earth.

When he opened his eyes, which had remained closed in prayerful meditation during his rapid descent, he found himself in a vast vault, bespangled overhead with luminous points like the starred firmament. It was also lighted by a yellow glow that seemed to proceed from a mighty sea or lake that occupied the centre of the chamber. Around this subterranean sea dusky figures flitted, bearing ladles filled with the yellow fluid, which they had replenished from its depths. From this lake diverging streams of the same mysterious flood penetrated like mighty rivers the cavernous distance. As they walked by the banks of this glittering Styx, Father José perceived how the liquid stream at certain places became solid. The ground was strewn with glittering flakes. One of these the Padre picked up and curiously examined. It was virgin gold.

An expression of discomfiture overcast the good Father's face at this discovery; but there was trace neither of malice nor satisfaction in the stranger's air, which was still of serious and fateful contemplation. When Father José recovered his equanimity, he said, bitterly,—

"This, then, Sir Devil, is your work! This is your deceitful lure for the weak souls of sinful nations! So would you replace the Christian grace of holy Spain!"

"This is what must be," returned the stranger, gloomily. " But listen, Sir Priest. It lies with you to avert the issue for a time. Leave me here in peace. Go back to Castile, and take with you your bells, your images, and your missions. Continue here, and you only precipitate results. Stay! promise me you will do this, and you shall not lack that which will render your old age an ornament and a blessing;" and the stranger motioned significantly to the lake.

It was here, the legend discreetly relates, that the Devil showed—as he always shows sooner or later— his cloven hoof. The worthy Padre, sorely perplexed by this threefold vision, and, if the truth must be told, a little nettled at this wresting away of the glory of holy Spanish discovery, had shown some hesitation. But the unlucky bribe of the Enemy of Souls touched his Castilian spirit. Starting back in deep disgust, he brandished his crucifix in the face of the unmasked Fiend, and in a voice that made the dusky vault resound, cried,—

"Avaunt thee, Sathanas! Diabolus, I defy thee! What! wouldst thou bribe me,—me, a brother of the Sacred Society of the Holy Jesus, Licentiate of Cordova and Inquisitor of Guadalaxara? Thinkest thou to buy me with thy sordid treasure? Avaunt!"

What might have been the issue of this rupture, and how complete might have been the triumph of the Holy Father over the Arch-Fiend, who was recoiling aghast at these sacred titles and the flourishing symbol, we can never know, for at that moment the crucifix slipped through his fingers.

Scarcely had it touched the ground before Devil and Holy Father simultaneously cast themselves toward it. In the struggle they clinched, and the pious José, who was as much the superior of his antagonist in bodily as in spiritual strength, was about to treat the Great Adversary to a back somersault, when he suddenly felt the long nails of the stranger piercing his flesh. A new fear seized his heart, a numbing chillness crept through his body, and he struggled to free himself, but in vain. A strange roaring was in his ears; the lake and cavern danced before his eyes and vanished; and with a loud cry he sank senseless to the ground.

When he recovered his consciousness he was aware of a gentle swaying motion of his body. He opened his eyes, and saw it was high noon, and that he was being carried in a litter through the valley. He felt stiff, and, looking down, perceived that his arm was tightly bandaged to his side.

He closed his eyes and after a few words of thankful prayer, thought how miraculously he had been preserved, and made a vow of candlesticks to the blessed Saint José. He then called in a faint voice, and presently the penitent Ignacio stood beside him.

The joy the poor fellow felt at his patron's returning consciousness for some time choked his utterance. He could only ejaculate, "A miracle! Blessed Saint José, he lives!" and kiss the Padre's bandaged hand. Father José, more intent on his last night's experience, waited for his emotion to subside, and asked where he had been found.

"On the mountain, your Reverence, but a few *varas* from where he attacked you."

"How?—you saw him then?" asked the Padre, in unfeigned astonishment.

"Saw him, your Reverence! Mother of God, I should think I did! And your Reverence shall see him too, if he ever comes again within range of Ignacio's arquebuse."

"What mean you, Ignacio?" said the Padre, sitting bolt-upright in his litter.

"Why, the bear, your Reverence,—the bear, Holy Father, who attacked your worshipful person while you were meditating on the top of yonder mountain."

"Ah!" said the Holy Father, lying down again. "Chut, child! I would be at peace."

When he reached the Mission, he was tenderly cared for, and in a few weeks was enabled to resume those duties from which, as will be seen, not even the machinations of the Evil One could divert him. The news of his physical disaster spread over the country; and a letter to the Bishop of Guadalaxara contained a confidential and detailed account of the good Father's spiritual temptation. But in some way the story leaked out; and long after José was gathered to his fathers, his mysterious encounter formed the theme of thrilling and whispered narrative. The mountain was generally shunned. It is true that Señor Joaquin Pedrillo afterward located a grant near the base of the mountain; but as Señora Pedrillo was known to be a termagant half-breed, the Señor was not supposed to be over-fastidious.

Such is the Legend of Monte del Diablo. As I said before, it may seem to lack essential corroboration. The discrepancy between the Father's narrative and the actual climax has given rise to some scepticism on the part of ingenious quibblers. All such I would simply refer to that part of the report of Señor Julio Serro, Sub-Prefect of San Pablo, before whom attest of the above was made. Touching this matter, the worthy Prefect observes, "That although the body of Father José doth show evidence of grievous conflict in the flesh, yet that is no proof that the Enemy of Souls, who could assume the figure of a decorous elderly *caballero*, could not at the same time transform himself into a bear for his own vile purposes."

THE RIGHT EYE OF THE COMMANDER.

The year of grace 1797 passed away on the coast of California in a southwesterly gale. The little bay of San Carlos, albeit sheltered by the headlands of the blessed Trinity, was rough and turbulent; its foam clung quivering to the seaward wall of the Mission garden; the air was filled with flying sand and spume, and as the Señor Comandante, Hermenegildo Salvatierra, looked from the deep embrasured window of the Presidio guard-room, he felt the salt breath of the distant sea buffet a color into his smoke-dried cheeks.

The Commander, I have said, was gazing thoughtfully from the window of the guard-room. He may have been reviewing the events of the year now about to pass away. But, like the garrison at the Presidio, there was little to review; the year, like its predecessors, had been uneventful,—the days had slipped by in a delicious monotony of simple duties, unbroken by incident or interruption. The regularly recurring feasts and saints' days, the half-yearly courier from San Diego, the rare transport-ship and rarer foreign vessel, were the mere details of his patriarchal life. If there was no achievement, there was certainly no failure. Abundant harvests and patient industry amply supplied the wants of Presidio and Mission. Isolated from the family of nations, the wars which shook the world concerned them not so much as the last earthquake; the struggle that emancipated their sister colonies on the other side of the continent to them had no suggestiveness. In short, it was that glorious Indian summer of California history, around which so much poetical haze still lingers,—that bland, indolent autumn of Spanish rule, so soon to be followed by the wintry storms of Mexican independence and the reviving spring of American conquest.

The Commander turned from the window and walked toward the fire that burned brightly on the deep oven-like hearth. A pile of copy-books, the work of the Presidio school, lay on the table. As he turned over the leaves with a paternal interest, and surveyed the fair round Scripture text,—the first pious pot-hooks of the pupils of San Carlos, an audible commentary fell from his lips: "'Abimelech took her from Abraham'—ah, little one, excellent!—'Jacob sent to see his brother' —body of Christ! that up-stroke of thine, Paquita, is marvellous; the Governor shall see it!" A film of honest pride dimmed the Commander's left eye,—the right, alas! twenty years before had been sealed by an Indian arrow. He rubbed it softly with the sleeve of his leather jacket, and continued; "'The Ishmaelites having arrived—'"

He stopped, for there was a step in the court-yard, a foot upon the threshold, and a stranger entered. With the instinct of an old soldier, the Commander, after one glance at the intruder, turned quickly toward the wall, where his trusty Toledo hung, or should have been hanging. But it was not there, and as he recalled that the last time he had seen that weapon it was being ridden up and down the gallery by Pepito, the infant son of Bautista, the tortilio-maker, he blushed and then contented himself with frowning upon the intruder.

But the stranger's air, though irreverent, was decidedly peaceful. He was unarmed, and wore the ordinary cape of tarpauling and sea-boots of a mariner. Except a villanous smell of codfish, there was little about him that was peculiar.

His name, as he informed the Commander, in Spanish that was more fluent than elegant or precise, —his name was Peleg Scudder. He was master of the schooner "General Court," of the port of Salem, in Massachusetts, on a trading-voyage to the South Seas, but now driven by stress of weather into the bay of San Carlos. He begged permission to ride out the gale under the headlands of the blessed Trinity, and no more. Water he did not need, having taken in a supply at Bodega. He knew the strict surveillance of the Spanish port regulations in regard to foreign vessels, and would do nothing against the severe discipline and good order of the settlement. There was a slight tinge of sarcasm in his tone as he glanced toward the desolate parade-ground of the Presidio and the open unguarded gate. The fact was that the sentry, Felipe Gomez, had discreetly retired to shelter at the beginning of the storm, and was then sound asleep in the corridor.

The Commander hesitated. The port regulations were severe, but he was accustomed to exercise individual authority, and beyond an old order issued ten years before, regarding the American ship "Columbia," there was no precedent to guide him. The storm was severe, and a sentiment of humanity urged him to grant the stranger's request. It is but just to the Commander to say, that his inability to enforce a refusal did not weigh with his decision. He would have denied with equal disregard of consequences that right to a seventy-four gun ship which he now yielded so gracefully to this Yankee trading-schooner. He stipulated only, that there should be no communication between the ship and shore. "For yourself, Señor Captain," he continued, "accept my hospitality. The fort is yours as long as you shall grace it with your distinguished presence;" and with old-fashioned courtesy, he made the semblance of withdrawing from the guard-room.

Master Peleg Scudder smiled as he thought of the half-dismantled fort, the two mouldy brass cannon, cast in Manila a century previous, and the shiftless garrison. A wild thought of accepting the Commander's offer literally, conceived in the reckless spirit of a man who never let slip an offer for trade, for a moment filled his brain, but a timely reflection of the commercial unimportance of the transaction checked him. He only took a capacious quid of tobacco, as the Commander gravely drew a settle before the fire, and in honor of his guest untied the black silk handkerchief that bound his grizzled brows.

What passed between Salvatierra and his guest that night it becomes me not, as a grave chronicler of the salient points of history, to relate. I have said that Master Peleg Scudder was a fluent talker, and under the influence of divers strong waters, furnished by his host, he became still more loquacious. And think of a man with a twenty years' budget of gossip! The Commander learned, for the first time, how Great Britain lost her colonies; of the French Revolution; of the great Napoleon, whose achievements, perhaps, Peleg colored more highly than the Commander's superiors would have liked. And when Peleg turned questioner, the Commander was at his mercy. He gradually made himself master of the gossip of the Mission and Presidio, the "small-beer" chronicles of that pastoral age, the conversion of the heathen, the Presidio schools, and- even asked the Commander how he had lost his eye! It is said that at this point of the conversation Master Peleg produced from about his person divers small trinkets, kick-shaws and new-fangled trifles, and even forced some of them upon his host. It is further alleged that under the malign influence of Peleg and several glasses of *aguardiente*, the Commander lost somewhat of his decorum, and behaved in a manner unseemly for one in his position, reciting high-flown Spanish poetry, and even piping in a thin, high voice, divers madrigals and heathen canzonets of an amorous complexion; chiefly in regard to a "little one" who was his, the Commander's, "soul"! These allegations, perhaps unworthy the notice of a serious chronicler, should be received with great caution, and are introduced here as simple hearsay. That the Commander, however, took a handkerchief and attempted to show his guest the mysteries of the *sembi cuacua*, capering in an agile but indecorous manner about the apartment, has been denied. Enough for the purposes of this narrative, that at midnight Peleg assisted his host to bed with many protestations of undying friendship, and then, as the gale had abated, took his leave of the Presidio and hurried aboard the "General Court." When the day broke the ship was gone.

I know not if Peleg kept his word with his host. It is said that the holy fathers at the Mission that night heard a loud chanting in the plaza, as of the heathens singing psalms through their noses; that for many days after an odor of salt codfish prevailed in the settlement; that a dozen hard nutmegs, which were unfit for spice or seed, were found in the possession of the wife of the baker, and that several bushels of shoe-pegs, which bore a pleasing resemblance to oats, but were quite inadequate to the purposes of provender, were discovered in the stable of the blacksmith. But when the reader reflects upon the sacredness of a Yankee trader's word, the stringent discipline of the Spanish port regulations, and the proverbial indisposition of my countrymen to impose upon the confidence of a simple people, he will at once reject this part of the story.

A roll of drums, ushering in the year 1798, awoke the Commander. The sun was shining brightly, and the storm had ceased. He sat up in bed, and through the force of habit rubbed his left eye. As the remembrance of the previous night came back to him, he jumped from his couch and ran to the window. There was no ship in the bay. A sudden thought seemed to strike him, and he rubbed both of his eyes. Not content with this, he consulted the metallic mirror which hung beside his crucifix. There was no mistake; the Commander had a visible second eye,—a right one,—as good, save for the purposes of vision, as the left.

Whatever might have been the true secret of this transformation, but one opinion prevailed at San Carlos.

It was one of those rare miracles vouchsafed a pious Catholic community as an evidence to the heathen, through the intercession of the blessed San Carlos himself. That their beloved Commander, the temporal defender of the Faith, should be the recipient of this miraculous manifestation was most fit and seemly. The Commander himself was reticent; he could not tell a falsehood,—he dared not tell the truth. After all, if the good folk of San Carlos believed that the powers of his right eye were actually restored, was it wise and discreet for him to undeceive them? For the first time in his life the Commander thought of policy,—for the first time he quoted that text which has been the lure of so many well-meaning but easy Christians, of being "all things to all men." Infeliz Hermenegildo Salvatierra!

For by degrees an ominous whisper crept through the little settlement. The Right Eye of the Commander, although miraculous, seemed to exercise a baleful effect upon the beholder. No one could look at it without winking. It was cold, hard, relentless and unflinching. More than that, it seemed to be endowed with a dreadful prescience,—a faculty of seeing through and into the inarticulate thoughts of those it looked upon. The soldiers of the garrison obeyed the eye rather than the voice of their commander, and answered his glance rather than his lips in questioning. The servants could not evade the ever-watchful, but cold attention that seemed to pursue them. The children of the Presidio School smirched their copy-books under the awful supervision, and poor Paquita, the prize pupil, failed utterly in that marvellous up-stroke when her patron stood beside her. Gradually distrust, suspicion, self-accusation, and timidity took the place of trust, confidence, and security throughout San Carlos. Whenever the Right Eye of the Commander fell, a shadow fell with it.

Nor was Salvatierra entirely free from the baleful influence of his miraculous acquisition. Unconscious of its effect upon others, he only saw in their actions evidence of certain things that the crafty Peleg had hinted on that eventful New Year's eve. His most trusty retainers stammered, blushed, and faltered before him. Self-accusations, confessions of minor faults and delinquencies, or extravagant excuses and apologies met his mildest inquiries. The very children that he loved—his pet pupil, Paquita—seemed to be conscious of some hidden sin. The result of this constant irritation showed itself more plainly. For the first half-year the Commander's voice and eye were at variance. He was still kind, tender, and thoughtful in speech. Gradually, however, his voice took upon itself the hardness of his glance and its sceptical, impassive quality, and as the year again neared its close it was plain that the Commander had fitted himself to the eye, and not the eye to the Commander.

It may be surmised that these changes did not escape the watchful solicitude of the Fathers. Indeed, the few who were first to ascribe the right eye of Salvatierra to miraculous origin and the special grace of the blessed San Carlos, now talked openly of witchcraft and the agency of Luzbel, the evil one. It would have fared ill with Hermenegildo Salvatierra had he been aught but Commander or amenable to local authority. But the reverend father, Friar Manuel de Cortes, had no power over the political executive, and all attempts at spiritual advice failed signally. He retired baffled and confused from his first interview with the Commander, who seemed now to take a grim satisfaction in the fateful power of his glance. The holy father contradicted himself, exposed the fallacies of his own arguments, and even, it is asserted, committed himself to several undoubted heresies. When the Commander stood up at mass, if the officiating priest caught that sceptical and searching eye, the service was inevitably ruined. Even the power of the Holy Church seemed to be lost, and the last hold upon the affections of the people and the good order of the settlement departed from San Carlos.

As the long dry summer passed, the low hills that surrounded the white walls of the Presidio grew more and more to resemble in hue the leathern jacket of the Commander, and Nature herself seemed to have borrowed his dry, hard glare. The earth was cracked and seamed with drought; a blight had fallen upon the orchards and vineyards, and the rain, long delayed and ardently prayed for, came not. The sky was as tearless as the right eye of the Commander. Murmurs of discontent, insubordination, and plotting among the Indians reached his ears; he only set his teeth the more firmly, tightened the knot of his black silk handkerchief, and looked up his Toledo.

The last day of the year 1798 found the Commander sitting, at the hour of evening prayers, alone in the guard-room. He no longer attended the services of the Holy Church, but crept away at such times to some solitary spot, where he spent the interval in silent meditation. The firelight played upon the low beams and rafters, but left the bowed figure of Salvatierra in darkness. Sitting thus, he felt a small hand touch his arm, and, looking down, saw the figure of Paquita, his little Indian pupil, at his knee. "Ah, littlest of all," said the Commander, with something of his old tenderness, lingering over the endearing diminutives of his native speech,—"sweet one, what doest thou here? Art thou not afraid of him whom every one shuns and fears?"

"No," said the little Indian, readily, "not in the dark. I hear your voice,—the old voice; I feel your touch,—the old touch; but I see not your eye, Señor Comandante. That only I fear,—and that, O Señor, O my father," said the child, lifting her little arms towards his,—"that I know is not thine own!"

The Commander shuddered and turned away. Then, recovering himself, he kissed Paquita gravely on the forehead and bade her retire. A few hours later, when silence had fallen upon the Presidio, he sought his own couch and slept peacefully.

At about the middle watch of the night a dusky figure crept through the low embrasure of the Commander's apartment. Other figures were flitting through the parade-ground, which the Commander might have seen had he not slept so quietly. The intruder stepped noiselessly to the couch and listened to the sleeper's deep-drawn inspiration. Something glittered in the firelight as the savage lifted his arm; another moment and the sore perplexities of Hermenegildo Salvatierra would have been over, when suddenly the savage started and fell back in a paroxysm of terror. The Commander slept peacefully, but his right eye, widely opened, fixed and unaltered, glared coldly on the would-be assassin. The man fell to the earth in a fit, and the noise awoke the sleeper.

To rise to his feet, grasp his sword, and deal blows thick and fast upon the mutinous savages who now thronged the room, was the work of a moment. Help opportunely arrived, and the undisciplined Indians were speedily driven beyond the walls, but in the scuffle the Commander received a blow upon his right eye, and, lifting his hand to that mysterious organ, it was gone. Never again was it found, and never again, for bale or bliss, did it adorn the right orbit of the Commander.

With it passed away the spell that had fallen upon San Carlos. The rain returned to invigorate the languid soil, harmony was restored between priest and soldier, the green grass presently waved over the sere hillsides, the children flocked again to the side of their martial preceptor, a *Te Deum* was sung in the Mission Church, and pastoral content once more smiled upon the gentle valleys of San Carlos. And far southward crept the "General Court" with its master, Peleg Scudder, trafficking in beads and peltries with the Indians, and offering glass eyes, wooden legs, and other Boston notions to the chiefs.

THE LEGEND OF DEVIL'S POINT.

On the northerly shore of San Francisco Bay, at a point where the Golden Gate broadens into the Pacific stands a bluff promontory. It affords shelter from the prevailing winds to a semicircular bay on the east. Around this bay the hillside is bleak and barren, but there are traces of former habitation in a weather-beaten cabin and deserted corral. It is said that these were originally built by an enterprising squatter, who for some unaccountable reason abandoned them shortly after. The "Jumper" who succeeded him disappeared one day, quite as mysteriously. The third tenant, who seemed to be a man of sanguine, hopeful temperament, divided the property into building lots, staked off the hillside, and projected the map of a new metropolis. Failing, however, to convince the citizens of San Francisco that they had mistaken the site of their city, he presently fell into dissipation and despondency. He was frequently observed haunting the narrow strip of beach at low tide, or perched upon the cliff at high water. In the latter position a sheep-tender one day found him, cold and pulseless, with a map of his property in his hand, and his face turned toward the distant sea.

Perhaps these circumstances gave the locality its infelicitous reputation. Vague rumors were bruited of a supernatural influence that had been exercised on the tenants. Strange stories were circulated of the origin of the diabolical title by which the promontory was known. By some it was believed to be haunted by the spirit of one of Sir Francis Drake's sailors who had deserted his ship in consequence of stories told by the Indians of gold discoveries, but who had perished by starvation on the rocks. A *vaquero* who had once passed a night in the ruined cabin, related how a strangely dressed and emaciated figure had knocked at the door at midnight and demanded food. Other story-tellers, of more historical accuracy, roundly asserted that Sir Francis himself had been little better than a pirate, and had chosen this spot to conceal quantities of ill-gotten booty, taken from neutral bottoms, and had protected his hiding-place by the orthodox means of hellish incantation and diabolic agencies. On moonlight nights a shadowy ship was sometimes seen standing off-and-on, or when fogs encompassed sea and shore the noise of oars rising and falling in their row-locks could be heard muffled and indistinctly during the night. Whatever foundation there might have been for these stories, it was certain that a more weird and desolate-looking spot could not have been selected for their theatre. High hills, verdureless and enfiladed with dark cañadas, cast their gaunt shadows on the tide. During a greater portion of the day the wind, which blew furiously and incessantly, seemed possessed with a spirit of fierce disquiet and unrest. Toward nightfall the seafog crept with soft step through the portals of the Golden Gate, or stole in noiseless marches down the hillside, tenderly soothing the wind-buffeted face of the cliff, until sea and sky were hid together. At such times the populous city beyond and the nearer settlement seemed removed to an infinite distance. An immeasurable loneliness settled upon the cliff. The creaking of a windlass, or the monotonous chant of sailors on some unseen, outlying ship, came faint and far, and full of mystic suggestion.

About a year ago a well-to-do middle-aged broker of San Francisco found himself at nightfall the sole occupant of a "plunger," encompassed in a dense fog, and drifting toward the Golden Gate. This unexpected termination of an afternoon's sail was partly attributable to his want of nautical skill, and partly to the effect of his usually sanguine nature. Having given up the guidance of his boat to the wind and tide, he had trusted too implicitly for that reaction which his business experience assured him was certain to occur in all affairs, aquatic as well as terrestrial. "The tide will turn soon," said the broker, confidently, "or something will happen." He had scarcely settled himself back again in the stern-sheets, before the bow of the plunger, obeying some mysterious impulse, veered slowly around and a dark object loomed up before him. A gentle eddy carried the boat further in shore, until at last it was completely embayed under the lee of a rocky point now faintly discernible through the fog. He looked around him in the vain hope of recognizing some familiar headland. The tops of the high hills which rose on either side were hidden in the fog. As the boat swung around, he succeeded in fastening a line to the rocks, and sat down again with a feeling of renewed confidence and security.

It was very cold. The insidious fog penetrated his tightly buttoned coat, and set his teeth to chattering in spite of the aid he sometimes drew from a pocket-flask. His clothes were wet and the stern-sheets were covered with spray. The comforts of fire and shelter continually rose before his fancy as he gazed wistfully on the rocks. In sheer despair he finally drew the boat toward the most accessible part of the cliff and essayed to ascend. This was less difficult than it appeared, and in a few moments he had gained the hill above. A dark object at a little distance attracted his attention, and on approaching it proved to be a deserted cabin. The story goes on to say, that having built a roaring fire of stakes pulled from the adjoining corral, with the aid of a flask of excellent brandy, he managed to pass the early part of the evening with comparative comfort.

There was no door in the cabin, and the windows were simply square openings, which freely admitted the searching fog. But in spite of these discomforts, —being a man of cheerful, sanguine temperament,— he amused himself by poking the fire, and watching the ruddy glow which the flames threw on the fog from the open door. In this innocent occupation a great weariness overcame him, and he fell asleep.

He was awakened at midnight by a loud "halloo," which seemed to proceed directly from the sea. Thinking it might be the cry of some boatman lost in the fog, he walked to the edge of the cliff, but the thick veil that covered sea and land rendered all objects at the distance of a few feet indistinguishable. He heard, however, the regular strokes of oars rising and falling on the water. The halloo was repeated. He was clearing his throat to reply, when to his surprise an answer came apparently from the very cabin he had quitted. Hastily retracing his steps, he was the more amazed, on reaching the open door, to find a stranger warming himself by the fire. Stepping back far enough to conceal his own person, he took a good look at the intruder.

He was a man of about forty, with a cadaverous face. But the oddity of his dress attracted the broker's attention more than his lugubrious physiognomy. His legs were hid in enormously wide trousers descending to his knee, where they met long boots of sealskin. A pea-jacket with exaggerated cuffs, almost as large as the breeches, covered his chest, and around his waist a monstrous belt, with a buckle like a dentist's sign, supported two trumpet-mouthed pistols and a curved hanger. He wore a long queue, which depended half-way down his back. As the firelight fell on his ingenuous countenance the broker observed with some concern that this queue was formed, entirely of a kind of tobacco, known as pigtail or twist. Its effect, the broker remarked, was much heightened when in a moment of thoughtful abstraction the apparition bit off a portion of it, and rolled it as a quid into the cavernous recesses of his jaws.

Meanwhile, the nearer splash of oars indicated the approach of the unseen boat. The broker had barely time to conceal himself behind the cabin before a number of uncouth-looking figures clambered up the hill toward the ruined rendezvous. They were dressed like the previous comer, who, as they passed through the open door, exchanged greetings with each in antique phraseology, bestowing at the same time some familiar nickname. Flash-in-the-Pan, Spitter-of-Frogs, Malmsey Butt, Latheyard-Will, and Mark-the-Pinker, were the few *sobriquets* the broker remembered. Whether these titles were given to express some peculiarity of their owner he could not tell, for a silence followed as they slowly ranged themselves upon the floor of the cabin in a semicircle around their cadaverous host.

At length Malmsey Butt, a spherical-bodied man-of-war's-man, with a rubicund nose, got on his legs somewhat unsteadily, and addressed himself to the company. They had met that evening, said the speaker, in accordance with a time-honored custom. This was simply to relieve that one of their number who for fifty years had kept watch and ward over the locality where certain treasures had been buried. At this point the broker pricked up his ears. "If so be, camarados and brothers all," he continued, "ye are ready to receive the report of our excellent and well-beloved brother, Master Slit-the-Weazand, touching his search for this treasure, why, marry, to't and begin."

A murmur of assent went around the circle as the speaker resumed his seat. Master Slit-the-Weazand slowly opened his lantern jaws, and began. He had spent much of his time in determining the exact location of the teasure. He believed—nay, he could state positively—that its position was now settled. It was true he had done some trifling little business outside. Modesty forbade his mentioning the particulars, but he would simply state that of the three tenants who had occupied the cabin during the past ten years, none were now alive. [Applause, and cries of "Go to! thou wast always a tall fellow!" and the like.]

Mark-the-Pinker next arose. Before proceeding to business he had a duty to perform in the sacred name of Friendship. It ill became him to pass an eulogy upon the qualities of the speaker who had preceded him, for he had known him from "boyhood's hour." Side by side they had wrought together in the Spanish war. For a neat hand with a toledo he challenged his equal, while how nobly and beautifully he had won his present title of Slit-the-Weazand, all could testify. The speaker, with some show of emotion, asked to be pardoned if he dwelt too freely on passages of their early companionship; he then detailed, with a fine touch of humor, his comrade's peculiar manner of slitting the ears and lips of a refractory Jew, who had been captured in one of their previous voyages. He would not weary the patience of his hearers, but would briefly propose that the report of Slit-the-Weazand be accepted, and that the thanks of the company be tendered him.

A beaker of strong spirits was then rolled into the hut, and cans of grog were circulated freely from hand to hand. The health of Slit-the-Weazand was proposed in a neat speech by Mark-the-Pinker, and responded to by the former gentleman in a manner that drew tears to the eyes of all present. To the broker, in his concealment, this momentary diversion from the real business of the meeting occasioned much anxiety. As yet nothing had been said to indicate the exact locality of the treasure to which they had mysteriously alluded. Fear restrained him from open inquiry, and curiosity kept him from making good his escape during the orgies which followed.

But his situation was beginning to become critical. Flash-in-the-Pan, who seemed to have been a man of choleric humor, taking fire during some hotly contested argument, discharged both his pistols at the breast of his opponent. The balls passed through on each side immediately below his arm-pits, making a clean hole, through which the horrified broker could see the firelight behind him. The wounded man, without betraying any concern, excited the laughter of the company, by jocosely putting his arms akimbo, and inserting his thumbs into the orifices of the wounds, as if they had been arm-holes. This having in a measure restored good-humor, the party joined hands and formed a circle preparatory to dancing. The dance was commenced by some monotonous stanzas hummed in a very high key by one of the party, the rest joining in the following chorus, which seemed to present a familiar sound to the broker's ear.

> "Her Majestie is very sicke,
> Lord Essex hath ye measles,
> Our Admiral hath licked ye French—
> Poppe! saith ye weasell!"

At the regular recurrence of the last line, the party discharged their loaded pistols in all directions, rendering the position of the unhappy broker one of extreme peril and perplexity.

When the tumult had partially subsided, Flash-in-the-Pan called the meeting to order, and most of the revellers returned to their places, Malmsey Butt, however, insisting upon another chorus, and singing at the top of his voice:—

> "I am ycleped J. Keyser—I was born at Spring, hys Garden,
> My father toe make me ane clerke erst did essaye,
> But a fico for ye offis—I spurn ye losels offeire;
> For I fain would be ane butcher by'r ladykin alwaye."

Flash-in-the-Pan drew a pistol from his belt, and bidding some one gag Malmsey Butt with the stock of it, proceeded to read from a portentous roll of parchment that he held in his hand. It was a semi-legal document, clothed in the quaint phraseology of a bygone period. After a long preamble, asserting their loyalty as lieges of Her most bountiful Majesty and Sovereign Lady the Queen, the document declared that they then and there took possession of the promontory, and all the treasure trove therein contained, formerly buried by Her Majesty's most faithful and devoted Admiral Sir Francis Drake, with the right to search, discover, and appropriate the same; and for the purpose thereof they did then and there form a guild or corporation to so discover, search for, and disclose said treasures, and by virtue thereof they solemnly subscribed their names. But at this moment the reading of the parchment was arrested by an exclamation from the assembly, and the broker was seen frantically struggling at the door in the strong arms of Mark-the-Pinker.

"Let me go!" he cried, as he made a desperate attempt to reach the side of Master Flash-in-the-Pan. "Let me go! I tell you, gentlemen, that document is not worth the parchment it is written on. The laws of the State, the customs of the country, the mining ordinances, are all against it. Don't, by all that's sacred, throw away such a capital investment through ignorance and informality. Let me go! I assure you, gentlemen, professionally, that you have a big thing, — a remarkably big thing, and even if I ain't in it, I'm not going to see it fall through. Don't, for God's sake, gentlemen, I implore you, put your names to such a ridiculous paper. There isn't a notary—"

He ceased. The figures around him, which were beginning to grow fainter and more indistinct, as he went on, swam before his eyes, flickered, reappeared again, and finally went out. He rubbed his eyes and gazed around him. The cabin was deserted. On the hearth the red embers of his fire were fading away in the bright beams of the morning sun, that looked aslant through the open window. He ran out to the cliff. The sturdy sea-breeze fanned his feverish cheeks, and tossed the white caps of waves that beat in pleasant music on the beach below. A stately merchantman with snowy canvas was entering the Gate. The voices of sailors came cheerfully from a bark at anchor below the point. The muskets of the sentries gleamed brightly on Alcatraz, and the rolling of drums swelled on the breeze. Farther on, the hills of San Francisco, cottage-crowned and bordered with wharves and warehouses, met his longing eye.

Such is the Legend of Devil's Point. Any objections to its reliability may be met with the statement, that the broker who tells the story has since incorporated a company under the title of Flash-in-the-Pan Gold and Silver Treasure Mining Company," and that its shares are already held at a stiff figure. A copy of the original document is said to be on record in the office of the company, and on any clear day the locality of the claim may be distinctly seen from the hills of San Francisco.

THE ADVENTURE OF PADRE VICENTIO.

A LEGEND OF SAN FRANCISCO.

ONE pleasant New Year's Eve, about forty years ago, Padre Vicentio was slowly picking his way across the sand-hills from the Mission Dolores. As he climbed the crest of the ridge beside Mission Creek, his broad, shining face might have been easily mistaken for the beneficent image of the rising moon, so bland was its smile and so indefinite its features. For the Padre was a man of notable reputation and character; his ministration at the mission of San José had been marked with cordiality and unction; he was adored by the simple-minded savages, and had succeeded in impressing his individuality so strongly upon them that the very children were said to have miraculously resembled him in feature.

As the holy man reached the loneliest portion of the road, he naturally put spurs to his mule as if to quicken that decorous pace which the obedient animal had acquired through long experience of its master's habits. The locality had an unfavorable reputation. Sailors—deserters from whaleships—had been seen lurking about the outskirts of the town, and low scrub oaks which everywhere beset the trail might have easily concealed some desperate runaway. Besides these material obstructions, the devil, whose hostility to the church was well known, was said to sometimes haunt the vicinity in the likeness of a spectral whaler, who had met his death in a drunken bout, from a harpoon in the hands of a companion. The ghost of this unfortunate mariner was frequently observed sitting on the hill toward the dusk of evening, armed with his favourite weapon and a tub containing a coil of line, looking out for some belated traveller on whom to exercise his professional skill. It is related that the good Father José Maria of the Mission Dolores had been twice attacked by this phantom sportsman; that once, on returning from San Francisco, and panting with exertion from climbing the hill, he was startled by a stentorian cry of "There she blows!" quickly followed by a hurtling harpoon, which buried itself in the sand beside him; that on another occasion he narrowly escaped destruction, his serapa having been transfixed by the diabolical harpoon and dragged away in triumph. Popular opinion seems to have been divided as to the reason for the devil's particular attention to Father José, some asserting that the extreme piety of the Padre excited the Evil One's animosity, and others that his adipose tendency simply rendered him, from a professional view-point, a profitable capture.

Had Father Vicentio been inclined to scoff at this apparition as a heretical innovation, there was still the story of Concepcion, the Demon Vaquero, whose terrible *riata* was fully as potent as the whaler's harpoon. Concepcion, when in the flesh, had been a celebrated herder of cattle and wild horses, and was reported to have chased the devil in the shape of a fleet *pinto* colt all the way from San Luis Obispo to San Francisco, vowing not to give up the chase until he had overtaken the disguised Arch-Enemy. This the devil prevented by resuming his own shape, but kept the unfortunate vaquero to the fulfilment of his rash vow; and Concepcion still scoured the coast on a phantom steed, beguiling the monotony of his eternal pursuit by lassoing travellers, dragging them at the heels of his unbroken mustang until they were eventually picked up, half-strangled, by the road-side. The Padre listened attentively for the tramp of this terrible rider. But no footfall broke the stillness of the night; even the hoofs of his own mule sank noiselessly in the shifting sand. Now and then a rabbit bounded lightly by him, or a quail ran into the bushes. The melancholy call of plover from the adjoining marshes of Mission Creek came to him so faintly and fitfully that it seemed almost a recollection of the past rather than a reality of the present.

To add to his discomposure one of those heavy sea-fogs peculiar to the locality began to drift across the hills and presently encompassed him. While endeavoring to evade its cold embraces, Padre Vicentio incautiously drove his heavy spurs into the flanks of his mule as that puzzled animal was hesitating on the brink of a steep declivity. Whether the poor beast was indignant at this novel outrage, or had been for some time reflecting on the evils of being priest-ridden, has not transpired; enough that he suddenly threw up his heels, pitching the reverend man over his head, and, having accomplished this feat, coolly dropped on his knees and tumbled after his rider.

Over and over went the Padre, closely followed by his faithless mule. Luckily the little hollow which received the pair was of sand that yielded to the superincumbent weight, half burying them without further injury. For some moments the poor man lay motionless, vainly endeavoring to collect his scattered senses. A hand irreverently laid upon his collar, and a rough shake, assisted to recall his consciousness. As the Padre staggered to his feet he found himself confronted by a stranger.

Seen dimly through the fog, and under circumstances that to say the least were not prepossessing, the new-comer had an inexpressibly mysterious and brigand-like aspect. A long boat-cloak concealed his figure, and a slouched hat hid his features, permitting only his eyes to glisten in the depths. With a deep groan the Padre slipped from the stranger's grasp and subsided into the soft sand again.

"Gad's life!" said the stranger, pettishly, "hast no more bones in thy fat carcass than a jelly-fish? Lend a hand, here! Yo, heave ho!" and he dragged the Padre into an upright position. "Now, then, who and what art thou?"

The Padre could not help thinking that the question might have more properly been asked by himself; but with an odd mixture of dignity and trepidation he began enumerating his different titles, which were by no means brief, and would have been alone sufficient to strike awe in the bosom of an ordinary adversary. The stranger irreverently broke in upon his formal phrases, and assuring him that a priest was the very person he was looking for, coolly replaced the old man's hat, which had tumbled off, and bade him accompany him at once on an errand of spiritual counsel to one who was even then lying in extremity. "To think," said the stranger, "that I should stumble upon the very man I was seeking! Body of Bacchus! but this is lucky! Follow me quickly, for there is no time to lose."

Like most easy natures the positive assertion of the stranger, and withal a certain authoritative air of command, overcame what slight objections the Padre might have feebly nurtured during this remarkable interview. The spiritual invitation was one, also, that he dared not refuse; not only that; but it tended somewhat to remove the superstitious dread with which he had begun to regard the mysterious stranger. But, following at a respectful distance, the Padre could not help observing with a thrill of horror that the stranger's footsteps made no impression on the sand, and his figure seemed at times to blend and incorporate itself with the fog, until the holy man was obliged to wait for its reappearance. In one of these intervals of embarrassment he heard the ringing of the far-off Mission bell, proclaiming the hour of midnight. Scarcely had the last stroke died away before the announcement was taken up and repeated by a multitude of bells of all sizes, and the air was filled with the sound of striking clocks and the pealing of steeple chimes. The old man uttered a cry of alarm. The stranger sharply demanded the cause. "The bells! did you not hear them?" gasped Padre Vicentio. "Tush! tush!" answered the stranger, "thy fall hath set triple bob-majors ringing in thine ears. Come on!"

The Padre was only too glad to accept the explanation conveyed in this discourteous answer. But he was destined for another singular experience. When they had reached the summit of the eminence now known as Russian Hill, an exclamation again burst from the Padre. The stranger turned to his companion with an impatient gesture; but the Padre heeded him not. The view that burst upon his sight was such as might well have engrossed the attention of a more enthusiastic temperament. The fog had not yet reached the hill, and the long valleys and hillsides of the embarcadero below were glittering with the light of a populous city. "Look!" said the Padre, stretching his hand over the spreading landscape. "Look, dost thou not see the stately squares and brilliantly lighted avenues of a mighty metropolis. Dost thou not see, as it were, another firmament below?"

"Avast heaving, reverend man, and quit this folly," said the stranger, dragging the bewildered Padre after him. "Behold rather the stars knocked out of thy hollow noddle by the fall thou hast had. Prithee, get over thy visions and rhapsodies, for the time is wearing apace."

The Padre humbly followed without another word. Descending the hill toward the north, the stranger leading the way, in a few moments the Padre detected the wash of waves, and presently his feet struck the firmer sand of the beach. Here the stranger paused, and the Padre perceived a boat lying in readiness hard by. As he stepped into the stern sheets, in obedience to the command of his companion, he noticed that the rowers seemed to partake of the misty incorporeal texture of his companion, a similarity that became the more distressing when he perceived also that their oars in pulling together made no noise. The stranger, assuming the helm, guided the boat on quietly, while the fog, settling over the face of the water and closing around them, seemed to interpose a muffled wall between themselves and the rude jarring of the outer world. As they pushed further into this penetralia, the Padre listened anxiously for the sound of creaking blocks and the rattling of cordage, but no vibration broke the veiled stillness or disturbed the warm breath of the fleecy fog. Only one incident occurred to break the monotony of their mysterious journey. A one-eyed rower, who sat in front of the Padre, catching the devout father's eye, immediately grinned such a ghastly smile, and winked his remaining eye with such diabolical intensity of meaning that the Padre was constrained to utter a pious ejaculation, which had the disastrous effect of causing the marine Cocles to "catch a crab," throwing his heels in the air and his head into the bottom of the boat. But even this accident did not disturb the gravity of the rest of the ghastly boat's crew.

When, as it seemed to the Padre, ten minutes had elapsed, the outline of a large ship loomed up directly across their bow. Before he could utter the cry of warning that rose to his lips, or brace himself against the expected shock, the boat passed gently and noiselessly through the sides of the vessel, and the holy man found himself standing on the berth deck of what seemed to be an ancient caravel. The boat and boat's crew had vanished. Only his mysterious friend, the stranger, remained. By the light of a swinging lamp the Padre beheld him standing beside a hammock, whereon, apparently, lay the dying man to whom he had been so mysteriously summoned. As the Padre, in obedience to a sign from his companion, stepped to the side of the sufferer, he feebly opened his eyes and thus addressed him:—

"Thou seest before thee, reverend father, a helpless mortal, struggling not only with the last agonies of the flesh, but beaten down and tossed with sore anguish of the spirit. It matters little when or how I became what thou now seest me. Enough that my life has been ungodly and sinful, and that my only hope of absolution lies in my imparting to thee a secret which is of vast importance to the holy Church, and affects greatly her power, wealth, and dominion on these shores. But the terms of this secret and the conditions of my absolution are peculiar. I have but five minutes to live. In that time I must receive the extreme unction of the Church."

"And thy secret?" said the holy father.

"Shall be told afterwards," answered the dying man. "Come, my time is short. Shrive me quickly."

The Padre hesitated. "Couldst thou not tell this secret first?"

"Impossible!" said the dying man, with what seemed to the Padre a momentary gleam of triumph. Then, as his breath grew feebler, he called impatiently, "Shrive me! shrive me!"

"Let me know at least what this secret concerns?" suggested the Padre, insinuatingly.

"Shrive me first," said the dying man.

But the priest still hesitated, parleying with the sufferer until the ship's bell struck, when, with a triumphant, mocking laugh from the stranger, the vessel suddenly fell to pieces, amid the rushing of waters which at once involved the dying man, the priest, and the mysterious stranger.

The Padre did not recover his consciousness until high noon the next day, when he found himself lying in a little hollow between the Mission Hills, and his faithful mule a few paces from him, cropping the sparse herbage. The Padre made the best of his way home, but wisely abstained from narrating the facts mentioned above, until after the discovery of gold, when the whole of this veracious incident was related, with the assertion of the padre that the secret which was thus mysteriously snatched from his possession was nothing more than the discovery of gold, years since, by the runaway sailors from the expedition of Sir Francis Drake.

THE DEVIL AND THE BROKER.

A MEDIÆVAL LEGEND.

THE church clocks in San Francisco were striking ten. The Devil, who had been flying over the city that evening, just then alighted on the roof of a church near the corner of Bush and Montgomery Streets. It will be perceived that the popular belief that the Devil avoids holy edifices, and vanishes at the sound of a *Credo* or *Pater-noster*, is long since exploded. Indeed, modern scepticism asserts that he is not averse to these orthodox discourses, which particularly bear reference to himself, and in a measure recognize his power and importance.

I am inclined to think, however, that his choice of a resting-place was a good deal influenced by its contiguity to a populous thoroughfare. When he was comfortably seated, he began pulling out the joints of a small rod which he held in his hand, and which presently proved to be an extraordinary fishing-pole, with a telescopic adjustment that permitted its protraction to a marvellous extent. Affixing a line thereto, he selected a fly of a particular pattern from a small box which he carried with him, and, making a skilful cast, threw his line into the very centre of that living stream which ebbed and flowed through Montgomery Street.

Either the people were very virtuous that evening

or the bait was not a taking one. In vain the Devil whipped the stream at an eddy in front of the Occidental, or trolled his line into the shadows of the Cosmopolitan; five minutes passed without even a nibble. "Dear me!" quoth the Devil, "that's very singular; one of my most popular flies, too! Why, they'd have risen by shoals in Broadway or Beacon Street for that. Well, here goes another." And, fitting a new fly from his well-filled box, he gracefully recast his line.

For a few moments there was every prospect of sport. The line was continually bobbing and the nibbles were distinct and gratifying. Once or twice the bait was apparently gorged and carried off in the upper stories of the hotels to be digested at leisure. At such times the professional manner in which the Devil played out his line would have thrilled the heart of Izaak Walton. But his efforts were unsuccessful; the bait was invariably carried off without hooking the victim, and the Devil finally lost his temper. "I've heard of these San-Franciscans before," he muttered; "wait till I get hold of one,—that's all!" he added malevolently, as he rebaited his hook. A sharp tug and a wriggle foiled his next trial, and finally, with considerable effort, he landed a portly two-hundred-pound broker upon the church roof.

As the victim lay there gasping, it was evident that the Devil was in no hurry to remove the hook from his gills; nor did he exhibit in this delicate operation that courtesy of manner and graceful manipulation which usually distinguished him.

"Come," he said, gruffly, as he grasped the broker by the waistband, "quit that whining and grunting. Don't flatter yourself that you're a prize either. I was certain to have had you. It was only a question of time."

"It is not that, my lord, which troubles me," whined the unfortunate wretch, as he painfully wriggled his head, "but that I should have been fooled by such a paltry bait. What will they say of me down there? To have let 'bigger things' go by, and to be taken in by this cheap trick," he added, as he groaned and glanced at the fly which the Devil was carefully rearranging, "is what,—pardon me, my lord,—is what gets me!"

"Yes," said the Devil, philosophically, "I never caught anybody yet who didn't say that; but tell me, ain't you getting somewhat fastidious down there? Here is one of my most popular flies, the greenback," he continued, exhibiting an emerald-looking insect, which he drew from his box. "This, so generally considered excellent in election season, has not even been nibbled at. Perhaps your sagacity, which, in spite of this unfortunate *contre-temps*, no one can doubt," added the Devil, with a graceful return to his usual courtesy, "may explain the reason or suggest a substitute."

The broker glanced at the contents of the box with a supercilious smile. "Too old-fashioned, my lord,—long ago played out. Yet," he added, with a gleam of interest, "for a consideration I might offer something—ahem!—that would make a taking substitute for these trifles. Give me," he continued, in a brisk, business-like way, "a slight percentage and a bonus down, and I'm your man."

"Name your terms," said the Devil, earnestly.

"My liberty and a percentage on all you take, and the thing's done."

The Devil caressed his tail thoughtfully, for a few moments. He was certain of the broker any way, and the risk was slight. "Done!" he said.

"Stay a moment," said the artful broker. "There are certain contingencies. Give me your fishing-rod and let me apply the bait myself. It requires a skilful hand, my lord; even your well-known experience might fail. Leave me alone for half an hour, and if you have reason to complain of my success I will forfeit my deposit,—I mean my liberty."

The Devil acceded to his request, bowed, and withdrew. Alighting gracefully in Montgomery Street, he dropped into Meade & Co.'s clothing store, where, having completely equipped himself *à la mode*, he sallied forth intent on his personal enjoyment. Determining to sink his professional character, he mingled with the current of human life, and enjoyed, with that immense capacity for excitement peculiar to his nature, the whirl, bustle, and feverishness of the people, as a purely æsthetic gratification unalloyed by the cares of business. What he did that evening does not belong to our story. We return to the broker, whom we left on the roof.

When he made sure that the Devil had retired, he carefully drew from his pocket-book a slip of paper and affixed it on the hook. The line had scarcely reached the current before he felt a bite. The hook was swallowed. To bring up his victim rapidly, disengage him from the hook, and reset his line, was the work of a moment. Another bite and the same result. Another, and another. In a very few minutes the roof was covered with his panting spoil. The broker could himself distinguish that many of them were personal friends; nay, some of them were familiar frequenters of the building on which they were now miserably stranded. That the broker felt a certain satisfaction in being instrumental in thus misleading his fellow-brokers no one acquainted with human nature will for a moment doubt. But a stronger pull on his line caused him to put forth all his strength and skill. The magic pole bent like a coach-whip. The broker held firm, assisted by the battlements of the church. Again and again it was almost wrested from his hand, and again and again he slowly reeled in a portion of the tightening line. At last, with one mighty effort, he lifted to the level of the roof a struggling object. A howl like Pandemonium rang through the air as the broker successfully landed at his feet—the Devil himself!

The two glared fiercely at each other. The broker, perhaps mindful of his former treatment, evinced no haste to remove the hook from his antagonist's jaw. When it was finally accomplished, he asked quietly if the Devil was satisfied. That gentleman seemed absorbed in the contemplation of the bait which he had just taken from his mouth. "I am," he said, finally, "and forgive you; but what do you call this?"

"Bend low," replied the broker, as he buttoned up his coat ready to depart. The Devil inclined his ear. "I call it WILD CAT!"

THE OGRESS OF SILVER LAND;

OR,

THE DIVERTING HISTORY OF PRINCE BADFELLAH AND PRINCE BULLEBOYE.

IN the second year of the reign of the renowned Caliph Lo there dwelt in SILVER LAND, adjoining his territory, a certain terrible ogress. She lived in the bowels of a dismal mountain, where she was in the habit of confining such unfortunate travellers as ventured within her domain. The country for miles around was sterile and barren. In some places it was covered with a white powder, which was called in the language of the country AL KA LI, and was supposed to be the pulverized bones of those who had perished miserably in her service.

In spite of this, every year, great numbers of young men devoted themselves to the service of the ogress, hoping to become her godsons, and to enjoy the good fortune which belonged to that privileged class. For these godsons had no work to perform, neither at the mountain nor elsewhere, but roamed about the world with credentials of their relationship in their pockets, which they called STOKH, which was stamped with the stamp and sealed with the seal of the ogress, and which enabled them at the end of each moon to draw large quantities of gold and silver from her treasury. And the wisest and most favored of those godsons were the Princes BADFELLAH and BULLEBOYE. They knew all the secrets of the ogress, and how to wheedle and coax her. They were also the favorites of SOOPAH INTENDENT, who was her Lord High Chamberlain and Prime Minister, and who dwelt in SILVER LAND.

One day, SOOPAH INTENDENT said to his servants, "What is that which travels the most surely, the most secretly, and the most swiftly?"

And they all answered as one man, "LIGHTNING, my lord, travels the most surely, the most swiftly, and the most secretly!"

Then said SOOPAH INTENDENT, "Let Lightning carry this message secretly, swiftly, and surely to my beloved friends the Princes BADFELLAH and BULLEBOYE, and tell them that their godmother is dying, and bid them seek some other godmother or sell their STOKH ere it becomes *badjee*,—worthless."

"Bekhesm! On our heads be it!" answered the servants; and they ran to Lightning with the message, who flew with it to the City by the Sea, and delivered it, even at that moment, into the hands of the Princes BADFELLAH and BULLEBOYE.

Now the Prince BADFELLAH was a wicked young man; and when he had received this message he tore his beard and rent his garment and reviled his godmother, and his friend SOOPAH INTENDENT. But presently he arose, and dressed himself in his finest stuffs, and went forth into the bazaars and among the merchants, capering and dancing as he walked, and crying in a loud voice, "O, happy day! O, day worthy to be marked with a white stone!"

This he said cunningly, thinking the merchants and men of the bazaars would gather about him, which they presently did, and began to question him: "What news, O most worthy and serene Highness? Tell us, that we make merry too!"

Then replied the cunning prince, "Good news, O my brothers, for I have heard this day that my godmother in SILVER LAND is well." The merchants, who were not aware of the substance of the real message, envied him greatly, and said one to another: "Surely our brother the Prince BADFELLAH is favored by Allah above all men"; and they were about to retire, when the prince checked them, saying: "Tarry for a moment. Here are my credentials, or STOKH. The same I will sell you for fifty thousand sequins, for I have to give a feast to-day, and need much gold. Who will give fifty thousand?" And he again fell to capering and dancing. But this time the merchants drew a little apart, and some of the oldest and wisest said: "What dirt is this which the prince would have us swallow? If his godmother were well, why should he sell his STOKH? Bismillah! The olives are old and the jar is broken!" When Prince BADFELLAH perceived them whispering, his countenance fell, and his knees smote against each other through fear; but, dissembling again, he said: "Well, so be it! Lo, I have much more than shall abide with me, for my days are many and my wants are few. Say forty thousand sequins for my STOKH and let me depart in Allah's name. Who will give forty thousand sequins to become the godson of such a healthy mother?" And he again fell to capering and dancing, but not as gayly as before, for his heart was troubled. The merchants, however, only moved farther away. "Thirty thousand sequins," cried Prince BADFELLAH; but even as he spoke they fled before his face, crying: "His godmother is dead. Lo, the jackals are defiling her grave. Mashallah! he has no godmother." And they sought out PANIK, the swift-footed messenger, and bade him shout through the bazaars that the godmother of Prince BADFELLAH was dead. When he heard this, the prince fell upon his face, and rent his garments, and covered himself with the dust of the market-place. As he was sitting thus, a porter passed him with jars of wine on his shoulders, and the prince begged him to give him a jar, for he was exceeding thirsty and faint. But the porter said, "What will my lord give me first?" And the prince, in very bitterness of spirit, said, "Take this," and handed him his STOKII, and so exchanged it for a jar of wine.

Now the Prince BULLEBOYE was of a different disposition. When he received the message of SOOPAH INTENDENT he bowed his head, and said, "It is the will of God." Then he rose, and without speaking a word entered the gates of his palace. But his wife, the peerless MAREE JAHANN, perceiving the gravity of his countenance, said, "Why is my lord cast down and silent? Why are those rare and priceless pearls, his words, shut up so tightly between those gorgeous oyster-shells, his lips?" But to this he made no reply. Thinking further to divert him, she brought her lute into the chamber and stood before him, and sang the song and danced the dance of BEN KOTTON, which is called IBRAHIM'S DAUGHTER, but she could not lift the veil of sadness from his brow.

When she had ceased, the Prince BULLEBOYE arose and said, "Allah is great, and what am I, his servant, but the dust of the earth! Lo, this day has my godmother sickened unto death, and my STOKH become as a withered palm-leaf. Call hither my servants and camel-drivers, and the merchants that have furnished me with stuffs, and the beggars who have feasted at my table, and bid them take all that is here, for it is mine no longer!" With these words he buried his face in his mantle and wept aloud.

But MAREE JAHANN, his wife, plucked him by the sleeve. "Prithee, my lord," said she, "bethink thee of the BROKAH or scrivener, who besought thee but yesterday to share thy STOKH with him and gave thee his bond for fifty thousand sequins." But the noble Prince BULLEBOYE, raising his head, said: "Shall I sell to him for fifty thousand sequins that which I know is not worth a SOO MARKEE? For is not all the BROKAH'S wealth, even his wife and children, pledged on that bond? Shall I ruin him to save myself? Allah forbid! Rather let me eat the salt fish of honest penury, than the kibobs of dishonorable affluence; rather let me wallow in the mire of virtuous oblivion, than repose on the divan of luxurious wickedness."

When the prince had given utterance to this beautiful and edifying sentiment, a strain of gentle music was heard, and the rear wall of the apartment, which had been ingeniously constructed like a flat, opened and discovered the Ogress of SILVER LAND in the glare of blue fire, seated on a triumphal car attached to two ropes which were connected with the flies, in the very act of blessing the unconscious prince. When the walls closed again without attracting his attention, Prince BULLEBOYE arose, dressed himself in his coarsest and cheapest stuffs, and sprinkled ashes on his head, and in this guise, having embraced his wife, went forth into the bazaars. In this it will be perceived how differently the good Prince BULLEBOYE acted from the wicked Prince BADFELLAH, who put on his gayest garments to simulate and deceive.

Now when Prince BULLEBOYE entered the chief bazaar, where the merchants of the city were gathered in council, he stood up in his accustomed place, and all that were there held their breath, for the noble Prince BULLEBOYE was much respected. "Let the BROKAH, whose bond I hold for fifty thousand sequins, stand forth!" said the prince. And the BROKAH stood forth from among the merchants. Then said the prince: "Here is thy bond for fifty thousand sequins, for which I was to deliver unto thee one half of my STOKH. Know, then, O my brother,—and thou, too, O Aga of the BROKAHS,—that this my STOKH which I pledged to thee is worthless. For my godmother, the Ogress of SILVER LAND, is dying. Thus do I release thee from thy bond, and from the poverty which might overtake thee as it has even me, thy brother, the Prince BULLEBOYE." And with that the noble Prince BULLEBOYE tore the bond of the BROKAH into pieces and scattered it to the four winds.

Now when the prince tore up the bond there was a great commotion, and some said, "Surely the Prince BULLEBOYE is drunken with wine;" and others, "He is possessed of an evil spirit;" and his friends expostulated with him, saying, "What thou hast done is not the custom of the bazaars,—behold, it is not BIZ!" But to all the prince answered gravely, "It is right; on my own head be it!"

But the oldest and wisest of the merchants, they

who had talked with Prince BADFELLAH the same morning, whispered together, and gathered round the BROKAH whose bond the Prince BULLEBOYE had torn up. "Hark ye," said they, "our brother the Prince BULLEBOYE is cunning as a jackal. What bosh is this about ruining himself to save thee? Such a thing was never heard before in the bazaars. It is a trick, O thou mooncalf of a BROKAH! Dost thou not see that he has heard good news from his godmother, the same that was even now told us by the Prince BAD-FELLAH, his confederate, and that he would destroy thy bond for fifty thousand sequins because his STOKH is worth a hundred thousand! Be not deceived, O too credulous BROKAH! for this what our brother the prince doeth is not in the name of ALLAH, but of BIZ, the only god known in the bazaars of the city."

When the foolish BROKAH heard these things he cried, "Justice, O Aga of the BROKAHS,—justice and the fulfilment of my bond! Let the prince deliver unto me the STOKH. Here are my fifty thousand sequins." But the prince said, "Have I not told that my godmother is dying, and that my STOKH is valueless?" At this the BROKAH only clamored the more for justice and the fulfilment of his bond. Then the Aga of the BROKAHS said, "Since the bond is destroyed, behold thou hast no claim. Go thy ways!" But the BROKAH again cried, "Justice, my lord Aga! Behold, I offer the prince seventy thousand sequins for his STOKH!" But the prince said, "It is not worth one sequin!" Then the Aga said, "Bismillah! I cannot understand this. Whether thy godmother be dead, or dying, or immortal, does not seem to signify. Therefore, O prince, by the laws of BIZ and of ALLAH, thou art released. Give the BROKAH thy STOKH for seventy thousand sequins, and bid him depart in peace. On his own head be it!" When the prince heard this command, he handed his STOKH to the BROKAH, who counted out to him seventy thousand sequins. But the heart of the virtuous prince did not rejoice, nor did the BROKAH, when he found his STOKH was valueless; but the merchants lifted their hands in wonder at the sagacity and wisdom of the famous Prince BULLEBOYE. For none would believe that it was the law of ALLAH that the prince followed, and not the rules of BIZ.

CONDENSED NOVELS.

HANDSOME IS AS HANDSOME DOES.

By CH——S R——DE.

CHAPTER I.

THE Dodds were dead. For twenty year they had slept under the green graves of Kittery churchyard. The townfolk still spoke of them kindly. The keeper of the alehouse, where David had smoked his pipe, regretted him regularly, and Mistress Kitty, Mrs. Dodd's maid, whose trim figure always looked well in her mistress's gowns, was inconsolable. The Hardins were in America. Raby was aristocratically gouty; Mrs. Raby, religious. Briefly, then, we have disposed of—

1. Mr. and Mrs. Dodd (dead).
2. Mr. and Mrs. Hardin (translated).
3. Raby, *baron et femme.* (Yet I don't know about the former; he came of a long-lived family, and the gout is an uncertain disease.)

We have active at the present writing (*place aux dames*)—

1. Lady Caroline Coventry, niece of Sir Frederick.
2. Faraday Huxley Little, son of Henry and Grace Little, deceased.

Sequitur to the above, A HERO AND HEROINE.

CHAPTER II.

On the death of his parents, Faraday Little was taken to Raby Hall. In accepting his guardianship, Mr. Raby struggled stoutly against two prejudices: Faraday was plain-looking and sceptical.

"Handsome is as handsome does, sweetheart," pleaded Jael, interceding for the orphan with arms that were still beautiful. "Dear knows, it is not his fault if he does not look like—his father," she added with a great gulp. Jael was a woman, and vindicated her womanhood by never entirely forgiving a former rival.

"It's not that alone, madam," screamed Raby, "but, d—m it, the little rascal's a scientist,—an atheist, a radical, a scoffer! Disbelieves in the Bible, ma'am; is full of this Darwinian stuff about natural selection and descent. Descent, forsooth! In my day, madam, gentlemen were content to trace their ancestors back to gentlemen, and not to—monkeys!"

"Dear heart, the boy is clever," urged Jael.

"Clever!" roared Raby; "what does a gentleman want with cleverness?"

CHAPTER III.

Young Little *was* clever. At seven he had constructed a telescope; at nine, a flying-machine. At ten he saved a valuable life.

Norwood Park was the adjacent estate,—a lordly domain dotted with red deer and black trunks, but scrupulously kept with gravelled roads as hard and blue as steel. There Little was strolling one summer morning, meditating on a new top with concealed springs. At a little distance before him he saw the flutter of lace and ribbons. A young lady, a very young lady,—say of seven summers,—tricked out in the crying abominations of the present fashion, stood beside a low bush. Her nursery-maid was not present, possibly owing to the fact that John the footman was also absent.

Suddenly Little came towards her. "Excuse me, but do you know what those berries are?" He was pointing to the low bush filled with dark clusters of shining—suspiciously shining—fruit.

"Certainly; they are blueberries."

"Pardon me; you are mistaken. They belong to quite another family."

Miss Impudence drew herself up to her full height (exactly three feet nine and a half inches) and, curling an eighth of an inch of scarlet lip, said, scornfully, "*Your* family, perhaps."

Faraday Little smiled in the superiority of boyhood over girlhood.

"I allude to the classification. That plant is the belladonna, or deadly nightshade. Its alkaloid is a narcotic poison."

Sauciness turned pale. "I—have—just—eaten—some!" And began to whimper. "O dear, what shall I do?" Then did it, i. e. wrung her small fingers and cried.

"Pardon me one moment." Little passed his arm around her neck, and with his thumb opened widely the patrician-veined lids of her sweet blue eyes.

"Thank Heaven, there is yet no dilation of the pupil; it is not too late!" He cast a rapid glance around. The nozzle and about three feet of garden hose lay near him.

"Open your mouth, quick!"

It was a pretty, kissable mouth. But young Little meant business. He put the nozzle down her pink throat as far as it would go.

"Now, don't move."

He wrapped his handkerchief around a hoop-stick. Then he inserted both in the other end of the stiff hose. It fitted snugly. He shoved it in and then drew it back.

Nature abhors a vacuum. The young patrician was as amenable to this law as the child of the lowest peasant.

She succumbed. It was all over in a minute. Then she burst into a small fury.

"You nasty, bad—*ugly* boy."

Young Little winced, but smiled.

"Stimulants," he whispered to the frightened nursery-maid who approached; "good evening." He was gone.

CHAPTER IV.

THE breach between young Little and Mr. Raby was slowly widening. Little found objectionable features in the Hall. "This black oak ceiling and wainscoting is not as healthful as plaster; besides, it absorbs the light. The bedroom ceiling is too low; the Elizabethan architects knew nothing of ventilation. The color of that oak panelling which you admire is due to an excess of carbon and the exuvia from the pores of your skin—"

"Leave the house," bellowed Raby, "before the roof falls on your sacrilegious head!"

As Little left the house, Lady Caroline and a handsome boy of about Little's age entered. Lady Caroline recoiled, and then—blushed. Little glared; he instinctively felt the presence of a rival.

CHAPTER V.

LITTLE worked hard. He studied night and day. In five years he became a lecturer, then a professor.

He soared as high as the clouds, he dipped as low as the cellars of the London poor. He analyzed the London fog, and found it two parts smoke, one disease, one unmentionable abominations. He published a pamphlet, which was violently attacked. Then he knew he had done something.

But he had not forgotten Caroline. He was walking one day in the Zoological Gardens and he came upon a pretty picture,—flesh and blood too.

Lady Caroline feeding buns to the bears! An exquisite thrill passed through his veins. She turned her sweet face and their eyes met. They recollected their first meeting seven years before, but it was his turn to be shy and timid. Wonderful power of age and sex! She met him with perfect self-possession.

"Well meant, but indigestible I fear" (he alluded to the buns).

"A clever person like yourself can easily correct that" (she, the slyboots, was thinking of something else).

In a few moments they were chatting gayly. Little eagerly descanted upon the different animals; she listened with delicious interest. An hour glided delightfully away.

After this sunshine, clouds.

To them suddenly entered Mr. Raby and a handsome young man. The gentlemen bowed stiffly and looked vicious,—as they felt. The lady of this quartette smiled amiably, as she did not feel.

"Looking at your ancestors, I suppose," said Mr. Raby, pointing to the monkeys; "we will not disturb you. Come." And he led Caroline away.

Little was heart-sick. He dared not follow them. But an hour later he saw something which filled his heart with bliss unspeakable.

Lady Caroline, with a divine smile on her face, feeding the monkeys!

CHAPTER VI.

ENCOURAGED by love, Little worked hard upon his new flying-machine. His labors were lightened by talking of the beloved one with her French maid Thérèse, whom he had discreetly bribed. Mademoiselle Thérèse was venal, like all her class, but in this instance I fear she was not bribed by British gold. Strange as it may seem to the British mind, it was British genius, British eloquence, British thought, that brought her to the feet of this young *savan.*

"I believe," said Lady Caroline, one day, interrupting her maid in a glowing eulogium upon the skill of "M. Leetell,"—"I believe you are in love with this Professor." A quick flush crossed the olive cheek of Thérèse, which Lady Caroline afterward remembered.

The eventful day of trial came. The public were gathered, impatient and scornful as the pig-headed public are apt to be. In the open area a long cylindrical balloon, in shape like a Bologna sausage, swayed above the machine, from which, like some enormous bird caught in a net, it tried to free itself. A heavy rope held it fast to the ground.

Little was waiting for the ballast, when his eye caught Lady Caroline's among the spectators. The glance was appealing. In a moment he was at her side.

"I should like so much to get into the machine," said the arch-hypocrite, demurely.

"Are you engaged to marry young Raby," said Little, bluntly.

"As you please," she said with a courtesy; "do I take this as a refusal?"

Little was a gentleman. He lifted her and her lapdog into the car.

"How nice! it won't go off?"

"No, the rope is strong, and the ballast is not yet in."

A report like a pistol, a cry from the spectators, a thousand hands stretched to grasp the parted rope, and the balloon darted upward.

Only one hand of that thousand caught the rope, —Little's! But in the same instant the horror-stricken spectators saw him whirled from his feet and borne upward, still clinging to the rope, into space.

CHAPTER VII.*

Lady Caroline fainted. The cold watery nose of her dog on her cheek brought her to herself. She dared not look over the edge of the car; she dared not look up to the bellying monster above her, bearing her to death. She threw herself on the bottom of the car, and embraced the only living thing spared her,—the poodle. Then she cried. Then a clear voice came apparently out of the circumambient air:—

"May I trouble you to look at the barometer?"

She put her head over the car. Little was hanging at the end of a long rope. She put her head back again.

In another moment he saw her perplexed, blushing face over the edge,—blissful sight.

"O, please don't think of coming up! Stay there, do!"

Little stayed. Of course she could make nothing out of the barometer, and said so. Little smiled.

"Will you kindly send it down to me?"

But she had no string or cord. Finally she said, "Wait a moment."

Little waited. This time her face did not appear. The barometer came slowly down at the end of—a stay-lace.

The barometer showed a frightful elevation. Little looked up at the valve and said nothing. Presently he heard a sigh. Then a sob. Then, rather sharply,—

"Why don't you do something?"

* The right of dramatization of this and succeeding chapters is reserved by the writer.

CHAPTER VIII.

LITTLE came up the rope hand over hand. Lady Caroline crouched in the farther side of the car. Fido, the poodle, whined. "Poor thing," said Lady Caroline, "it's hungry."

"Do you wish to save the dog?" said Little.

"Yes."

"Give me your parasol."

She handed Little a good-sized affair of lace and silk and whalebone. (None of your "sun-shades.") Little examined its ribs carefully.

"Give me the dog."

Lady Caroline hurriedly slipped a note under the dog's collar, and passed over her pet.

Little tied the dog to the handle of the parasol and launched them both into space. The next moment they were slowly, but tranquilly, sailing to the earth.

"A parasol and a parachute are distinct, but not different. Be not alarmed, he will get his dinner at some farm-house."

"Where are we now?"

"That opaque spot you see is London fog. Those twin clouds are North and South America. Jerusalem and Madagascar are those specks to the right."

Lady Caroline moved nearer; she was becoming interested. Then she recalled herself and said freezingly, "How are we going to descend?"

"By opening the valve."

"Why don't you open it then?"

"BECAUSE THE VALVE-STRING IS BROKEN!"

CHAPTER IX.

Lady Caroline fainted. When she revived it was dark. They were apparently cleaving their way through a solid block of black marble. She moaned and shuddered.

"I wish we had a light."

"I have no lucifers," said Little. "I observe, however, that you wear a necklace of amber. Amber under certain conditions becomes highly electrical. Permit me."

He took the amber necklace and rubbed it briskly. Then he asked her to present her knuckle to the gem. A bright spark was the result. This was repeated for some hours. The light was not brilliant, but it was enough for the purposes of propriety, and satisfied the delicately minded girl.

Suddenly there was a tearing, hissing noise and a smell of gas. Little looked up and turned pale. The balloon, at what I shall call the pointed end of the Bologna sausage, was evidently bursting from increased pressure. The gas was escaping, and already they were beginning to descend. Little was resigned but firm.

"If the silk gives way, then we are lost. Unfortunately I have no rope nor material for binding it."

The woman's instinct had arrived at the same conclusion sooner than the man's reason. But she was hesitating over a detail.

"Will you go down the rope for a moment?" she said, with a sweet smile,

Little went down. Presently she called to him. She held something in her hand,—a wonderful invention of the seventeenth century, improved and perfected in this: a pyramid of sixteen circular hoops of light yet strong steel, attached to each other by cloth bands.

With a cry of joy Little seized them, climbed to the balloon, and fitted the elastic hoops over its conical end. Then he returned to the car.

"We are saved."

Lady Caroline, blushing, gathered her slim but antique drapery against the other end of the car.

CHAPTER X.

They were slowly descending. Presently Lady Caroline distinguished the outlines of Raby Hall. "I think I will get out here," she said.

Little anchored the balloon and prepared to follow her.

"Not so, my friend," she said, with an arch smile. "We must not be seen together. People might talk. Farewell."

Little sprang again into the balloon and sped away to America. He came down in California, oddly enough in front of Hardin's door, at Dutch Flat. Hardin was just examining a specimen of ore.

"You are a scientist; can you tell me if that is worth anything?" he said, handing it to Little.

Little held it to the light. "It contains ninety per cent of silver."

Hardin embraced him. "Can I do anything for you, and why are you here?"

Little told his story. Hardin asked to see the rope. Then he examined it carefully.

"Ah, this was cut, not broken!"

"With a knife?" asked Little.

"No. Observe both sides are equally indented. It was done with a *scissors!*"

"Just Heaven!" gasped Little. "Thérèse!"

CHAPTER XI.

LITTLE returned to London. Passing through London one day he met a dog-fancier. "Buy a nice poodle, sir?"

Something in the animal attracted his attention. "Fido!" he gasped.

The dog yelped.

Little bought him. On taking off his collar a piece of paper rustled to the floor. He knew the handwriting and kissed it. It ran:—

"TO THE HON. AUGUSTUS RABY:— I cannot marry you. If I marry any one" (sly puss) "it will be the man who has twice saved my life,—Professor Little.

"CAROLINE COVENTRY."

And she did.

LOTHAW;

OR,

THE ADVENTURES OF A YOUNG GENTLEMAN IN SEARCH OF A RELIGION.

By MR. BENJAMINS.

CHAPTER I.

"I REMEMBER him a little boy," said the Duchess. "His mother was a dear friend of mine; you know she was one of my bridesmaids."

"And you have never seen him since, mamma?" asked the oldest married daughter, who did not look a day older than her mother.

"Never; he was an orphan shortly after. I have often reproached myself, but it is so difficult to see boys."

This simple yet first-class conversation existed in the morning-room of Plusham, where the mistress of the palatial mansion sat involved in the sacred privacy of a circle of her married daughters. One dexterously applied golden knitting-needles to the fabrication of a purse of floss silk of the rarest texture, which none who knew the almost fabulous wealth of the Duke would believe was ever destined to hold in its silken meshes a less sum than £1,000,000; another adorned a slipper exclusively with seed pearls; a third emblazoned a page with rare pigments and the finest quality of gold leaf. Beautiful forms leaned over frames glowing with embroidery, and beautiful frames leaned over forms inlaid with mother-of-pearl. Others, more remote, occasionally burst into melody as they tried the passages of a new and exclusive air given to them in MS. by some titled and devoted friend, for the private use of the aristocracy alone, and absolutely prohibited for publication.

The Duchess, herself the superlative of beauty, wealth, and position, was married to the highest noble in the Three Kingdoms. Those who talked about such matters said that their progeny were exactly like their parents,—a peculiarity of the aristocratic and wealthy. They all looked like brothers and sisters, except their parents, who, such was their purity of blood, the perfection of their manners, and the opulence of their condition, might have been taken for their own children's elder son and daughter. The daughters, with one exception, were all married to the highest nobles in the land. That exception was the Lady Coriander, who, there being no vacancy above a marquis and a rental of £1,000,000, waited. Gathered around the refined and sacred circle of their breakfast-table, with their glittering coronets, which, in filial respect to their father's Tory instincts and their mother's Ritualistic tastes, they always wore on their regal brows, the effect was dazzling as it was refined. It was this peculiarity and their strong family resemblance which led their brother-in-law, the good-humored St. Addlegourd, to say that, "'Pon my soul, you know, the whole precious mob looked like a ghastly pack of court cards, you know." St. Addlegourd was a radical. Having a rent-roll of £15,000,000, and belonging to one of the oldest families in Britain, he could afford to be.

"Mamma, I've just dropped a pearl," said the Lady Coriander, bending over the Persian hearth-rug.

"From your lips, sweet friend," said Lothaw, who came of age and entered the room at the same moment.

"No, from my work. It was a very valuable pearl, mamma; papa gave Isaacs and Sons £50,000 for the two."

"Ah, indeed," said the Duchess, languidly rising; "let us go to luncheon."

"But your Grace," interposed Lothaw, who was still quite young, and had dropped on all-fours on the carpet in search of the missing gem, "consider the value—"

"Dear friend," interposed the Duchess, with infinite tact, gently lifting him by the tails of his dress-coat, "I am waiting for your arm."

CHAPTER II.

LOTHAW was immensely rich. The possessor of seventeen castles, fifteen villas, nine shooting-boxes, and seven town houses, he had other estates of which he had not even heard.

Everybody at Plusham played croquet, and none badly. Next to their purity of blood and great wealth, the family were famous for this accomplishment. Yet Lothaw soon tired of the game, and after seriously damaging his aristocratically large foot in an attempt to "tight croquet" the Lady Aniseed's ball, he limped away to join the Duchess.

"I'm going to the hennery," she said.

"Let me go with you, I dearly love fowls—broiled," he added, thoughtfully.

"The Duke gave Lady Montairy some large Cochins the other day," continued the Duchess, changing the subject with delicate tact.

> "Lady Montairy,
> Quite contrairy,
> How do your Cochins grow?"

sang Lothaw gayly.

The Duchess looked shocked. After a prolonged silence, Lothaw abruptly and gravely said:—

"If you please, ma'am, when I come into my property I should like to build some improved dwellings for the poor, and marry Lady Coriander."

"You amaze me, dear friend, and yet both your aspirations are noble and eminently proper," said the Duchess; "Coriander is but a child,—and yet," she added, looking graciously upon her companion, "for the matter of that, so are you."

CHAPTER III.

Mr. Putney Giles's was Lothaw's first grand dinner-party. Yet, by carefully watching the others, he managed to acquit himself creditably, and avoided drinking out of the finger-bowl by first secretly testing its contents with a spoon. The conversation was peculiar and singularly interesting.

"Then you think that monogamy is simply a

question of the thermometer?" said Mrs. Putney Giles to her companion.

"I certainly think that polygamy should be limited by isothermal lines," replied Lothaw.

"I should say it was a matter of latitude," observed a loud talkative man opposite. He was an Oxford Professor with a taste for satire, and had made himself very obnoxious to the company, during dinner, by speaking disparagingly of a former well-known Chancellor of the Exchequer,—a great statesman and brilliant novelist,—whom he feared and hated.

Suddenly there was a sensation in the room; among the females it absolutely amounted to a nervous thrill. His Eminence, the Cardinal, was announced. He entered with great suavity of manner, and, after shaking hands with everybody, asking after their relatives, and chucking the more delicate females under the chin with a high-bred grace peculiar to his profession, he sat down, saying, "And how do we all find ourselves this evening, my dears?" in several different languages, which he spoke fluently.

Lothaw's heart was touched. His deeply religious convictions were impressed. He instantly went up to this gifted being, confessed, and received absolution. "To-morrow," he said to himself, "I will partake of the communion, and endow the Church with my vast estates. For the present I'll let the improved cottages go."

CHAPTER IV.

As Lothaw turned to leave the Cardinal, he was struck by a beautiful face. It was that of a matron,

slim but shapely as an Ionic column. Her face was
Grecian, with Corinthian temples; Hellenic eyes that
looked from jutting eyebrows, like dormer-windows in
an Attic forehead, completed her perfect Athenian outline.
She wore a black frock-coat tightly buttoned over
her bloomer trousers, and a standing collar.

"Your Lordship is struck by that face," said a
social parasite.

"I am; who is she?"

"Her name is Mary Ann. She is married to an
American, and has lately invented a new religion."

"Ah!" said Lothaw eagerly, with difficulty restraining
himself from rushing toward her.

"Yes; shall I introduce you?"

Lothaw thought of Lady Coriander's High Church
proclivities, of the Cardinal, and hesitated: "No, I thank
you, not now."

CHAPTER V.

LOTHAW was maturing. He had attended two
woman's rights conventions, three Fenian meetings,
had dined at White's, and had danced *vis-à-vis* to a
prince of the blood, and eaten off of gold plates at
Crecy House.

His stables were near Oxford, and occupied more
ground than the University. He was driving over there
one day, when he perceived some rustics and menials
endeavoring to stop a pair of runaway horses attached
to a carriage in which a lady and gentleman were
seated. Calmly awaiting the termination of the accident,
with high-bred courtesy Lothaw forbore to interfere
until the carriage was overturned, the occupants

thrown out, and the runaways secured by the servants, when he advanced and offered the lady the exclusive use of his Oxford stables.

Turning upon him a face whose perfect Hellenic details he remembered, she slowly dragged a gentleman from under the wheels into the light and presented him with ladylike dignity as her husband, Major-General Camperdown, an American.

"Ah," said Lothaw, carelessly, "I believe I have some land there. If I mistake not, my agent, Mr. Putney Giles, lately purchased the State of—Illinois—I think you call it."

"Exactly. As a former resident of the city of Chicago, let me introduce myself as your tenant."

Lothaw bowed graciously to the gentleman, who, except that he seemed better dressed than most Englishmen, showed no other signs of inferiority and plebeian extraction.

"We have met before," said Lothaw to the lady as she leaned on his arm, while they visited his stables, the University, and other places of interest in Oxford. "Pray tell me, what is this new religion of yours?"

"It is Woman Suffrage, Free Love, Mutual Affinity, and Communism. Embrace it and me."

Lothaw did not know exactly what to do. She however soothed and sustained his agitated frame and sealed with an embrace his speechless form. The General approached and coughed slightly with gentlemanly tact.

"My husband will be too happy to talk with you further on this subject," she said with quiet dignity, as she regained the General's side. "Come with us to Oneida. Brook Farm is a thing of the past."

CHAPTER VI.

As Lothaw drove toward his country-seat, "The Mural Enclosure," he observed a crowd, apparently of the working class, gathered around a singular-looking man in the picturesque garb of an Ethiopian serenader. "What does he say?" inquired Lothaw of his driver.

The man touched his hat respectfully and said, "My Mary Ann."

"'My Mary Ann!'" Lothaw's heart beat rapidly. Who was this mysterious foreigner? He had heard from Lady Coriander of a certain Popish plot; but could he connect Mr. Camperdown with it?

The spectacle of two hundred men at arms who advanced to meet him at the gates of The Mural Enclosure drove all else from the still youthful and impressible mind of Lothaw. Immediately behind them, on the steps of the baronial halls, were ranged his retainers, led by the chief cook and bottle-washer, and head crumb-remover. On either side were two companies of laundry-maids, preceded by the chief crimper and fluter, supporting a long Ancestral Line, on which depended the family linen, and under which the youthful lord of the manor passed into the halls of his fathers. Twenty-four scullions carried the massive gold and silver plate of the family on their shoulders, and deposited it at the feet of their master. The spoons were then solemnly counted by the steward, and the perfect ceremony ended.

Lothaw sighed. He sought out the gorgeously gilded "Taj," or sacred mausoleum erected to his grandfather in the second story front room, and wept over the man he did not know. He wandered alone in his magnificent park, and then, throwing himself on a grassy bank, pondered on the Great First Cause, and the necessity of religion. "I will send Mary Ann a handsome present," said Lothaw, thoughtfully.

CHAPTER VII.

"EACH of these pearls, my Lord, is worth fifty thousand guineas," said Mr. Amethyst, the fashionable jeweler, as he lightly lifted a large shovelful from a convenient bin behind his counter.

"Indeed," said Lothaw, carelessly, "I should prefer to see some expensive ones."

"Some number sixes, I suppose," said Mr. Amethyst, taking a couple from the apex of a small pyramid that lay piled on the shelf. "These are about the size of the Duchess of Billingsgate's, but they are in finer condition. The fact is, her Grace permits her two children, the Marquis of Smithfield and the Duke of St. Giles,—two sweet pretty boys, my Lord,—to use them as marbles in their games. Pearls require some attention, and I go down there regularly twice a week to clean them. Perhaps your Lordship would like some ropes of pearls?"

"About half a cable's length," said Lothaw, shortly, "and send them to my lodgings."

Mr. Amethyst became thoughtful. "I am afraid I have not the exact number—that is—excuse me one moment. I will run over to the Tower and borrow a few from the crown jewels." And before Lothaw could prevent him, he seized his hat and left Lothaw alone.

His position certainly was embarrassing. He could not move without stepping on costly gems which had rolled from the counter; the rarest diamonds lay scattered on the shelves; untold fortunes in priceless emeralds lay within his grasp. Although such was the aristocratic purity of his blood and the strength of his religious convictions that he probably would not have pocketed a single diamond, still he could not help thinking that he might be accused of taking some. "You can search me, if you like," he said when Mr. Amethyst returned; "but I assure you, upon the honor of a gentleman, that I have taken nothing."

"Enough, my Lord," said Mr. Amethyst, with a low bow; "we never search the aristocracy."

CHAPTER VIII.

As Lothaw left Mr. Amethyst's, he ran against General Camperdown. "How is Mary Ann?" he asked hurriedly.

"I regret to state that she is dying," said the General, with a grave voice, as he removed his cigar from his lips, and lifted his hat to Lothaw.

"Dying!" said Lothaw, incredulously.

"Alas, too true!" replied the General. "The engagements of a long lecturing season, exposure in travelling by railway during the winter, and the imperfect nourishment afforded by the refreshments along the road, have told on her delicate frame. But she wants to see you before she dies. Here is the key of my lodging. I will finish my cigar out here."

Lothaw hardly recognized those wasted Hellenic outlines as he entered the dimly lighted room of the dying woman. She was already a classic ruin,—as wrecked and yet as perfect as the Parthenon. He grasped her hand silently.

"Open-air speaking twice a week, and saleratus bread in the rural districts, have brought me to this," she said feebly; "but it is well. The cause progresses. The tyrant man succumbs."

Lothaw could only press her hand.

"Promise me one thing. Don't—whatever you do —become a Catholic."

"Why?"

"The Church does not recognize divorce. And now embrace me. I would prefer at this supreme moment to introduce myself to the next world through the medium of the best society in this. Good by. When I am dead, be good enough to inform my husband of the fact."

CHAPTER IX.

LOTHAW spent the next six months on an Aryan island, in an Aryan climate, and with an Aryan race.

"This is an Aryan landscape," said his host, "and that is a Mary Ann statue." It was, in fact, a full-length figure in marble of Mrs. General Camperdown!

"If you please, I should like to become a Pagan," said Lothaw, one day, after listening to an impassioned discourse on Greek art from the lips of his host.

But that night, on consulting a well-known spiritual medium, Lothaw received a message from the late Mrs.

General Camperdown, advising him to return to England. Two days later he presented himself at Plusham.

"The young ladies are in the garden," said the Duchess. "Don't you want to go and pick a rose?" she added with a gracious smile, and the nearest approach to a wink that was consistent with her patrician bearing and aquiline nose.

Lothaw went and presently returned with the blushing Coriander upon his arm.

"Bless you, my children," said the Duchess. Then turning to Lothaw, she said: "You have simply fulfilled and accepted your inevitable destiny. It was morally impossible for you to marry out of this family. For the present, the Church of England is safe."

MUCK-A-MUCK.

A MODERN INDIAN NOVEL.

After COOPER.

CHAPTER I.

It was toward the close of a bright October day. The last rays of the setting sun were reflected from one of those sylvan lakes peculiar to the Sierras of California. On the right the curling smoke of an Indian village rose between the columns of the lofty pines, while to the left the log cottage of Judge Tompkins, embowered in buckeyes, completed the enchanting picture.

Although the exterior of the cottage was humble and unpretentious, and in keeping with the wildness of the landscape, its interior gave evidence of the cultivation and refinement of its inmates. An aquarium, containing goldfishes, stood on a marble centre-table at one end of the apartment, while a magnificent grand piano occupied the other. The floor was covered with a yielding tapestry carpet, and the walls were adorned with paintings from the pencils of Van Dyke, Rubens, Tintoretto, Michael Angelo, and the productions of the more modern Turner, Kensett, Church, and Bierstadt. Although Judge Tompkins had chosen the frontiers of civilization as his home, it was impossible for him to entirely forego the habits and tastes of his former life. He was seated in a luxurious arm-chair, writing at a mahogany *écritoire*, while his daughter, a lovely young girl of seventeen summers, plied her crochet-needle on an ottoman beside him. A bright fire of pine logs flickered and flamed on the ample hearth.

Genevra Octavia Tompkins was Judge Tompkins's only child. Her mother had long since died on the Plains. Reared in affluence, no pains had been spared with the daughter's education. She was a graduate of one of the principal seminaries, and spoke French with a perfect Benicia accent. Peerlessly beautiful, she was dressed in a white *moire antique* robe trimmed with *tulle*. That simple rosebud, with which most heroines exclusively decorate their hair, was all she wore in her raven locks.

The Judge was the first to break the silence.

"Genevra, the logs which compose yonder fire seem to have been incautiously chosen. The sibilation produced by the sap, which exudes copiously therefrom, is not conducive to composition."

"True, father, but I thought it would be preferable to the constant crepitation which is apt to attend the combustion of more seasoned ligneous fragments."

The Judge looked admiringly at the intellectual features of the graceful girl, and half forgot the slight annoyances of the green wood in the musical accents of his daughter. He was smoothing her hair tenderly, when the shadow of a tall figure, which suddenly darkened the doorway, caused him to look up.

CHAPTER II.

It needed but a glance at the new-comer to detect at once the form and features of the haughty aborigine, —the untaught and untrammelled son of the forest. Over one shoulder a blanket, negligently but gracefully thrown, disclosed a bare and powerful breast, decorated with a quantity of three-cent postage-stamps which he had despoiled from an Overland Mail stage a few weeks previous. A cast-off beaver of Judge Tompkins's, adorned by a simple feather, covered his erect head, from beneath which his straight locks descended. His right hand hung lightly by his side, while his left was engaged in holding on a pair of pantaloons, which the lawless grace and freedom of his lower limbs evidently could not brook.

"Why," said the Indian, in a low sweet tone,— "why does the Pale Face still follow the track of the Red Man? Why does he pursue him, even as *O-kee-chow*, the wild-cat, chases *Ka-ka*, the skunk? Why are the feet of *Sorrel-top*, the white chief, among the acorns of *Muck-a-Muck*, the mountain forest? Why," he repeated, quietly but firmly abstracting a silver spoon from the table—"why do you seek to drive him from the wigwams of his fathers? His brothers are already gone to the happy hunting-grounds. Will the Pale Face seek him there?" And, averting his face from the Judge, he hastily slipped a silver cake-basket beneath his blanket, to conceal his emotion.

"*Muck-a-Muck* has spoken," said Genevra, softly. "Let him now listen. Are the acorns of the mountain sweeter than the esculent and nutritious bean of the

Pale Face miner? Does my brother prize the edible qualities of the snail above that of the crisp and oleaginous bacon? Delicious are the grasshoppers that sport on the hillside,—are they better than the dried apples of the Pale Faces? Pleasant is the gurgle of the torrent, *Kish-Kish*, but is it better than the cluck-cluck of old Bourbon from the old stone bottle?"

"Ugh!" said the Indian,—"ugh! good. The White Rabbit is wise. Her words fall as the snow on Tootoonolo, and the rocky heart of Muck-a-Muck is hidden. What says my brother the Gray Gopher of Dutch Flat?"

"She has spoken, Muck-a-Muck," said the Judge, gazing fondly on his daughter. "It is well. Our treaty is concluded. No, thank you,—you need *not* dance the Dance of Snow Shoes, or the Moccasin Dance, the Dance of Green Corn, or the Treaty Dance. I would be alone. A strange sadness overpowers me."

"I go," said the Indian. "Tell your great chief in Washington, the Sachem Andy, that the Red Man is retiring before the footsteps of the adventurous Pioneer. Inform him, if you please, that westward the star of empire takes its way, that the chiefs of the Pi-Ute nation are for Reconstruction to a man, and that Klamath will poll a heavy Republican vote in the fall."

And folding his blanket more tightly around him, Muck-a-Muck withdrew.

CHAPTER III.

GENEVRA TOMPKINS stood at the door of the log-cabin, looking after the retreating Overland Mail stage which conveyed her father to Virginia City. "He may never return again," sighed the young girl as she glanced at the frightfully rolling vehicle and wildly careering horses,—"at least, with unbroken bones. Should he meet with an accident! I mind me now a fearful legend, familiar to my childhood. Can it be that the drivers on this line are privately instructed to despatch all passengers maimed by accident, to prevent tedious litigation? No, no. But why this weight upon my heart?"

She seated herself at the piano and lightly passed her hand over the keys. Then, in a clear mezzo-soprano voice, she sang the first verse of one of the most popular Irish ballads:—

> "O *Arrah, ma dheelish*, the distant *dudheen*
> Lies soft in the moonlight, *ma bouchal vourneen:*
> The springing *gossoons* on the heather are still,
> And the *cauberens* and *colleens* are heard on the hills."

But as the ravishing notes of her sweet voice died upon the air, her hands sank listlessly to her side. Music could not chase away the mysterious shadow from her heart. Again she rose. Putting on a white crape bonnet, and carefully drawing a pair of lemon-colored gloves over her taper fingers, she seized her parasol and plunged into the depths of the pine forest.

CHAPTER IV.

Genevra had not proceeded many miles before a weariness seized upon her fragile limbs, and she would fain seat herself upon the trunk of a prostrate pine, which she previously dusted with her handkerchief. The sun was just sinking below the horizon, and the scene was one of gorgeous and sylvan beauty. "How beautiful is Nature!" murmured the innocent girl, as, reclining gracefully against the root of the tree, she gathered up her skirts and tied a handkerchief around her throat. But a low growl interrupted her meditation. Starting to her feet, her eyes met a sight which froze her blood with terror.

The only outlet to the forest was the narrow path, barely wide enough for a single person, hemmed in by trees and rocks, which she had just traversed. Down this path, in Indian file, came a monstrous grizzly, closely followed by a California lion, a wildcat, and a buffalo, the rear being brought up by a wild Spanish bull. The mouths of the three first animals were distended with frightful significance; the horns of the last were lowered as ominously. As Genevra was preparing to faint, she heard a low voice behind her.

"Eternally dog-gone my skin ef this ain't the puttiest chance yet."

At the same moment, a long, shining barrel dropped lightly from behind her, and rested over her shoulder.

Genevra shuddered.

"Dern ye—don't move!"

Genevra became motionless.

The crack of a rifle rang through the woods. Three frightful yells were heard, and two sullen roars. Five animals bounded into the air and five lifeless bodies lay upon the plain. The well-aimed bullet had done its work. Entering the open throat of the grizzly, it had traversed his body only to enter the throat of the California lion, and in like manner the catamount, until it passed through into the respective foreheads of the bull and the buffalo, and finally fell flattened from the rocky hillside.

Genevra turned quickly. "My preserver!" she shrieked, and fell into the arms of Natty Bumpo, the celebrated Pike Ranger of Donner Lake.

CHAPTER V.

The moon rose cheerfully above Donner Lake. On its placid bosom a dug-out canoe glided rapidly, containing Natty Bumpo and Genevra Tompkins.

Both were silent. The same thought possessed each, and perhaps there was sweet companionship even in the unbroken quiet. Genevra bit the handle of her parasol and blushed. Natty Bumpo took a fresh chew of tobacco. At length Genevra said, as if in half-spoken revery:—

"The soft shining of the moon and the peaceful ripple of the waves seem to say to us various things of an instructive and moral tendency."

"You may bet yer pile on that, Miss," said her companion, gravely. "It's all the preachin' and psalm-singin' I've heern since I was a boy."

"Noble being!" said Miss Tompkins to herself,

glancing at the stately Pike as he bent over his paddle to conceal his emotion. "Reared in this wild seclusion, yet he has become penetrated with visible consciousness of a Great First Cause." Then, collecting herself, she said aloud: "Methinks 'twere pleasant to glide ever thus down the stream of life, hand in hand with the one being whom the soul claims as its affinity. But what am I saying?"—and the delicate-minded girl hid her face in her hands.

A long silence ensued, which was at length broken by her companion.

"Ef you mean you're on the marry," he said, thoughtfully, "I ain't in no wise partikler!"

"My husband," faltered the blushing girl; and she fell into his arms.

In ten minutes more the loving couple had landed at Judge Tompkins's.

CHAPTER VI.

A YEAR has passed away. Natty Bumpo was returning from Gold Hill, where he had been to purchase provisions. On his way to Donner Lake, rumors of an Indian uprising met his ears. "Dern their pesky skins, ef they dare to touch my Jenny," he muttered between his clenched teeth.

It was dark when he reached the borders of the lake. Around a glittering fire he dimly discerned dusky figures dancing. They were in war paint. Conspicuous among them was the renowned Muck-a-Muck. But why did the fingers of Natty Bumpo tighten convulsively around his rifle?

The chief held in his hand long tufts of raven

hair. The heart of the pioneer sickened as he recognized the clustering curls of Genevra. In a moment his rifle was at his shoulder, and with a sharp "ping," Muck-a-Muck leaped into the air a corpse. To knock out the brains of the remaining savages, tear the tresses from the stiffening hand of Muck-a-Muck, and dash rapidly forward to the cottage of Judge Tompkins, was the work of a moment.

He burst open the door. Why did he stand transfixed with open mouth and distended eyeballs? Was the sight too horrible to be borne? On the contrary, before him, in her peerless beauty, stood Genevra Tompkins, leaning on her father's arm.

"Ye'r not scalped, then!" gasped her lover.

"No. I have no hesitation in saying that I am not; but why this abruptness?" responded Genevra.

Bumpo could not speak, but frantically produced the silken tresses. Genevra turned her face aside.

"Why, that's her waterfall!" said the Judge.

Bumpo sank fainting to the floor.

The famous Pike chieftain never recovered from the deceit, and refused to marry Genevra, who died, twenty years afterwards, of a broken heart. Judge Tompkins lost his fortune in Wild Cat. The stage passes twice a week the deserted cottage at Donner Lake. Thus was the death of Muck-a-Muck avenged.

TERENCE DENVILLE.

By CH—L-S L.—V- R.

CHAPTER I.

My Home.

THE little village of Pilwiddle is one of the smallest and obscurest hamlets on the western coast of Ireland. On a lofty crag, overlooking the hoarse Atlantic, stands "Denville's Shot Tower"—a corruption by the peasantry of *D'Enville's Château*, so called from my great-grandfather, Phelim St. Remy d'Enville, who assumed the name and title of a French heiress with whom he ran away. To this fact my familiar knowledge and excellent pronunciation of the French language may be attributed, as well as many of the events which covered my after life.

The Denvilles were always passionately fond of field sports. At the age of four, I was already the boldest rider and the best shot in the country. When only eight, I won the St. Remy Cup at the Pilwiddle races,—riding my favorite bloodmare *Hellfire*. As I approached the stand amidst the plaudits of the assembled multitude, and cries of, "Thrue for ye, Masther Terence," and "O, but it's a Dinville!" there was a slight stir among the gentry, who surrounded the Lord Lieutenant, and other titled personages whom the race had attracted thither. "How young he is,—a mere child; and yet how noble-looking," said a sweet low voice, which thrilled my soul.

I looked up and met the full liquid orbs of the Hon. Blanche Fitzroy Sackville, youngest daughter of the Lord Lieutenant. She blushed deeply. I turned pale and almost fainted. But the cold, sneering tones of a masculine voice sent the blood back again into my youthful cheek.

"Very likely the ragged scion of one of these banditti Irish gentry, who has taken naturally to 'the road.' He should be at school—though I warrant me his knowledge of Terence will not extend beyond his own name," said Lord Henry Somerset, aid-de-camp to the Lord Lieutenant.

A moment and I was perfectly calm, though cold as ice. Dismounting, and stepping to the side of the speaker, I said in a low, firm voice:—

"Had your Lordship read Terence more carefully, you would have learned that banditti are sometimes proficient in other arts beside horsemanship," and I touched his holster significantly with my hand. I had not read Terence myself, but with the skilful audacity of my race I calculated that a vague allusion, coupled with a threat, would embarrass him. It did.

"Ah—what mean you?" he said, white with rage.

"Enough, we are observed," I replied; "Father Tom will wait on you this evening; and to-morrow morning, my lord, in the glen below Pilwiddle we will meet again."

"Father Tom—glen!" ejaculated the Englishman,

with genuine surprise. "What? do priests carry challenges and act as seconds in your infernal country?"

"Yes!" I answered, scornfully, "why should they not? Their services are more often necessary than those of a surgeon," I added significantly, turning away.

The party slowly rode off, with the exception of the Hon. Blanche Sackville, who lingered for a moment behind. In an instant I was at her side. Bending her blushing face over the neck of her white filly, she said hurriedly:—

"Words have passed between Lord Somerset and yourself. You are about to fight. Don't deny it—but hear me. You will meet him—I know your skill of weapons. He will be at your mercy. I entreat you to spare his life!"

I hesitated. "Never!" I cried passionately; "he has insulted a Denville!"

"Terence," she whispered, "Terence—*for my sake?*"

The blood rushed to my cheeks, and her eyes sought the ground in bashful confusion.

"You love him then?" I cried, bitterly.

"No, no," she said, agitatedly, "no, you do me wrong. I—I—cannot explain myself. My father!— the Lady Dowager Sackville—the estate of Sackville— the borough—my uncle, Fitzroy Somerset. Ah! what am I saying? Forgive me. O Terence," she said, as her beautiful head sank on my shoulder, "you know not what I suffer!"

I seized her hand and covered it with passionate

kisses. But the high-bred English girl, recovering something of her former *hauteur*, said hastily, "Leave me, leave me, but promise!"

"I promise," I replied, enthusiastically; "I *will* spare his life!"

"Thanks, Terence,—thanks!" and disengaging her hand from my lips she rode rapidly away.

The next morning, the Hon. Captain Henry Somerset and myself exchanged nineteen shots in the glen, and at each fire I shot away a button from his uniform. As my last bullet shot off the last button from his sleeve, I remarked quietly, "You seem now, my lord, to be almost as ragged as the gentry you sneered at," and rode haughtily away.

CHAPTER II.

The Fighting fifty-sixth.

WHEN I was nineteen years old my father sold the *Château d'Enville* and purchased my commission in the "Fifty-sixth" with the proceeds. "I say, Denville," said young McSpadden, a boy-faced ensign, who had just joined, "you'll represent the estate in the Army, if you won't in the House." Poor fellow, he paid for his meaningless joke with his life, for I shot him through the heart the next morning. "You're a good fellow, Denville," said the poor boy faintly, as I knelt beside him: "good by!" For the first time since my grandfather's death I wept. I could not help thinking that I would have been a better man if Blanche—but why proceed? Was she not now in Florence—the belle of the English Embassy?

But Napoleon had returned from Elba. Europe was in a blaze of excitement. The Allies were preparing to resist the Man of Destiny. We were ordered from Gibraltar home, and were soon again *en route* for Brussels. I did not regret that I was to be placed in active service. I was ambitious, and longed for an opportunity to distinguish myself. My garrison life in Gibraltar had been monotonous and dull. I had killed five men in duel, and had an affair with the colonel of my regiment, who handsomely apologized before the matter assumed a serious aspect. I had been twice in love. Yet these were but boyish freaks and follies. I wished to be a man.

The time soon came,—the morning of Waterloo. But why describe that momentous battle, on which the fate of the entire world was hanging? Twice were the Fifty-sixth surrounded by French cuirassiers, and twice did we mow them down by our fire. I had seven horses shot under me, and was mounting the eighth, when an orderly rode up hastily, touched his cap, and, handing me a despatch, galloped rapidly away.

I opened it hurriedly and read:—

"LET PICTON ADVANCE IMMEDIATELY ON THE RIGHT."

I saw it all at a glance. I had been mistaken for a general officer. But what was to be done? Picton's division was two miles away, only accessible through a heavy cross fire of artillery and musketry. But my mind was made up.

In an instant I was engaged with an entire squadron of cavalry, who endeavored to surround me. Cutting my way through them, I advanced boldly upon a battery and sabred the gunners before they could bring their pieces to bear. Looking around, I saw that I had in fact penetrated the French centre. Before I was well aware of the locality, I was hailed by a sharp voice in French,—

"Come here, sir!"

I obeyed, and advanced to the side of a little man in a cocked hat.

"Has Grouchy come?"

"Not yet, sire," I replied,—for it was the Emperor.

"Ha!" he said suddenly, bending his piercing eyes on my uniform; "a prisoner?"

"No, sire," I said, proudly.

"A spy?"

I placed my hand upon my sword, but a gesture from the Emperor bade me forbear.

"You are a brave man," he said.

I took my snuff-box from my pocket, and, taking a pinch, replied by handing it, with a bow, to the Emperor.

His quick eye caught the cipher on the lid.

"What! a D'Enville? Ha! this accounts for the purity of your accent. Any relation to Roderick d'Enville?"

"My father, sire."

"He was my schoolfellow at the *École Polytechnique*. Embrace me!" And the Emperor fell upon my neck in the presence of his entire staff. Then, recovering himself, he gently placed in my hand his own magnificent snuff-box, in exchange for mine, and hanging upon my breast the cross of the Legion of Honor which he took from his own, he bade one of his Marshals conduct me back to my regiment.

I was so intoxicated with the honor of which I had been the recipient, that on reaching our lines I uttered a shout of joy and put spurs to my horse. The intelligent animal seemed to sympathize with my feelings, and fairly flew over the ground. On a rising eminence a few yards before me stood a gray-haired officer, surrounded by his staff. I don't know what possessed me, but putting spurs to my horse, I rode at him boldly, and with one bound cleared him, horse and all. A shout of indignation arose from the assembled staff. I wheeled suddenly, with the intention of apologizing, but my mare misunderstood me, and, again dashing forward, once more vaulted over the head of the officer, this time unfortunately uncovering him by a vicious kick of her hoof. "Seize him!" roared the entire army. I was seized. As the soldiers led me away, I asked the name of the gray-haired officer. "That—why, that's the DUKE OF WELLINGTON!"

I fainted.

* * * * * *

For six months I had brain-fever. During my illness ten grapeshot were extracted from my body which I had unconsciously received during the battle. When I opened my eyes I met the sweet glance of a Sister of Charity.

"Blanche!" I stammered feebly.

"The same," she replied.

"You here?"

"Yes, dear; but hush! It's a long story. You see, dear Terence, your grandfather married my great-aunt's sister, and your father again married my grandmother's niece, who, dying without a will, was, according to the French law—"

"But I do not comprehend," I said.

"Of course not," said Blanche, with her old sweet smile; "you've had brain-fever; so go to sleep."

I understood, however, that Blanche loved me; and I am now, dear reader, Sir Terence Sackville, K. C. B., and Lady Blanche is Lady Sackville.

SELINA SEDILIA.

By MISS M. E. B—DD—N and MRS. H—N—Y W—D.

CHAPTER I.

THE sun was setting over Sloperton Grange, and reddened the window of the lonely chamber in the western tower, supposed to be haunted by Sir Edward Sedilia, the founder of the Grange. In the dreamy distance arose the gilded mausoleum of Lady Felicia Sedilia, who haunted that portion of Sedilia Manor, known as "Stiff-uns Acre." A little to the left of the Grange might have been seen a mouldering ruin, known as "Guy's Keep," haunted by the spirit of Sir Guy Sedilia, who was found, one morning, crushed by one of the fallen battlements. Yet, as the setting sun gilded these objects, a beautiful and almost holy calm seemed diffused about the Grange.

The Lady Selina sat by an oriel window, overlooking the park. The sun sank gently in the bosom of the German Ocean, and yet the lady did not lift her beautiful head from the finely curved arm and diminutive hand which supported it. When darkness finally shrouded the landscape she started, for the sound of horse-hoofs clattered over the stones of the avenue. She had scarcely risen before an aristocratic young man fell on his knees before her.

"My Selina!"

"Edgardo! You here?"

"Yes, dearest."

"And—you—you—have—seen nothing?" said the lady in an agitated voice and nervous manner, turning her face aside to conceal her emotion.

"Nothing—that is nothing of any account," said Edgardo. "I passed the ghost of your aunt in the park, noticed the spectre of your uncle in the ruined keep, and observed the familiar features of the spirit of your great-grandfather at his usual post. But nothing beyond these trifles, my Selina. Nothing more, love, absolutely nothing."

The young man turned his dark liquid orbs fondly upon the ingenuous face of his betrothed.

"My own Edgardo!—and you still love me? You still would marry me in spite of this dark mystery which surrounds me? In spite of the fatal history of my race? In spite of the ominous predictions of my aged nurse?"

"I would, Selina;" and the young man passed his arm around her yielding waist. The two lovers gazed at each other's faces in unspeakable bliss. Suddenly Selina started.

"Leave me, Edgardo! leave me! A mysterious something—a fatal misgiving—a dark ambiguity—an equivocal mistrust oppresses me. I would be alone!"

The young man arose, and cast a loving glance on the lady. "Then we will be married on the seventeenth."

"The seventeenth," repeated Selina, with a mysterious shudder.

They embraced and parted. As the clatter of hoofs

in the court-yard died away, the Lady Selina sank into the chair she had just quitted.

"The seventeenth," she repeated slowly, with the same fateful shudder. "Ah!—what if he should know that I have another husband living? Dare I reveal to him that I have two legitimate and three natural children? Dare I repeat to him the history of my youth? Dare I confess that at the age of seven I poisoned my sister, by putting verdigris in her cream-tarts,—that I threw my cousin from a swing at the age of twelve? That the lady's-maid who incurred the displeasure of my girlhood now lies at the bottom of the horse-pond? No! no! he is too pure,—too good,—too innocent, to hear such improper conversation!" and her whole body writhed as she rocked to and fro in a paroxysm of grief.

But she was soon calm. Rising to her feet, she opened a secret panel in the wall, and revealed a slow-match ready for lighting.

"This match," said the Lady Selina, "is connected with a mine beneath the western tower, where my three children are confined; another branch of it lies under the parish church, where the record of my first marriage is kept. I have only to light this match and the whole of my past life is swept away!" She approached the match with a lighted candle.

But a hand was laid upon her arm, and with a shriek the Lady Selina fell on her knees before the spectre of Sir Guy.

CHAPTER II.

"Forbear, Selina," said the phantom in a hollow voice.

"Why should I forbear?" responded Selina haughtily, as she recovered her courage. "You know the secret of our race?"

"I do. Understand me,—I do not object to the eccentricities of your youth. I know the fearful destiny which, pursuing you, led you to poison your sister and drown your lady's-maid. I know the awful doom which I have brought upon this house! But if you make way with these children—"

"Well," said the Lady Selina, hastily.

"They will haunt you!"

"Well, I fear them not," said Selina, drawing her superb figure to its full height.

"Yes, but, my dear child, what place are they to haunt? The ruin is sacred to your uncle's spirit. Your aunt monopolizes the park, and, I must be allowed to state, not unfrequently trespasses upon the grounds of others. The horse-pond is frequented by the spirit of your maid, and your murdered sister walks these corridors. To be plain, there is no room at Sloperton Grange for another ghost. I cannot have them in my room,—for you know I don't like children. Think of this, rash girl, and forbear! Would you, Selina," said the phantom, mournfully,—"would you force your great-grandfather's spirit to take lodgings elsewhere?"

Lady Selina's hand trembled; the lighted candle fell from her nerveless fingers.

"No," she cried passionately; "never!" and fell fainting to the floor.

CHAPTER III.

EDGARDO galloped rapidly towards Sloperton. When the outline of the Grange had faded away in the darkness, he reined his magnificent steed beside the ruins of Guy's Keep.

"It wants but a few minutes of the hour," he said, consulting his watch by the light of the moon. "He dare not break his word. He will come." He paused, and peered anxiously into the darkness. "But come what may, she is mine," he continued, as his thoughts reverted fondly to the fair lady he had quitted. "Yet if she knew all. If she knew that I were a disgraced and ruined man,—a felon and an outcast. If she knew that at the age of fourteen I murdered my Latin tutor and forged my uncle's will. If she knew that I had three wives already, and that the fourth victim of misplaced confidence and my unfortunate peculiarity is expected to be at Sloperton by to-night's train with her baby. But no; she must not know it. Constance must not arrive. Burke the Slogger must attend to that.

"Ha! here he is! Well?"

These words were addressed to a ruffian in a slouched hat, who suddenly appeared from Guy's Keep.

"I be's here, measter," said the villain, with a disgracefully low accent and complete disregard of grammatical rules.

"It is well. Listen: I'm in possession of facts that will send you to the gallows. I know of the murder of Bill Smithers, the robbery of the toll-gate-keeper, and the making away of the youngest daughter of Sir Reginald de Walton. A word from me, and the officers of justice are on your track."

Burke the Slogger trembled.

"Hark ye! serve my purpose, and I may yet save you. The 5.30 train from Clapham will be due at Sloperton at 9.25. *It must not arrive!*"

The villain's eyes sparkled as he nodded at Edgardo.

"Enough,—you understand; leave me!"

CHAPTER IV.

ABOUT half a mile from Sloperton Station the South Clapham and Medway line crossed a bridge over Sloperton-on-Trent. As the shades of evening were closing, a man in a slouched hat might have been seen carrying a saw and axe under his arm, hanging about the bridge. From time to time he disappeared in the shadow of its abutments, but the sound of a saw and axe still betrayed his vicinity. At exactly nine o'clock he reappeared, and, crossing to the Sloperton side, rested his shoulder against the abutment and gave a shove. The bridge swayed a moment, and then fell with a splash into the water, leaving a space of one hundred feet between the two banks. This done, Burke the Slogger,—for it was he,—with a fiendish chuckle seated himself on the divided railway track and awaited the coming of the train.

A shriek from the woods announced its approach. For an instant Burke the Slogger saw the glaring of a red lamp. The ground trembled. The train was going with fearful rapidity. Another second and it had reached the bank. Burke the Slogger uttered a fiendish laugh. But the next moment the train leaped across the chasm, striking the rails exactly even, and, dashing out the life of Burke the Slogger, sped away to Sloperton.

The first object that greeted Edgardo, as he rode up to the station on the arrival of the train, was the body of Burke the Slogger hanging on the cow-catcher; the second was the face of his deserted wife looking from the windows of a second-class carriage.

CHAPTER V.

A NAMELESS terror seemed to have taken possession of Clarissa, Lady Selina's maid, as she rushed into the presence of her mistress.

"O my lady, such news!"

"Explain yourself," said her mistress, rising.

"An accident has happened on the railway, and a man has been killed."

"What—not Edgardo!" almost screamed Selina.

"No, Burke the Slogger!" your ladyship.

"My first husband!" said Lady Selina, sinking on her knees. "Just Heaven, I thank thee!"

CHAPTER VI.

The morning of the seventeenth dawned brightly over Sloperton. "A fine day for the wedding," said the sexton to Swipes, the butler of Sloperton Grange. The aged retainer shook his head sadly. "Alas! there's no trusting in signs!" he continued. "Seventy-five years ago, on a day like this, my young mistress—" But he was cut short by the appearance of a stranger.

"I would see Sir Edgardo," said the new-comer, impatiently.

The bridegroom, who, with the rest of the wedding-train, was about stepping into the carriage to proceed to the parish church, drew the stranger aside.

"It's done!" said the stranger, in a hoarse whisper.

"Ah! and you buried her?"

"With the others!"

"Enough. No more at present. Meet me after the ceremony, and you shall have your reward."

The stranger shuffled away, and Edgardo returned to his bride. "A trifling matter of business I had forgotten, my dear Selina; let us proceed." And the young man pressed the timid hand of his blushing bride as he handed her into the carriage. The cavalcade rode out of the court-yard. At the same moment, the deep bell on Guy's Keep tolled ominously.

CHAPTER VII.

Scarcely had the wedding-train left the Grange, than Alice Sedilia, youngest daughter of Lady Selina, made her escape from the western tower, owing to a lack of watchfulness on the part of Clarissa. The innocent child, freed from restraint, rambled through the lonely corridors, and finally, opening a door, found herself in her mother's boudoir. For some time she amused herself by examining the various ornaments and elegant trifles with which it was filled. Then, in pursuance of a childish freak, she dressed herself in her mother's laces and ribbons. In this occupation she chanced to touch a peg which proved to be a spring that opened a secret panel in the wall. Alice uttered a cry of delight as she noticed what, to her childish fancy, appeared to be the slow-match of a fire-work. Taking a lucifer match in her hand she approached the fuse. She hesitated a moment. What would her mother and her nurse say?

Suddenly the ringing of the chimes of Sloperton parish church met her ear. Alice knew that the sound signified that the marriage party had entered the church, and that she was secure from interruption. With a childish smile upon her lips, Alice Sedilia touched off the slow-match.

CHAPTER VIII.

At exactly two o'clock on the seventeenth, Rupert Sedilia, who had just returned from India, was thoughtfully descending the hill toward Sloperton manor. "If I can prove that my aunt Lady Selina was married before my father died, I can establish my claim to Sloperton Grange," he uttered, half aloud. He paused, for a sudden trembling of the earth beneath his feet, and a terrific explosion, as of a park of artillery, arrested his progress. At the same moment he beheld a dense cloud of smoke envelop the churchyard of Sloperton, and the western tower of the Grange seemed to be lifted bodily from its foundation. The air seemed filled with falling fragments, and two dark objects struck the earth close at his feet. Rupert picked them up. One seemed to be a heavy volume bound in brass.

A cry burst from his lips.

"The Parish Records." He opened the volume hastily. It contained the marriage of Lady Selina to "Burke the Slogger."

The second object proved to be a piece of parchment. He tore it open with trembling fingers. It was the missing will of Sir James Sedilia!

CHAPTER IX.

When the bells again rang on the new parish church of Sloperton it was for the marriage of Sir Rupert Sedilia and his cousin, the only remaining members of the family.

Five more ghosts were added to the supernatural population of Sloperton Grange. Perhaps this was the reason why Sir Rupert sold the property shortly afterward, and that for many years a dark shadow seemed to hang over the ruins of Sloperton Grange.

THE NINETY-NINE GUARDSMEN.

By AL—X—D—R D—M—S.

CHAPTER I.

Showing the Quality of the Customers of the Innkeeper of Provins.

TWENTY years after, the gigantic innkeeper of Provins stood looking at a cloud of dust on the highway.

This cloud of dust betokened the approach of a traveller. Travellers had been rare that season on the highway between Paris and Provins.

The heart of the innkeeper rejoiced. Turning to Dame Perigord, his wife, he said, stroking his white apron:—

"St. Denis! make haste and spread the cloth. Add a bottle of Charlevoix to the table. This traveller, who rides so fast, by his pace must be a Monseigneur."

Truly the traveller, clad in the uniform of a musketeer, as he drew up to the door of the hostelry, did not seem to have spared his horse. Throwing his reins to the landlord, he leaped lightly to the ground. He was a young man of four-and-twenty, and spoke with a slight Gascon accent.

"I am hungry, *Morbleu!* I wish to dine!"

The gigantic innkeeper bowed and led the way to

a neat apartment, where a table stood covered with tempting viands. The musketeer at once set to work. Fowls, fish, and *pâtés* disappeared before him. Perigord sighed as he witnessed the devastations. Only once the stranger paused.

"Wine!" Perigord brought wine. The stranger drank a dozen bottles. Finally he rose to depart. Turning to the expectant landlord, he said:—

"Charge it."

"To whom, your highness?" said Perigord, anxiously.

"To his Eminence!"

"Mazarin!" ejaculated the innkeeper.

"The same. Bring me my horse," and the musketeer, remounting his favorite animal, rode away.

The innkeeper slowly turned back into the inn. Scarcely had he reached the courtyard before the clatter of hoofs again called him to the doorway. A young musketeer of a light and graceful figure rode up.

"*Parbleu*, my dear Perigord, I am famishing. What have you got for dinner?"

"Venison, capons, larks, and pigeons, your excellency," replied the obsequious landlord, bowing to the ground.

"Enough!" The young musketeer dismounted and entered the inn. Seating himself at the table replenished by the careful Perigord, he speedily swept it as clean as the first comer.

"Some wine, my brave Perigord," said the graceful young musketeer, as soon as he could find utterance.

Perigord brought three dozen of Charlevoix. The young man emptied them almost at a draught.

"By-by, Perigord," he said lightly, waving his hand, as, preceding the astonished landlord, he slowly withdrew.

"But, your highness,—the bill," said the astounded Perigord.

"Ah, the bill. Charge it!"

"To whom?"

"The Queen!"

"What, Madame?"

"The same. Adieu, my good Perigord." And the graceful stranger rode away. An interval of quiet succeeded, in which the innkeeper gazed wofully at his wife. Suddenly he was startled by a clatter of hoofs, and an aristocratic figure stood in the doorway.

"Ah," said the courtier good-naturedly. "What, do my eyes deceive me? No, it is the festive and luxurious Perigord. Perigord, listen. I famish. I languish. I would dine."

The innkeeper again covered the table with viands. Again it was swept clean as the fields of Egypt before the miraculous swarm of locusts. The stranger looked up.

"Bring me another fowl, my Perigord."

"Impossible, your excellency; the larder is stripped clean."

"Another flitch of bacon, then."

"Impossible, your highness; there is no more."

"Well, then, wine!"

The landlord brought one hundred and forty-four bottles. The courtier drank them all.

"One may drink if one cannot eat," said the aristocratic stranger, good-humoredly.

The innkeeper shuddered.

The guest rose to depart. The innkeeper came slowly forward with his bill, to which he had covertly added the losses which he had suffered from the previous strangers.

"Ah, the bill. Charge it."

"Charge it! to whom?"

"To the King," said the guest.

"What! his Majesty?"

"Certainly. Farewell, Perigord."

The innkeeper groaned. Then he went out and took down his sign. Then remarked to his wife:—

"I am a plain man, and don't understand politics. It seems, however, that the country is in a troubled state. Between his Eminence the Cardinal, his Majesty the King, and her Majesty the Queen, I am a ruined man."

"Stay," said Dame Perigord, "I have an idea."

"And that is—"

"Become yourself a musketeer."

CHAPTER II.

The Combat.

ON leaving Provins the first musketeer proceeded to Nangis, where he was reinforced by thirty-three followers. The second musketeer, arriving at Nangis at the same moment, placed himself at the head of thirty-three more. The third guest of the landlord of Provins arrived at Nangis in time to assemble together thirty-three other musketeers.

The first stranger led the troops of his Eminence.
The second led the troops of the Queen.
The third led the troops of the King.

The fight commenced. It raged terribly for seven hours. The first musketeer killed thirty of the Queen's troops. The second musketeer killed thirty of the King's troops. The third musketeer killed thirty of his Eminence's troops.

By this time it will be perceived the number of musketeers had been narrowed down to four on each side.

Naturally the three principal warriors approached each other.

They simultaneously uttered a cry.
"Aramis!"
"Athos!"
"D'Artagnan!"

They fell into each other's arms.

"And it seems that we are fighting against each other, my children," said the Count de la Fere, mournfully.

"How singular!" exclaimed Aramis and D'Artagnan.

"Let us stop this fratricidal warfare," said Athos.

"We will!" they exclaimed together.

"But how to disband our followers?" queried D'Artagnan.

Aramis winked. They understood each other. "Let us cut 'em down!"

They cut 'em down. Aramis killed three. D'Artagnan three. Athos three.

The friends again embraced. "How like old times," said Aramis. "How touching!" exclaimed the serious and philosophic Count de la Fere.

The galloping of hoofs caused them to withdraw from each other's embraces. A gigantic figure rapidly approached.

"The innkeeper of Provins!" they cried, drawing their swords.

"Perigord, down with him!" shouted D'Artagnan.

"Stay," said Athos.

The gigantic figure was beside them. He uttered a cry.

"Athos, Aramis, D'Artagnan!"

"Porthos!" exclaimed the astonished trio.

"The same." They all fell in each other's arms.

The Count de la Fere slowly raised his hands to

Heaven. "Bless you! Bless us, my children! However different our opinion may be in regard to politics, we have but one opinion in regard to our own merits. Where can you find a better man than Aramis?"

"Than Porthos?" said Aramis.

"Than D'Artagnan?" said Porthos.

"Than Athos?" said D'Artagnan.

CHAPTER III.

Showing how the King of France went up a Ladder.

THE King descended into the garden. Proceeding cautiously along the terraced walk, he came to the wall immediately below the windows of Madame. To the left were two windows, concealed by vines. They opened into the apartments of La Valliere.

The King sighed.

"It is about nineteen feet to that window," said the King. "If I had a ladder about nineteen feet long, it would reach to that window. This is logic."

Suddenly the King stumbled over something. "St. Denis!" he exclaimed, looking down. It was a ladder, just nineteen feet long.

The King placed it against the wall. In so doing, he fixed the lower end upon the abdomen of a man who lay concealed by the wall. The man did not utter a cry or wince. The King suspected nothing. He ascended the ladder.

The ladder was too short. Louis the Grand was not a tall man. He was still two feet below the window.

"Dear me!" said the King.

Suddenly the ladder was lifted two feet from below. This enabled the King to leap in the window. At the farther end of the apartment stood a young girl, with red hair and a lame leg. She was trembling with emotion.

"Louise!"

"The King!"

"Ah, my God, mademoiselle."

"Ah, my God, sire."

But a low knock at the door interrupted the lovers. The King uttered a cry of rage; Louise one of despair.

The door opened and D'Artagnan entered.

"Good evening, sire," said the musketeer.

The King touched a bell. Porthos appeared in the doorway.

"Good evening, sire."

"Arrest M. D'Artagnan."

Porthos looked at D'Artagnan, and did not move.

The King almost turned purple with rage. He again touched the bell. Athos entered.

"Count, arrest Porthos and D'Artagnan."

The Count de la Fere glanced at Porthos and D'Artagnan, and smiled sweetly.

"*Sacre!* Where is Aramis?" said the King, violently.

"Here, sire," and Aramis entered.

"Arrest Athos, Porthos, and D'Artagnan."

Aramis bowed and folded his arms.

"Arrest yourself!"

Aramis did not move.

The King shuddered and turned pale. "Am I not King of France?"

"Assuredly, sire, but we are also severally, Porthos, Aramis, D'Artagnan, and Athos."

"Ah!" said the King.

"Yes, sire."

"What does this mean?"

"It means, your Majesty," said Aramis, stepping forward, "that your conduct as a married man is highly improper. I am an Abbé, and I object to these improprieties. My friends here, D'Artagnan, Athos, and Porthos, pure-minded young men, are also terribly shocked. Observe, sire, how they blush!"

Athos, Porthos, and D'Artagnan blushed.

"Ah," said the King, thoughtfully. "You teach me a lesson. You are devoted and noble young gentlemen, but your only weakness is your excessive modesty. From this moment I make you all Marshals and Dukes, with the exception of Aramis."

"And me, sire?" said Aramis.

"You shall be an Archbishop!"

The four friends looked up and then rushed into each other's arms. The King embraced Louise de la Valliere, by way of keeping them company. A pause ensued. At last Athos spoke:—

"Swear, my children, that, next to yourselves, you will respect—the King of France; and remember that 'Forty years after' we will meet again."

END OF VOL. I.

PRINTING OFFICE OF THE PUBLISHER.

www.ingramcontent.com/pod-product-compliance
Lightning Source LLC
Chambersburg PA
CBHW030807230426
43667CB00008B/1102